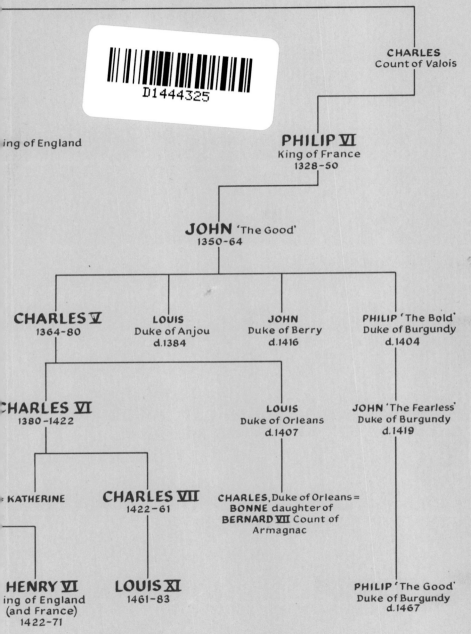

CHARLES
Count of Valois

ing of England

PHILIP VI
King of France
1328-50

JOHN 'The Good'
1350-64

CHARLES V
1364-80

LOUIS
Duke of Anjou
d.1384

JOHN
Duke of Berry
d.1416

PHILIP 'The Bold'
Duke of Burgundy
d.1404

CHARLES VI
1380-1422

LOUIS
Duke of Orleans
d.1407

JOHN 'The Fearless'
Duke of Burgundy
d.1419

KATHERINE

CHARLES VII
1422-61

CHARLES, Duke of Orleans =
BONNE daughter of
BERNARD VII Count of
Armagnac

HENRY VI
ing of England
(and France)
1422-71

LOUIS XI
1461-83

PHILIP 'The Good'
Duke of Burgundy
d.1467

ASTRIAN   ARMAGNAC   BURGUNDIAN

Henry V

A fifteenth century portrait of Henry V.

HENRY V

A BIOGRAPHY

Harold F. Hutchison

EYRE & SPOTTISWOODE
LONDON

© *Harold F. Hutchison 1967*
First published 1967
by Eyre & Spottiswoode (Publishers) Ltd
11 New Fetter Lane, London EC4
Printed in Great Britain by
Cox & Wyman Ltd, Fakenham, Norfolk

TO
CHRISTINA, KATE, CLAIRE
AND MARK

Contents

Illustrations

ILLUSTRATIONS

The end-piece to the last chapter (*page 225*) shows Henry V's signature, *from a letter in the Public Record Office, Exchequer Rolls E28/34*

MAPS
drawn by W. H. Bromage

TABLES

ACKNOWLEDGEMENTS

The author and publishers gratefully acknowledge the following for permission to reproduce copyright photographs:

The Trustees of the National Portrait Gallery for frontispiece; The Trustees of the British Museum for plates 1a, 1b, 5a, 5b; The National Monuments Record for plate 2 (Crown copyright) and plate 3; The Dean and Chapter of Westminster Abbey for plates 4, 11a, 11b; The Rev. A. H. Rodgers of St George's Church, Trotton for plate 6; A.C.I., Brussels, and the Koningklijk Museum, Antwerp, for plate 7; The Bibliothèque National, Paris, for plate 8; A. E. Entwhistle Esq., and the Dean and Chapter of Canterbury Cathedral for plate 9; Albert W. Kerr Esq., for plate 10; The Trustees of the Victoria and Albert Museum for plate 12; and the Public Record Office for the signature of Henry V on page 225.

FOREWORD

O nce upon a time, there was a famous prince who became King Henry V of England. In his youth he was gay, wilful and riotous, but the moment he became king he was changed into a paragon of all the kingly virtues. His evil boon-companions – including a pot-bellied braggart named Falstaff – were disowned, the Chief Justice who had once sentenced him to gaol for brawling was handsomely rewarded. He proceeded to display to an admiring Europe superb skill in generalship and surprising zeal for implacable justice. This King Henry won a great battle against the French at Agincourt and was granted the hand of the daughter of the king of France in marriage . . .

So, the legends linked with the name of Henry of Monmouth have been woven by the genius of William Shakespeare into a tapestry which was a glowing backcloth to the Elizabethan age. In our own day, the magic of the cinema has added further authenticity to Shakespeare's great patriotic dramas, and the legends have remained more potent than the facts of Henry's story. Our schoolbooks have no room to go deeply into the truth behind the legends, our theatre programmes never warn audiences that what they hear or see may be false, and even our major historians are neither certain nor agreed about their verdicts on Henry as a man and Henry as a king.

I have therefore felt that a reconsideration of facts which are now uncontested would not be a waste of effort. Legends must be put in their proper place and corrected where necessary. The conquest of Normandy, the siege-warfare of 1417–22 which displayed far greater generalship than the desperate raid to Agincourt, and the diplomacy which ended the Papal Schism and achieved the astounding Treaty of Troyes all deserve the careful attention of the historian even though they may be ignored by the dramatist. And there is always room for a reassessment of personality and achievement in the light of new research. The only portrait we have of Henry tells us nothing of the secret of

FOREWORD

his undoubted personal popularity, and the Elizabethans' hero-king – both fascinating and repellent to a modern eye – leaves us searching for the true reasons for his fame.

In this attempt to achieve a believable portrait of Henry of Monmouth and his times I have found no new original sources, but the rich sources from both sides of the Channel which are available deserve constant re-interpretation, and I have diligently studied them. And to all those modern scholars who have tilled these fields before me I owe a heavy debt. I wish especially to mention the classic works of Dr J. H. Wylie and Professor W. T. Waugh, of C. L. Kingsford, of my old tutor Professor R. B. Mowat, and the more recent and invaluable studies of Professor R. A. Newhall and Professor E. F. Jacob.

Finally, I must record that this book could never have been completed without the understanding, the encouragement and the secretarial efficiency of my wife.

HAROLD F. HUTCHISON
Froxfield, 1967

Henry V

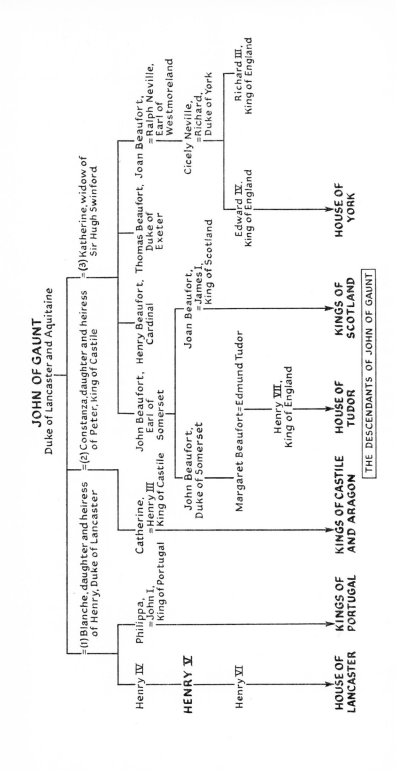

THE DESCENDANTS OF JOHN OF GAUNT

Chapter 1

THE YOUNG LORD HENRY

HENRY OF MONMOUTH was born on September 16th, 1387, in the castle of Monmouth in the southern Marches of Wales. That there was some dispute before the exact date of his birth was established is not surprising.[1] His grandfather, it is true, was the renowned John of Gaunt – that 'time honour'd Lancaster' who was the eldest uncle of King Richard II and fourth son of King Edward III. His father Henry Bolingbroke, earl of Derby, duke of Hereford and future King Henry IV, was not in the direct line of royal descent, and, when his first son was born, he was certainly not suspected of having designs on the throne. At his birth, therefore, Henry of Monmouth was of no greater importance than a dozen other kinsmen of the reigning monarch. Yet, twelve years later his father was crowned king of England, twenty-five years later he himself succeeded to the throne, and thirty-five years later he was to die not only undisputed and idolized king of England but regent of and heir to the kingdom of France, with a son who was actually to be crowned king of France as well as of England and to hold his titles for nearly forty years. About such a birth and such a destiny later writers were to weave many romantic and inspiring legends, but the only solid fact concerning Henry of Monmouth's babyhood contained in contemporary records is that he was nursed by one Johanna Waring, and the only touching memorial is a cradle now preserved in the London Museum which was reputedly rocked by the devoted Johanna.[2]

We do know something more of Henry of Monmouth's forebears. His mother was the Lady Mary de Bohun. She and her elder sister Eleanor were co-heiresses to the large estates which the Norman de Bohuns had acquired after the Conquest and had subsequently enlarged into three earldoms. Mary had been destined for the convent rather than the court, but, when her sister Eleanor became affianced to John of Gaunt's ambitious younger brother Thomas of Woodstock, duke of Gloucester, Gaunt had curbed Gloucester's plans for aggrandisement through marriage by taking Mary from her cloister and marrying her to his own son and heir. She brought Bolingbroke half the de Bohun estates, the earldoms of Hereford, Essex and Northampton, and subsequently four distinguished sons and two daughters. She was to die at the early age of twenty-four, and it is a tribute to her that her husband was to remain a widower for eight years. She was buried with great pomp at Leicester, and only two months after his accession her eldest son ordered a handsome effigy for her tomb.[3]

Bolingbroke was already famed through western Europe as a redoubtable soldier and jouster. A few months after the birth of his son and heir he showed his generalship in the campaign which so quickly ended in the rout of Richard II's friends at the skirmish of Radcot Bridge. Three years later he distinguished himself in the 'crusades' of the Teutonic Knights at Danzig and at Königsberg. While Gaunt was busy founding dynasties in the Spanish peninsula, Bolingbroke was visiting Bohemia, Hungary, Venice, Rhodes and Cyprus, and actually completed a pilgrimage to Jerusalem. As a boy, therefore, Henry of Monmouth saw very little of his father although he must have heard of his exploits. From both his parents he inherited traditions of military prowess, and much of the astuteness and efficiency which his father was to display as monarch was to be reflected in the ruthlessness and discipline which Henry of Monmouth – to the surprise of his contemporaries – was to show in later years.

Henry of Monmouth was only seven years of age when in July 1394 he lost his mother; and until the usurpation of 1399 there is no detailed factual evidence as to how he was educated. His youth was spent in the so-called 'Quiet Years' of the reign of Richard II. Between the bloody episode of the Lords Appellant in 1388 and the fateful drama of the Lists of Coventry ten years later England enjoyed a productive period of peace.

Court patronage encouraged Chaucer to write his *Canterbury Tales*. Froissart, admiring King Richard's French as they chatted over the handsome volume of his chronicles of chivalry which he had presented to the king, was at home in the English court. There was a blossoming of the arts and crafts which has bequeathed the noblest timber roof in Europe over West-minster Hall, the soaring ecclesiastical architecture of Yevele and his contemporaries, some of our best brasses and effigies, and in the Wilton diptych and the first authentic portrait of any English king two important contributions to the history of medieval painting.

Such achievements, it is true, reflected the culture and the greater magnificence of the courts of France, Burgundy and Italy, but they were the first significant flowerings of an indigenous English culture. It was a peaceful and fruitful inter-lude between two tragic crises, and what monkish chroniclers condemned as luxury and extravagance, and what war-loving barons despised as effeminate and useless, can be recognized now as the first beginnings of our English renaissance.

In this fascinating milieu Henry of Monmouth would have received the normal education of a young medieval nobleman. John Hardyng, who was later to accompany Henry V on his first French campaign, tells us what that involved.[4] He would begin with school at four years of age where he learned his letters; after six he would study language and learn to sit at meat 'semely'; at ten or twelve he would learn to 'revelle daunce and synge and speke of gentelnesse'; at fourteen he would hunt the deer and learn 'hardynesse', for to hunt and slay the deer and see them bleed 'hardyment gyffith to his corage', and in outwitting game he would sharpen his own wits; at sixteen he would learn the arts of war and the techniques of jousting, riding, besieging of castles, setting of night-watches, and every day would practise sword-play with his men . . .

His special tutor was his uncle Henry Beaufort, the second illegitimate son of John of Gaunt by his mistress the Lady Katherine Swynford, and one of the most brilliant political ecclesiastics of the age. Beaufort's astonishing career had begun with a prebendal stall at Lincoln in his teens and was to be followed by the episcopal thrones of Lincoln and Winchester.

He and his brothers were legitimized by Richard II in 1397 and his splendid and surviving memorials are still at the cathedral and the hospital of St Cross at Winchester. The young Henry of Monmouth could have had no abler tutor, and in addition he quickly found especial favour in the eyes of King Richard – he could not have spent his boyhood in more fortunate or more enlightened surroundings.

Some dim sidelights on Henry's youth are provided by a Westminster monk[5] who was very close to him. Apparently Henry spent his spare time in hunting, falconry, fishing, riding and walking abroad; but he did not neglect the 'learned counsels of his elders', and we are told that King Richard was very fond of him and showed him many favours. In the accounts of the duchy of Lancaster there is evidence of some cultural activity. The sum of eightpence was paid to one Adam Gastron for harp strings for 'the young Lord Henry' when he was ten years old, and seven books of grammar contained in one volume were bought for him in London at a cost of four shillings. On the other hand, the same accounts note that one Stephen Furbour received one shilling for a new scabbard for Henry's sword, and that the cost of three-quarters of an ounce of tissue of black silk bought in London from one Margaret Stranson for another of his swords was one shilling and sixpence. Necessary military training did not preclude the gentler art of minstrelsy and the peaceful pursuit of at least the elements of learning.[6] There is even a legend that the young Lord Henry was at The Queen's College, Oxford. It probably stems from the fact that his tutor Henry Beaufort was in 1398 in residence at Queen's as chancellor of the university, but Beaufort was only there for a brief six months and at that time his pupil could only have been eleven years old.[7] There is no evidence to support the legend, and The Queen's College has had to forgo the tourist attraction of a memorial window which during the nineteenth century attempted to lend it credence.

The only other item concerning Henry of Monmouth's boyhood to be gleaned from the sparse contemporary records is that when he was eight years old he was seriously ill. The receiver of the duchy of Lancaster recorded in the spring of 1395 the charge of 6s. 8d. for Thomas Pye and a horse hired at

London, March 18th, to carry him to Leicester with all speed, on account of the illness of the young Lord Henry. As his father was to die at the age of forty-six of an obscure but foul disease[8] which some chroniclers called leprosy, and he himself was to die in his bed at the early age of thirty-five – his medical heredity was none too good.

In the year 1398 Henry of Monmouth saw his father banished. Yet when the trial by combat at Coventry, between Mowbray duke of Norfolk and Bolingbroke, duke of Hereford, gave Richard II his carefully prepared opportunity to take final revenge for the defeat, execution, and exile of Richard's friends of ten years before, he did not allow his hatred of the father to prejudice his affection for the son. When Richard so dramatically stopped the duel and banished both contestants, Bolingbroke's eldest son was retained close to the king. In the following year Richard embarked on his second expedition to Ireland, and he took the young Lord Henry with him, partly as protégé and partly as hostage for Bolingbroke's loyalty. During his father's exile, Henry of Monmouth was allotted an annual income of £500[9] – a not ungenerous allowance.

It is fortunate for us that a Frenchman named Creton accompanied Richard's Irish expedition. He was more minstrel than soldier, and, having developed a great respect for Richard, he composed in his honour an invaluable metrical record of what he saw and felt about the expedition and the subsequent usurpation of the English throne which helps to counterbalance the biased accounts of the Lancastrian chroniclers. He tells us that in the middle of the Irish campaign Richard signalized his regard for Henry of Monmouth by conferring on him the order of knighthood, and, expressly in his honour, conferred the same rank on ten of his companions-in-arms. He describes Henry as a 'fair young and handsome bachelor' and quotes Richard's accolade – 'my fair cousin, henceforth be gallant and bold, for unless you conquer you will have little name for valour'.[10] The future King Henry V was to remember at least the latter part of the injunction.

When Richard II was compelled to forgo his Irish ambitions and hurry back to England to meet the invasion of Bolingbroke, the young Lord Henry was summoned to the royal presence and reproached with the treason of his father. According to the chronicler Otterbourne his reply was bold and to the point – 'In truth, my gracious king and lord, I am sincerely grieved by these tidings, and, as I conceive, you are fully assured of my innocence in this proceeding of my father.'[11] Richard accepted the denial, but before he left Ireland he consigned Henry of Monmouth and Humphrey, the young son of the murdered duke of Gloucester, to safekeeping in the castle of Trim in Meath. On returning to England, Richard found himself a king without an army, and within three fateful months a simple knight imprisoned in the Lancastrian fortress of Pontefract.

The usurpation of the English throne by Bolingbroke only concerns this story in its effect on the young Lord Henry. He was only twelve years old at the revolution of 1399, and he knew the deposed monarch better than he knew his own father. It must have been with very mixed feelings that Henry of Monmouth suddenly found himself heir to the usurper. Yet, twelve years of age at this period was nearer to sixteen in modern times. He was already a knight thanks to his royal patron, he had already seen something of guerrilla warfare in the bogs and woods of medieval Ireland, and he had already experienced the doubts and fears of imprisonment in a castle far from his native land. His youth was soon over.

Bolingbroke's first thought as king was to commission a sea-captain of Chester – one Henry Dryhurst – to proceed immediately to Ireland to bring his eldest son home, together with the young Humphrey of Gloucester.[12] Humphrey died of an illness on the voyage,[13] and we do not know precisely when or where the young Lord Henry joined his father. We do know that no time was lost in presenting Henry of Monmouth with all the titles and panoply proper to the heir to the throne. On Sunday, October 12th, 1399, Bolingbroke, now King Henry IV, ignoring the accolades of his predecessor, knighted his four sons together with forty-five other esquires.[14] Next day Henry of Monmouth carried the unpointed sword 'curtana' – the symbol of mercy – at his father's coronation. In the first parliament of the new reign immediately after the coronation it was announced by the new chancellor, Archbishop Arundel, that the king was to create his eldest son prince of Wales, duke of Cornwall and earl of Chester. On October 23rd Henry of Monmouth was made duke of Aquitaine, and on November 8th he was duly invested with the glamorous titles promised by Arundel.[15] The ceremony was impressive. The new king seated on the throne summoned his eldest son to the presence, placed a golden coronet adorned with pearls on his head, a ring on his finger and a golden rod in his hand, and it is significant that the attendant commons requested that their presence and agreement should be specifically recorded. Two days later the new prince was created duke of Lancaster, and the widespread estates and the formidable palatinate powers of that duchy were finally linked to the English crown.[16] Prince Henry's *cursus honorum* was both spectacular and rapid.

After so much excitement and ceremonial the new king and his family retired to spend the Christmas feast of 1399 resting and recuperating at the royal castle of Windsor. On Twelfth Night there was to be a magnificent 'mumming', and it was at this juncture that Richard's friends and supporters had planned a counter-stroke. A plot had been hatched by the Hollands, half brothers of the ex-king, Edward, earl of Rutland and son of the duke of York, the earl of Salisbury, the former Archbishop Walden and other nobles and clerics to storm Windsor Castle, capture Bolingbroke and his sons dead or alive, and restore Richard of Bordeaux to the throne of his ancestors. The plot very nearly succeeded, and only failed through the treachery of Rutland who betrayed the plot to his father who in turn warned the royal family. Windsor Castle was duly stormed, but Henry IV and his sons had just had time to escape to the friendly shelter of the walls of the city of London. From there the new king speedily mobilized an army, and after a check at Colnbrook he pursued the now disheartened conspirators westwards to Cirencester. There the townsfolk had begun a butchery which Henry IV ruthlessly completed, and the young prince of Wales's first introduction to affairs of state involved all the brutalities of medieval retribution. The rout at Cirencester[17] and the subsequent executions were quickly followed by the death of Richard of Bordeaux in Pontefract's castle dungeon, and whether that was a case of wilful murder or shameful neglect or suicidal starvation is a controversy which belongs to the history of the prince's father, and it is a controversy which can never now be decided. From the young prince's point of view he had lost a royal friend, and it was his own father who was suspected of murder. There is evidence that his father's conscience was uneasy on two counts[18] – his usurpation of the throne and the death of an anointed king – but there is no evidence that the prince in any way bore his father ill-will for the events of 1399. The corpse of Richard – if it was his corpse – was sealed in lead, revealing only the face, and brought to London. After two days' public exposure at St Paul's, the body was buried without state ceremony in the priory of King's Langley in Hertfordshire.

Politically the death of Richard II had been badly mishandled by a statesman who in so many other ways was both cautious and astute. The legend that Richard had escaped from Pontefract, and that the corpse at King's Langley was a fraud, pursued Henry IV throughout his reign, and even outlived him to worry his son. It might have been wiser for Henry IV to have tried Richard openly and executed him publicly. That the prince of Wales was not an unmoved observer of these tragic events is proved by the fact that one of his earliest acts as king was to do signal honour to the remains of his royal patron, but it is a pointer to his future political realism that before that graceful act he waited until his father was in the grave.

Henry of Monmouth's boyhood had been exciting. If he had not actually witnessed the Lists of Coventry at least he must have heard of them – his father was one of the protagonists. He had lost his mother and seen his father exiled before he was twelve years of age. He had learned something of the arts of peace at the court of the friendly monarch who was implacably and understandably his father's enemy. He had seen something of the hardships of soldiering in the wild terrain beyond the Irish 'pale'. He had heard of his father's desperate invasion and of its speedy and overwhelming success which had led to the bold usurpation of the English throne. He had been released from imprisonment to stand at his father's side through the long and magnificent ceremonial of coronation.[19] He had survived the first ill-fated attempt to upset the new dynasty, and, although he had seen the astonishing rewards that awaited rebels who succeeded beyond their dreams, he had also seen the grim fate that awaited rebels who failed. The new prince of Wales was old beyond his years.

Chapter 2

BACKGROUND

P RINCE HENRY was about to step on to a stage which
was European as well as English. His father knew
Europe well, and he himself was to spend most of his
reign in France and to be involved in the diplomacy of
European kings, popes, cardinals and emperors. What
was the pattern and make-up of this early fifteenth-century
Europe?[1]

In Prince Henry's day the kingdom of France still did not
include Navarre, Rousillon, Provence and the English bridgeheads at Calais and in Aquitaine. Its royal dukes had been permitted to build up a system of semi-independent 'appanages'
which were a constant threat to centralized monarchy. The
house of Burgundy, for example, was as powerful in Flanders
and Brabant as it was in its ancestral duchy round Dijon, and
the dukedom of Brittany with its own Celtic language was not
united to the French crown until over a century later.

Italy, north of the kingdom of Naples, was divided between
the Papal States which stretched from Rome to Ravenna, such
independent city-states as Siena, Florence, Genoa and Venice,
and such independent duchies as Savoy and Milan. To Prince
Henry, Italy was the proper home of the Pope, and of those
foreign traders and merchants from Genoa, Lombardy, Florence and Venice who brought to a remote England the luxuries
and spices of the very different Mediterranean and Oriental
worlds.

By the lake of Lucerne lay a new nation-state little more than
a century old. The burghers of the Swiss cantons of Uri,
Schwyz and Unterwalden had united in 1291, and at the battles
of Morgarten in 1315 and of Sempach in 1386 they had proved
that free Swiss pikemen and halberdiers feared neither Burgun-

dian nor Austrian, and already the foundations of modern Switzerland were secure.

With Scandinavia in remote times England had had the closest links – Canute had included England in his Scandinavian empire. But in Prince Henry's day Scandinavia was merely a market where salt herrings could be exchanged for furs, and where, only a few years before, Norway, Sweden and Denmark had been united under a Danish king – a distant and detached semi-barbarian monarchy not yet equipped to play a significant part in European politics. On the other hand, English traders were beginning to penetrate the southern and eastern shores of the Baltic sea, and the Hanseatic League of German cities already had one of its most important depots in the walled steelyard[2] in London where the 'Easterlings', or German traders had many valuable extra-territorial rights and privileges.

At the south-west corner of Europe, the Spanish peninsula was divided between the kingdoms of Navarre, of Castile, of Aragon, of Portugal and in the south the Moorish Emirate of Granada. Thanks to Prince Henry's grandfather, John of Gaunt, England had the closest links with Portugal and Castile. Gaunt's daughter Philippa had been married to King John of Portugal, his daughter Katherine had been married to King Henry of Castile, and he himself had had claims on the throne of Castile through his second wife, Costanza. It was not until the end of the fifteenth century that Castile and Aragon were united in a single kingdom under Ferdinand and Isabella, that Navarre was joined to France, and that the Moors were finally driven back into Africa across the Straits of Gibraltar. Prince Henry's grandfather had been known as 'my lord of Spain'; he himself sought and found greater glory nearer home.

At the heart of Europe was still the Holy Roman Empire. Over two centuries before Henry's day, Frederick Barbarossa's spectacular genius had begun the creation of a *pax Germanica* which would stretch from the North Sea to the Mediterranean, from the Rhine to the Vistula. Under Barbarossa's grandson, that *stupor mundi* Frederick II, a further attempt had been made to link Sicily and Naples in one great empire with what was later called Germany and Austria, the Netherlands, Bohemia, Switzerland, northern Italy and the southern lands of Burgundy.

Both attempts had been wrecked on the rock of St Peter, and both emperors had been thwarted by the obstinacy of Italian city-states and the power of a universal Church. The Holy Roman Empire was now but the ghost of ancient Rome. Its ill-defined borders had been contracted under pressures from popes, from the separatist interests of electoral princes, from citizen armies and family spheres of influence, to include merely the kingdom of Bohemia, the archdukedom of Austria, and the nominal overlordship of a kaleidoscope of conflicting interests and rival hegemonies. Modern Germany, like modern Italy, dates from the nineteenth and not the fifteenth century, and yet, such is the power of legend and history, it was to be one of Prince Henry's greatest moments when he welcomed to our shores the Luxembourg prince who had been elected King of the Romans and later was acknowledged as Emperor of the Holy Roman Empire.

Prince Henry's Europe was not yet safe. It was no longer seriously threatened by the Muslim invasion of Spain, but it was very much threatened by the aggression of the Ottoman Turks. The Ottomans had by-passed Constantinople, where the last remnant of the ancient Byzantine Empire of the east was to survive only for a precarious fifty years, and were now threatening western Europe along the line of the river Danube. The last crusade of Christian chivalry against Muslim Saracens had petered out over a century before, and when Prince Henry's father had gone crusading he had matched his arms not against the Muslim but against barbarian Letts and Esthonians. In 1396, when Prince Henry was nine, the Ottoman Turks under their celebrated Sultan Bayazid had crushingly defeated a great crusading army from the west, which included the future Emperor Sigismund, at the battle of Nicopolis. The Mongol Tamerlane, by defeating and capturing Bayazid on the plains of Angora in 1402, saved western Europe from an invasion it was ill-prepared to withstand, and it was fortunate for the west that Tamerlane's main preoccupations were in the east.

There, then, in outline is the European picture which faced Prince Henry – a Europe where a new kind of nation-state was in the making. And there were three loyalties in Henry's narrow world which still overrode political and geographical allegiances – the Church, feudalism, and the universities.

The Roman Church was the real heir to the ancient Roman Empire. Its Latin language was the *lingua franca* of medieval Europe, and in spite of a 'Babylonish Captivity' which had shackled the pope to a French Avignon since 1309, and in spite of the fact that from 1378 there had been one pope in Avignon and another in Rome, the Church was still the core of an international European civilization. The Church still stood for the essential unity of Christendom even though its component parts were beginning to think of going their several ways. It had kept the lamps of learning alight through the Dark Ages, it had brightened the twilight of the Middle Ages, and at all times it had fostered the peaceful arts of carving, needlework, painting, illumination, and architecture. Its enormous wealth had tempted the neediness of civil authorities, its papal pretensions to universal dominion had already roused the criticisms of nationalistic reformers and independent philosophers, its abuses had created heretics in France, England and Bohemia; but nevertheless it was still the one universal Christian Church. Orthodox critics could criticize but still remain loyal, and the ambition of all good Christians was to see the Church re-unified and reformed rather than to see it rejected and overthrown.

Feudalism, in its social rather than its economic aspects, was the second great unifying phenomenon of the Middle Ages. It had its local variations, but fundamentally it was a European international system, which, based on land tenure and personal services of both a military and an economic nature, cut across merely political frontiers and divided European society into horizontal rather than vertical strata. An English baron of the previous century had been as near to a French baron as to English burghers close to his castle walls. When John of Gaunt, the greatest English lord of his day, needed a refuge from rebelling English peasants in 1381, and when his feudal enemy, the earl of Northumberland, had shut the gates of Bamburgh castle against him, he found honourable refuge and safety with his feudal peers but ancestral enemies in Scotland. When Prince Henry's father had been banished he found a hospitable welcome at the court of France in spite of the fact that Richard's queen was a French princess. All medieval English kings were directly descended from a Norman duke, and the language of court and castle was Norman–French. Henry II had ruled an empire which was more French than English, and he was buried not at Westminster but at Fontevrault. His son, Richard Coeur de Lion had hardly ever lived in England either before or after his accession, and his most famous memorial was his 'saucy castle' on the Seine. When English barons brought King John to the fateful meadows of Runnymede it was the son of a French king who helped them to victory. Simon de Montfort, whom some would name as the founder of English liberties, was a Frenchman. The stalls of the knights of the Garter at Windsor are still emblazoned in Norman–French, and in the escutcheons of all our kings and queens the lilies of France remained quartered with the leopards of England from the days of the Angevins to the days of the Hanoverians. Prince Henry's England was very close to Europe.

In the medieval universities – a very medieval invention – was a third phenomenon which in origin was international. Inspired by the early medical university of Salerno and the great legal university of Bologna there had grown up in Paris and in Oxford universities devoted to learning in all its branches, which had nothing to do with warring aristocracies but were meeting the need for educated lawyers, doctors, clergy, and administrators. Now, in spite of their common use of Latin and their easy interchange of travelling students and teachers, they were developing an independence of outlook and a freedom of thought and expression which, coupled with the development of native literary languages, was soon to convert them into bulwarks of a national feeling which stemmed from the fact that their scholars were for the most part of humble local origin. Prince Henry may never have been an Oxford scholar but it is significant that later legend maintained that he was, and it is equally significant that in Paris and in Oxford, although the students were controlled by a bishop's chancellor, both were organized into 'nations'. Oxford, and soon Cambridge, was becoming as English as Paris was becoming French.

No institutions are static, and Henry's day was a period when the process of change was accelerating rapidly. The feudal castle still stood, but the power of gunpowder was beginning to threaten its walls. The great abbeys and churches still proclaimed a unity, but the Church was already divided and its dogmas questioned. And the many cities and towns of medieval Europe were forcing grounds for the growth of a new spirit – the spirit of nationalism – which was to change Europe speedily and irrevocably.

The towns had bought their liberties and their privileges from needy barons and impoverished monarchs – they were fortified islands of freedom in a sea of decaying feudalism. In Italy and Germany they had become powerful enough to build city-states. In France, Flanders and England they had found a national unity in their highly organized economies, and it was largely through the national trading guilds that Englishmen were realizing their Englishness. During the Peasants' Revolt of 1381 the citizens of London had turned on the foreign Flemings and Lombards with such fury that it was the only incident of the Revolt which rated a mention in the benign pages of Chaucer.[3] The feudal aristocracies of England and of France shared many fellow feelings and common traditions but in both countries a new feeling of hatred for the foreigner, because he was a foreigner, was welling up from below. In both countries the separate languages of the common man were ousting the universal Latin of court and Church. In 1362, English had been decreed compulsory in our courts of law; a few years later the English parliament had been opened in the English tongue for the first time; and when Prince Henry's father had challenged the crown of England he had done so *in materna lingua* as the chroniclers put it – in plain English. The England of Langland, Chaucer and Gower had developed a literary language by which a new national spirit could be expressed, and outside court circles there was a flourishing native English which owed little to the Norman–French of monarchs and barons. By the time Prince Henry inherited the throne he owed a great deal of his popularity to his mastery of the pithy, salty, forthright language of the common people.[4]

Even our English Church was not as Roman or as international as its theory would make it appear. The unity of

Christendom was still a potent ideal, but the Schism had revealed a tragic split at the top and cracks were very visible down below. But the greatest threat to the international unity of the Church was not from rival popes and intriguing cardinals allied to warring civil potentates, it was rather from scholars whose logic questioned the mysteries of ecclesiastical miracles, and their followers, who, like Wyclif's 'poor preachers', tested dogma in terms of common sense, and were now provided with a Holy Writ in a language they could speak, read and understand. And there were many Englishmen in all ranks of society who resented the yearly drain of English wealth to an overseas Church and listened to the logic of reformers who were very close to heresy. In southern France the great Pope Innocent III had wiped out the Albigensian heresy with appalling efficiency, but in England the Lollardy of the followers of Wyclif was never wiped out. In Bohemia the beliefs of Huss were to survive both stake and cannon, and throughout Europe the papal bull *Unam Sanctam*, which in 1302 had declared that it was 'altogether necessary to salvation for every human creature to be subject to the Roman pontiff',[5] had been attacked with increasing vehemence and authority from within and without the Church.

Prince Henry grew up as orthodox in his outlook as his father – who sanctioned the first burning of heretics in England – but he was as firm as his ancestors in rejecting the political implications and the ecclesiastical arrogance of those who still hankered after the objectives of Pope Innocent III – Henry's Catholic church was to be Roman in doctrine but very English in administration and control.

The British Isles of Henry's day were still geographically on the outer edge of the western civilized world. But in the thirteenth century, England had produced the Franciscan friar, Roger Bacon, who had anticipated a great deal of that experimental philosophy which was to be the basis of the future European renaissance, and Duns Scotus had successfully matched his Scottish dialectic against the system of Thomas Aquinas. In the early fourteenth century William of Ockham and Richard Fitz-Ralph, archbishop of Armagh, had begun to criticize the Church, and at the century's end Wyclif and his followers were undermining it with a new logic, a native Bible and the impetus of popular support. In the fields of thought and philosophy, England had already made a very significant contribution to Europe. In the arts and crafts England had a splendid record. All over the land were great cathedrals, abbeys, churches and castles which proclaimed the skills of native craftsmen in stone, in wood, in frescoes, in stained glass and in brass engraving. In literature, if Italy had already produced her Dante, Petrarch and Boccaccio, England had produced her Chaucer and Langland, and if in the 'fine art' of painting she was still lagging behind Italy, France and Flanders her *opus anglicanum* – the needlework of the tapestry makers – was celebrated throughout Europe.[6] In the arts of war English knights and English archers at the great victories of Crécy, Poitiers, Sluys and Nájera had demonstrated to all Europe that England could be a formidable foe or a valuable ally.[7] In the skills of commerce English merchants and English sea-captains were reaching the Baltic and the Mediterranean, English wool and cloth were famed and unrivalled, and Sheffield steel was already equalling the products of Damascus and Toledo. Prince Henry had no reason to be ashamed of his inheritance.

In 1399 Prince Henry's father was named, as Edward III and Richard II had been named, not only king of England but also king of France and lord of Ireland. The history of his second title is the history of the Hundred Years War and a spectacular portion of that history is a major part of this book. The history of the third title is more briefly told.[8]

Only three of our medieval kings were able to concern themselves with Irish affairs – Henry II, John and Richard II. The first had created the Irish 'pale' within whose ill-defined boundaries on the east of Ireland Anglo–Norman barons were presented with estates and lordships which in fact gave them little more than good hunting and much guerrilla warfare, but which in theory were governed under a viceroy with a semblance of those instruments of taxation and justice which in England were now being concentrated in parliament. Beyond the 'pale' was an Ireland of petty kingships and clan rivalry which was not far removed from barbarism. John, as his father's viceroy, had made sensible efforts to impose order in the 'pale' and to control the savage hinterland beyond. Richard II had made two serious attempts to make his title *seigneur d'Irland* more meaningful, but rebellion in England had cut short an effort which promised well. When Henry IV seized the throne of England he inherited an Ireland still unsubdued but an Ireland so poor, so ill-armed and so unorganized that it was never a menace to his sovereignty, and throughout his reign he was too much occupied with rebels within his own proper realm to be able to bother with rebels across the Irish Sea.

The principality of Wales, however, was a thornier problem too close at hand to be ignored. West Wales was separated from England by the Welsh March, where great Anglo–Norman lords were in reality petty princelings with royal licence to levy dues and taxes and dispense a very rough justice from their border strongholds. The prince of Wales had very little real authority over these marcher lords, but west of the March, where the population was wholly Welsh, he was the head of an occupying power whose law was the law of England, and whose sovereignty was imposed on a subject race by the garrisons of the great Edwardian castles. Yet Welsh nationality had survived – its final suppression was to be a training ground for the future victor of Agincourt.

Scotland was still an independent kingdom. Its highlands were too wild and inaccessible to be of any consequence, but in its lowlands, although a Norman feudalism had been imposed on the Celtic Scots, there had developed a truly Scottish nationality, which, even if divided and handicapped by internal jealousies, was at one in regarding the north of England as legitimate raiding ground and the English as hereditary enemies. In the early years of the reign of Henry IV the Scots were not slow to give assistance to those who still considered Henry a usurper, and they perpetuated the legend that Richard II had escaped from Pontefract to Scotland. But, apart from the usual border raiding, a national campaign of Scots against English was rendered difficult when the young heir to the Scottish throne fell into Henry IV's hands by accident. The Scots staged no major invasion of England during the reigns of Henry IV or of his son; they were content to send occasional contingents to help Welsh or English rebels or to reinforce England's enemies in France.

And how did England herself stand when Prince Henry's father 'in the name of Fadir Son and Holy Gost' challenged the realm of England and its crown? The last successful invasion by a foreign race was as far away from the days of Bolingbroke and his son as the restoration of Charles II is from our own time. While the English baronage had maintained its chivalrous links with France it is nevertheless true that an English England had been consolidating itself for three hundred years, and although it had had its share of civil war and rebellion it had seen no successful national enemies since William the Norman. Defeat by the Scots at Bannockburn had been avenged by the victory of English longbows at Neville's Cross, and the great victories of Edward III and the Black Prince had founded a tradition of English military supremacy on the Continent which was based not on the mounted chivalry of feudalism but on the sturdy virtues of native archers led by knights who were not ashamed to dismount and stand to fight side by side with their social inferiors. Even on the sea – where warfare was still military rather than naval – English sea-captains, who had learned their rough trade in many a piratical Channel raid, had shown their superiority at the battle of Sluys. When Chaucer's pilgrims wended their way to Canterbury they were a distinctively English cavalcade. His prioress spoke French but only with a very English accent, and his miller, his wife of Bath and even his friars were as English as he was himself. Even the gloomy verses of Langland have for background the Malvern Hills and a village life which are still very much a part of the English scene.[9]

The England of 1400 was rooted in the soil – its economics were based on the agriculture of the manor.[10] But it was an agriculture which, like so much else, was in process of change. Since the Black Death of 1349 had wiped out at least a third of the population, the static feudal system, whereby villeins were *ascripti glebae*, 'owned nothing but their bellies'[11] and paid for the security of their strip holdings by doing compulsory work for their lords, had been considerably modified. Many villeins had been able to buy their freedom, and lords who lacked servile tenants were glad to offer wages to free labourers, and to 'commute' traditional labour services for much-needed cash. At focal points in a landscape which was either rural manor or forest, which belonged to king or lord and had its separate and savage legal code of protection, there were now islands of freedom in towns and cities. These fortified markets were buying their privileges with the profits of their trading, and using their command of ready cash to build up a trade in wool and cloth of such dimensions that they were able to lend financial assistance – at a handsome profit – to needy monarchs and warring barons, and to achieve an importance which is symbolized even today by the woolsack which is the seat of our Lords Chancellor.[12] The fairly simple social pyramid in which kings and barons were based on a substratum of rural serfs was now a false analogy. A class of free yeomen farmers who as knights of the shire had now been given a share in local justice and national parliamentary representation, a class of free labourers and free craftsmen who now had their own protection behind stout walls and in city guilds, and a class of merchants whose control of the great wool and cloth trade had given them financial control of the national economy had very much changed the picture. England was no longer a purely rural community; it was a curious complex in which primitive subsistence agriculture went hand in hand with the first beginnings of a capitalist system based on large-scale sheep rearing, urban industry and international trade.

In matters of religion also, the clear-cut outlines of the thirteenth century were now blurred and confused. England was still a religious society – every manor had its priest, and the countryside was already rich in great ecclesiastical buildings. But the abuses of priests who neglected their flocks to become civil servants, and of clerical landlords who were adamantly opposed to any winds of change, had provided soil for the 'tares' of the Lollards,[13] and a rich Church, flayed by the satire of a Langland and slashed by the wit of a Chaucer, was not only attacked by near-heretics but envied by orthodox and needy governments – even John of Gaunt had lent his support to one of the earliest movements for the expropriation of at least some of the Church's riches in the interests of an empty national treasury.[14]

And there was yet another new class of society which added to the complexity of the medieval scene – the lawyers. Throughout the previous century they had been growing in importance and organizing themselves from the shelter of their London Inns. A lawless society, in which even peaceful townsfolk were wise to carry short-swords, displayed the paradox that there was almost a mania for litigation especially in all matters concerning tenures and inheritances. A great corpus of common law had been built up which needed interpretation and application, and the growing complexities of national government needed men who knew their precedents, who could state a case, and who were the real architects of what was to become a peculiarly English constitution. One of the first violent acts of the rioters of 1381 had been to burn the records of the Inns of Court in the 'great chimney' of the Temple – it had been a very misguided act but it had also been a tribute to an importance which even common folk had begun dimly to appreciate.

In 1400, therefore, English society was in a state of flux. It was still a medieval monarchy in theory and in practice. Even Wat Tyler had wanted to retain King Richard, even though he himself was to be the Lord Tyler and John Ball his archbishop. Richard II had aired views of a divine right of kings which in a sense were correctly traditional, and yet contained a prophetic touch of that 'new monarchy' which men were to accept under the Tudors.[15] Bolingbroke had usurped the throne by force of arms, yet later lawyers were able to read into the situation a semblance of what was to become parliamentary control. Kings still became kings by hereditary right, by the sanction of their peers, and with the benediction of sacred oil; it was only incidentally that they owed their thrones to the will of the people. The instrument for recording and reckoning with that will had been slowly developing in the governmental machinery of the medieval 'parliament'. Throughout the previous century the commons of England had been summoned from time to time to the king's council – primarily to provide part of the finance which enabled an oligarchy to govern and its armies to make war. They had seized the opportunity to make the granting of money conditional on at least some attention being paid to their ambitions and grievances. Where the wealthy Church in its convocations had been content to offer subsidies which might pay for a blind eye to privileges and abuses, the wealthy commons of England, through their knights of the shire and their burgesses from towns and cities, were now determined to have a much greater say in matters of state. But it is not true to say that Henry Bolingbroke began what one distinguished historian has called 'the Lancastrian constitutional experiment'[16] – the English constitution which emerged through the centuries was not created, devised or imagined, it simply developed from precedent to precedent. Henry IV and his son were not architects of democracy, they were simply medieval kings who were compelled, largely for financial reasons, to appreciate and accept the new and growing power of the third 'estate'.

When Henry of Monmouth at a very early age became the heir to the English throne he was living in an England which in most outward appearances was unchanged from the England of his great-grandfather Edward III. Affairs of state were still governed by the king and his peers, and the power of the feudal 'magnates'[17] was vast and widespread. In spite of statutes of Livery and Maintenance[18] the great lords of England were powerful enough to overawe local justice, and, if they thought fit, to raise armies against their king. In their great castles they held great state and obeyed a code of chivalry, which however picturesque and Christian in its symbolism, relegated the folk of England to a subjection which was still near to serfdom. But below the surface in the Church were the roots of reformation; interpolated into the established aristocracy were *novi homines* who had bought, married and deserved their careers from trade to privilege and power; in addition to a king's council of great lords there was now a body of commons with wealth and influence behind it which could no longer be ignored; and a society which for centuries had given pride of place to a ruthless if chivalrous military caste had now been invaded by a class of ecclesiastical and legal civil servants who owed their positions to their brains rather than to their heritage or their swords.[19]

Both Henry IV and his son were realists – they dealt with new problems on their merits – but there is no evidence that either of them appreciated that their England was *not* the England of Edward III. For the fourteen troubled years of Henry IV's reign there was not much time or opportunity to do more than establish a new dynasty firmly on the throne, and the son played a useful part in helping his father successfully to accomplish this. But neither father nor son could lead a newly-emerging nation along new-fashioned roads – they were as conservative as their ancestors when around them was a ferment which they could neither recognize nor understand. Before the fifteenth century was out, the discovery of the Americas, the invention of printing, the development of gunpowder, the harvests of the European Renaissance and the phenomenon of great nation-states were to relegate Prince Henry and his father to paragons of a world which had passed away.

Chapter 3

TWO PRINCES OF
WALES

'THEN AROSE DUKE HENRY. His eldest son, who humbly knelt before him, he made Prince of Wales and gave him the land; but I think he must conquer it if he will have it: for in my opinion the Welsh would on no account allow him to be their lord, for the sorrow, evil and disgrace which the English, together with his father, had brought upon King Richard.' Thus the contemporary French minstrel-knight Creton referred to Henry of Monmouth's first appointment.[1] It was a shrewd appraisal of a threatening situation. During the previous reign a remarkable personal victory had been achieved by Richard II. He had recruited his famous bodyguard from those Cheshire archers who had learned their skill from neighbours in the Welsh Marches, and, when the rest of England seemed all against him, he had still been able to count on the loyalty of the Welsh. In the crisis of 1399 his advance party under the earl of Salisbury had been able to muster a considerable Welsh army to support him in North Wales. It was not Richard's fault that, owing to the treachery of at least one of his closest friends and the difficulties of Welsh communications, he arrived at Conway Castle too late to recall the scattered Welsh, whom Salisbury had hoped to lead in his cause but whose patience had understandably evaporated in the absence of their monarch and of any news from him. The loyalty of the Welsh to Richard II boded ill for the duke who had usurped his throne, and for the son who so quickly had been appointed prince of their Wales.

The prince, now thirteen years old, had not been slow to realize

38

what was due to his new rank and dignity. In the minutes of the Privy Council early in the year 1400 the council is requested by the prince 'to consider how my lord the Prince is utterly destitute of every kind of appointment relative to his household ... that is to say, his chapels, chambers, halls, wardrobe, pantry, buttery, kitchen, scullery, saucery, almonry, anointry, and generally all things requisite for his establishment'.[2] Presumably these considerable needs were reasonably well satisfied, but a personal household of princely appointments mattered little at this juncture – he was immediately faced with a Welsh rebellion which was to occupy him for a third of his eventful life.

Geographically and racially Wales of the early fifteenth century was roughly the Wales of our modern atlases. Politically it was much more complicated. The Normans had found it easier to conquer southern and central Wales than the north, and except in Pembrokeshire the superimposition of Norman lords had left the native Celtic institutions and language undisturbed. When Henry of Monmouth became prince of Wales he inherited a precarious settlement which dated from Edward I's statute of Rhuddlan in 1284.[3] Edward had finally defeated Llewelyn ap Griffith, the last prince of Wales, and by this statute had established an English enclave in North Wales. It comprised the shires of Anglesea, Caernarvon and Merioneth – and later of Flint, Cardigan and Carmarthen – in the direct control of his son the prince of Wales. Caernarvon was the capital of this principality; it had its own council, its own independent chancery and exchequer, and its justice was a tactful mixture of English law and Welsh custom. The rest of Wales, as we know it, was the almost absolute property of the Lords Marcher – for the most part the descendants of the original Norman invaders. Under Edward I they had been compelled to do homage for their privileges to the prince of Wales but since Edward III's day they owed allegiance directly to the English crown.

The great fortresses of Caernarvon, Harlech, Criccieth, Conway, Rhuddlan and Beaumaris, whose ruins still dominate North Wales, held down the principality, and each of a hundred or more Lords Marcher had his own lesser stronghold in central and southern Wales. In the wars of Edward III the Welsh fighting spirit had found opportunity both for and against the English in France. The famous English longbow, which wrought such havoc at Crécy and was to be the secret of English military successes for a century, was borrowed from the Welsh archer, and it is in the early stages of the Hundred Years War that we first hear of the leek as a Welsh national emblem. On the other hand Owen the Red, the brother of Llewelyn ap Griffith, was one of Edward III's doughtiest opponents on the French side. In the fourteenth century Welsh fighting men went abroad for exercise while at home there was so-called peace – an English peace of subjugation in a land where the bards still flourished and kept alive that spirit of Welsh nationality which still awaited a native leader.

Henry of Monmouth, English prince of Wales, was now to meet in Owen Glendower, Welsh prince of Wales, the leader of the last great effort of the Welsh to win back their independence.

Owen Glendower's early life is as obscure as his end, but for thirteen years he kept his standard flying and earned the respect, and finally the pardon, of the young English prince to whom he taught so much. He was no barbarian. He was descended from the Welsh princes of both Powys and Gwynedd, and was a well-to-do landed gentleman of about forty-one when circumstances put him at the head of the last Welsh national rising. His lands were on either side of the Berwyn Mountains in North Wales – at Glyndyfrdwy, which was in the valley of the Dee between Llangollen and Corwen, and at Cynllaith Owain not far from Oswestry and nearer the border. He had a house at Carrog in Glyndyfrdwy and a considerable fortified mansion at Sycharth where his ancestors had been Lords Marcher for three or four generations. As a young man he had been trained in law at the courts of Westminster,[4] he had accompanied King Richard II on his campaign of 1385 against the Scots, he had become an esquire to the earl of Arundel, and his allegiance during the English 'troubles' of 1399 had been given to Bolingbroke rather than to Richard, and although there is no concrete evidence there is at least a legend that he had actually accompanied Bolingbroke on his crusading adventures in the Baltic states.

In 1383 Glendower had married the daughter of Sir David Hanmer whose estates were in Flint and who was a highly respected justice of the King's Bench. In 1386 he had given evidence on behalf of Grosvenor in a famous law-suit between the Lords Scrope and Grosvenor, which was concerned with a highly technical matter of heraldic coats-of-arms and had lasted nearly five years.[5] There is nothing in this career to suggest the rebel, but, unfortunately for Henry IV, his accession coincided with a local dispute between Glendower and a neighbour, Reginald Lord Grey of Ruthin, which in its sequel was to set all Wales aflame. The dispute concerned a piece of land near Glendower's Deeside home which was claimed by both parties but which had been forcibly occupied by Lord Grey. A dispute which in more civilized areas would have been reasonably settled in a court of law had become a bloodthirsty struggle of local raid and counter-raid. To complicate such a tense situation Henry IV in the summer of 1400 summoned Glendower to perform his feudal duties and accompany him on an expedition against the Scots.

The royal summons was unfortunately, or unwisely, dispatched through the Lord Grey with whom Glendower was already in dispute, and it either never reached Glendower or it arrived too late. Glendower was branded as a knight who had failed in his feudal duty,[6] and the private war between him and Grey was soon sparked into a rebellion against Henry IV which was to last until the end of the reign. The preliminary skirmishes were sufficiently alarming to cause Henry IV to decide on an immediate expedition to Wales. In September 1400 an English army, which included the young Prince Henry, marched rapidly through North Wales as far as the Menai Straits. Glendower and his men disappeared into the fastnesses of Snowdonia, his estates were confiscated, and within a month the king was back in London under the impression that the disturbances had been settled. He left the prince behind at Chester with instructions to keep his principality in order, and he arranged for a council under the leadership of Lord Henry Percy – 'Hotspur' – to give him all necessary authority, aid and advice.[7]

Henry IV and his councillors seem to have had no idea that a major rebellion was afoot. They thought little of a race described by one chronicler as 'bare-footed churls' and referred to in one of the king's letters as *de petit reputacion*.[8] Prince Henry was quickly to realize that his father and his father's advisers had grossly underestimated the abilities of Glendower and had no conception of the latent power of the Welsh national spirit.

In the Rolls of Parliament for February 21st, 1401, we find that the commons of England were better informed than their lords – they warn the king that he might soon be faced with a full-scale war in Wales.[9] But the Welsh did not 'rise as one man'. Their revolt had its origins in a petty land dispute, and it was some time before Glendower found himself willy-nilly at the head of a national rising. For months Welsh students at both Oxford and Cambridge had been returning to Wales, and Welsh labourers too had been deserting their English masters and streaming back to their homes. By the middle of the year 1401 the whole of North Wales was in open revolt, and Glendower found himself at its head with powerful support from the family of Tudor, whose strength was in Anglesey and whose descendants were one day to supersede both Lancastrians and Yorkists on the English throne.[10]

It was to be a bitter and savage guerrilla warfare for the most part, and the savagery was common to both sides. In the chronicle of Adam of Usk the ravaging of the countryside he knew so well is impartially described. He tells us that after one raid the English carried off a thousand Welsh children of both sexes to be their servants, and that Glendower in a counter-raid not only seized the prince of Wales' baggage train but 'cruelly harried the countryside with fire and sword'.[11] And there is a gruesome story in Walsingham's chronicle which shows that Welsh women in their treatment of defeated Englishmen could be bestial enough to shock even a cynical medieval morality.[12] King Henry and his son were no more merciful than Glendower. A man 'of gentle birth and bountiful' was taken prisoner, and, 'because he was well disposed to the said Owen', he was at the king's command drawn, hanged, beheaded and quartered. The chronicler is at pains to add that this especially savage sentence was at the express command of the king, and that it was carried out in the actual presence of both the king and his eldest son.[13] The 'young Lord Henry' at the age of thirteen was early and forthrightly blooded.

Towards the end of the year 1401 there is evidence that Glendower might have been ready to come to terms with Hotspur and Prince Henry's council, providing that he was granted a free pardon with some guarantees of its genuineness. Hotspur seems to have had a great respect for the Welshman, but his advisers had none – they counselled that Glendower should be murdered during the peace parleys. Hotspur to his credit replied that 'it was not in keeping with his rank to use the oath of fealty as a means of deception',[14] and the negotiations were abandoned. On November 2nd, 1401, Owen Glendower raised his standard – a golden dragon on a white field – outside the walls of Caernarvon Castle: full-scale national rebellion began.[15] At this early stage, Prince Henry was only titular ruler of the principality – he was governed immediately by Hotspur and his council at Chester and remotely but firmly by his father at Westminster. Both the prince and Hotspur were frequently complaining of lack of funds and men, and the garrisons of the English castles were absurdly inadequate – Conway had but fifteen men-at-arms and sixty archers, and Caernarvon only twenty men-at-arms and eighty archers.[16] When Hotspur, angry at inadequate material and financial support, resigned his commission in Wales and departed for his northern estates, Henry IV appointed Hugh le Despenser as his successor, and when Despenser suddenly died the prince's nominations for a successor were ignored. On the other hand, the young prince seems to have respected and liked Hotspur's successor – Despenser's death was 'a great weight of sorrow to my heart'; and there is a charming letter extant which shows how concerned he was for the health of his chancellor at Chester who was suffering grievously from sciatica.[17] But it was not until the spring of 1403 that the prince of Wales took full command – on March 7th on the recommendation of the king's council the prince was declared to be his father's lieutenant on the Marches of Wales.[18]

Meanwhile Glendower had been making progress. He had written letters[19] to the petty kings of Ireland and to the king of Scotland with a view to concerted attacks on the English usurper, and based his appeal to Robert III of Scotland on their common ancestry in Brutus of ancient Rome. The pedigree was fanciful but the threat to England was serious. In January 1402 Glendower defeated the forces of his personal enemy, Lord Grey of Ruthin, and in April in a second local victory he actually captured him. Ransom was granted at the steep price of 10,000 marks, and in paying it Grey was financially ruined.[20] Shortly afterwards a much more important prisoner was led into Glendower's camp – Sir Edmund Mortimer. Mortimer was a great Marcher lord and uncle to the young earl of March, who was the rightful heir to Richard II although at this time a willing hostage at the court of Henry IV. The English king refused to ransom Mortimer on the grounds that he had no money to spare for Welsh rebels, but there were also suggestions that he suspected Mortimer's loyalty. In the event the suggestions were proved correct – Mortimer made his peace with Glendower and married one of his daughters,[21] and we still have the letter in which he announces the decision to his tenantry and asks for their help in fighting the usurper and attempting to establish his own nephew on the English throne.[22] This was a major political achievement by Glendower – henceforth his rebellion had the prestige attached to a formidable baronial opposition in England.

But there were no decisive victories on either side. There were no pitched battles of any consequence, and although Glendower had some narrow personal escapes his guerrilla tactics and his knowledge of the Welsh mountains kept him safe. In August 1402 Henry IV undertook another invasion in force. He divided his expedition into three units – one under himself, one under the earl of Arundel and one under Prince Henry. They never saw their enemies, and the skill of the Welsh mountaineers and the exigencies of Welsh weather were attributed to the black magic of the rebel Glendower.[23] But if the Welsh could not be found neither could the English be defeated – the rebellion smouldered on, and many of the English castles, in spite of inadequate garrisons, still held out. Occasionally, guerrilla tactics were succeeded by siege-warfare, and at the assault on Caernarvon Castle we read, in a letter which asks Henry IV for speedy help, that Glendower was assaulting 'with engines, sowes and ladders of great length' and with the useful assistance of French ships and men.[24]

It was a brutal warfare in which Prince Henry was learning his soldier's trade. In a revealing letter written by him before he was sixteen he displays all the sang-froid of a seasoned campaigner. He reports to the keepers of the Marches after a typical raid that he had burned Glendower's homes at Sycharth and Glyndyfrdwy, and adds casually that he had also captured 'a gentleman of the neighbourhood who offered five hundred pounds for his ransom to preserve his life and to be allowed two weeks for the purpose of raising money, but the offer was refused and he received the death'.[25] The gentleman of Wales foolishly assumed that he could appeal to the established code of chivalrous ransoming – unfortunately for him he was faced with a young prince who was learning to fight a very different kind of war. Yet it is a part answer to later charges of youthful irresponsibility and frivolity that in so harsh a situation Prince Henry never flinched, that he pawned his own jewels[26] to support his troops, and that his soldiering had even earned the unqualified approval of so experienced a campaigner as Hotspur.

Towards the end of the year 1402 Glendower's diplomacy had seemed to be bearing fruit in Scotland where the earl of Douglas, aided by some thirty French knights and other Border lords, had staged a major raid into England. It was halted on the river Till, and at the battle of Homildon Hill the Scots had been heavily defeated by the earl of Northumberland and his eldest son, Hotspur. The details of this foray are of little consequence to a life of Henry V, but it is important to note that the earl of Douglas had been taken prisoner by Hotspur and had quickly become his friend and ally, and that Hotspur's wife was the sister of the Mortimer who had married Glendower's daughter. Henry IV quite correctly, but ill-advisedly, claimed that so important a prisoner as a Douglas should be handed over to the crown. Hotspur refused on the grounds that a ransom for a Douglas might help to recompense him for his heavy and unpaid expenses in North Wales. The dispute added fuel to a fire which had started when Hotspur's father had helped Bolingbroke to his rightful dukedom of Lancaster only to find that he had actually placed him on the English throne. The Percys kept their forces under arms, refused to surrender their valuable prisoners, and Hotspur, when ordered back to Wales in the early summer of the year 1403, prepared for active defiance and armed rebellion. This was a major crisis in the reign of Henry IV in which the prince of Wales was to play an important part.

In July 1403 the Percy family sent its formal challenge to 'Henry of Lancaster', and Hotspur, his uncle Thomas Percy, earl of Worcester and at this time governor of the prince of Wales, and the earl of Douglas marched down from the northern territories to Chester, gathering their forces as they went and arranging for help from Cheshire archers and Welsh auxiliaries when they arrived. This was one moment when Owen Glendower could have struck decisively, and perhaps in helping to unseat Henry IV he might have seated himself on the throne of an independent Wales. Unfortunately for both the Percys and Glendower there was a lack of liaison and communications, which is not surprising when the transport conditions of the fifteenth century are borne in mind. Glendower never joined forces with the Percys.

The complex reasons behind the rebellion of the Percy family are part of the history of King Henry IV, and their details are beyond the purview of this book.[27] It suffices to state that the Percys accused Henry IV of having broken the oath which he swore to them when he landed at Ravenspur to claim only his rightful ducal inheritance; and yet he had gone on to usurp the throne. Added to this public indictment was the private grievance that the Percys' expenses in defending both the Scottish and the Welsh borders had not been properly met by the central exchequer. On the other hand, the Percys had received office and emoluments at Henry IV's accession, and they had certainly been better paid for their work on both the Scottish and Welsh borders than Henry's own son. The truth was that the Percys had been willing to curb a Richard II but they had found it impossible to stomach the sudden and unexpected self-promotion of a Bolingbroke. Now their patience was exhausted, and they pinned their hopes on a rising which might destroy the

46

usurper and restore the throne to a rightful heir – the young earl of March – who could be guided and controlled to their own advantage.

For the young prince of Wales there was only one course of action. His duty was to be at his father's side, and he promptly took what forces he could muster to Shrewsbury to await his father's arrival and face the Percys approaching from Chester. Henry IV was a master of speedy strategy. He was on his way to the north with a fair-sized army to deal with foraying Scots when he first heard news of the Percy rebellion, and he had reached Lichfield on July 20th. He and his men covered forty-five miles in the day, and joined up with his son's forces in Shrewsbury before Hotspur and the Percy army could arrive. It was a superb effort which deserved the overwhelming success which followed.

The encounter at Shrewsbury on July 21st, 1403, was Prince Henry's first major battle. Although there is much dispute as to the numbers engaged on both sides – estimates vary from 40,000 to a more likely 5,000 in each army – there is general agreement that the royal and rebel forces were evenly matched.[28] The rebels were led by Hotspur, his uncle Thomas Percy, earl of Worcester, and the Scottish earl of Douglas, and although there were some Welsh in the rebel ranks there was no Glendower. The royal army was in two divisions – the right commanded by the king and the left by the prince of Wales. Hotspur took up his position on a low hill named Hayteley Field some two miles north of Shrewsbury. His front was protected by a number of ponds, and a strong body of Welsh and Cheshire archers who had the advantage of shooting downhill. In the first hail of rebel arrows the prince of Wales was wounded – he was hit in the face but made light of his injury and continued the fight.[29] Despite the arrows, both royal wings charged up the incline, divided at the ponds, and joined again at the top in a desperate mêlée in which no quarter was given on either side. The fight lasted until nightfall and the casualties on both sides were heavy. It was alleged afterwards that the royalists adopted one subterfuge which shows how the code of chivalrous warfare had degenerated – several of the king's knights were disguised in the royal coat-armour, and the Douglas and Hotspur slew several supposed kings of England before Hotspur himself was slain and the Douglas taken prisoner. It has been estimated that at least 1,600 were killed on both sides, and that twice that number were wounded and never survived the brutal mercies of the local pillagers who worked throughout the night. Hotspur's corpse was dismembered and its head spiked on Micklegate Bar at York. Thomas Percy, who had been captured, was immediately tried and beheaded, and his head was set up on London Bridge. The defeat of the rebels was total and disastrous, and the battle of Shrewsbury, in its origins and in its bitterness, can be seen as the prototype of that later series of savage baronial battles which we now refer to as the Wars of the Roses.[30]

Henry, prince of Wales at sixteen years of age, had distinguished himself in a major battle both as leader and as warrior, and it was not his fault that his opponents at Shrewsbury were mostly his own peers and comrades-in-arms. His prowess and maturity were recognized by the fact that at so young an age he was now given the sole responsibility for carrying on the war against Glendower, and Glendower's prospects, although he had missed the opportunity of Shrewsbury, were still rosy; the prince had a heavy responsibility.

While the prince and his father were dealing with English rebels at Shrewsbury, Glendower was extending his sway into South Wales – he had even captured Carmarthen, and was still receiving useful help from French auxiliaries. In September of this same year, 1403, Henry IV attempted to follow up the victory of Shrewsbury by an extended expedition into South Wales. He reached and reoccupied Carmarthen but was compelled to withdraw 'for he had no money to conduct the expedition',[31] and he soon found himself fully occupied with the problem of how to deal with the earl of Northumberland, who since 1399 had been behind every opposition. The ageing head of the Percy family was still powerful enough to escape a verdict of treason from his peers – they decided to be content with the lesser charge of 'trespass'.[32] The wily old earl retired to his northern castles and the support of his friends beyond the Scottish border. Meanwhile, Glendower after several narrow escapes was still able to blockade such important castles as

Caernarvon, Harlech, Aberystwyth and Cardigan, and was still
supported by French ships and fighting men under one Jean
d'Espagne. Now assuming the title of prince of Wales, Glendower established himself with all the trappings of full sovereignty – he had his great and privy seal, his chancellor and his
ambassadors to foreign courts. 'In the fourth year of our princi-
pate', so ran his proud writ, he summoned a Welsh parliament
to Machynnlleth, or, as the chronicler put it, 'held or counterfeited or made pretence of holding parliaments',[33] and in June
1404 a solemn treaty was sealed at Paris between Glendower's
plenipotentiaries and the king of France for mutual alliance and
joint war against 'Henry of Lancaster'.[34] Throughout the year
1404 the English prince of Wales had the greatest difficulty in
holding Glendower in check. He found himself fighting a skilful
foe he could never see and a rebel leader so confident that he
even raided and harried Herefordshire.

In the early February of 1405 an abortive attempt was made
to link Glendower even more closely with those in England who
favoured the Mortimer succession. The Lady Despenser who
was the sister of the duke of York and the widow of that earl of
Gloucester who had been executed at Bristol after the rout of
Cirencester in 1400, had carried off the two Mortimer children
from Windsor and made for south Wales. The plot was discovered in time, and the children – one of whom was Richard
II's legitimate heir – were recaptured at Cheltenham. Apparently such eminent persons as Thomas Mowbray, the earl
marshal, the duke of York and even the archbishop of Canterbury were suspected of being implicated. The duke was imprisoned, the earl was pardoned and the archbishop was
exonerated.[35] The Despenser plot was a wretched failure – but
it proved that Glendower was not without friends at the English
court.

Glendower's rebellion now achieved its summit – the famous
Tripartite Indenture was agreed in the house of the arch-
deacon of Bangor. It was a 'league and confederation' between
the earl of Northumberland, Sir Edmund Mortimer and Owen
Glendower, and it proposed to divide England and Wales
between the three of them. Glendower was to have all Wales
with a boundary along the river Severn to Worcester, thence to

the source of the Trent and as far as the source of the Mersey 'and so along that river to the sea' – considerably more than modern Wales. The earl of Northumberland was to be given the whole of the north of England, and in addition the midland counties of Leicester, Northampton, Warwick, Norfolk. Mortimer was to have the worst of the bargain – he was to have the 'rest of England' but to sacrifice the ancestral properties of his family in the Marches of Wales.[36]

In the early summer of the year 1405, therefore, Owen Glendower seemed poised for final victory. He had the promise of further aid from France, and it was at this juncture that Henry IV was faced with a second rebellion in the north of England. It linked the archbishop of York with so important a magnate as the earl marshal and a bevy of northern lords whose prime allegiances were to the earl of Northumberland. There is no evidence that Glendower was in direct communication with this revolt, but there is clear evidence that Northumberland – who was a party to the Tripartite Indenture – was the real power behind it. Once again Henry IV showed his speed and his mettle in meeting a formidable rising, and his ruthlessness in dealing out punishment. The northern rebels were met by the earl of Westmorland's forces at Shipton Moor about six miles north-west of York. The rebel leaders, including Richard le Scrope, the archbishop of York, were tempted into a parley. They were immediately taken prisoner, and the king followed up this indecent stratagem with a farce of justice which so shocked his chief justice, Sir William Gascoigne, that he refused to take any part in the subsequent proceedings.

Archbishop Scrope, Thomas Mowbray the earl marshal, and Scrope's nephew Sir William Plumpton, were sentenced to death, and all three were promptly executed just outside the city walls of York. Bootham and Micklegate Bars were once more adorned with traitors' heads, but the archbishop's remains – soon to be revered as the relics of Saint Richard – were buried in York Minster, and the earl of Northumberland again sought refuge over the Scottish border. Once again Glendower had missed the critical moment for a major attack, and the prince of Wales could feel that at least his rear was safe in the care of a father powerful enough to execute even an archbishop, and no doubt he was flattered to hear that the executed earl marshal's castle of Framlingham in Suffolk had been allotted to him as a small reward for his labours in Wales.[37]

Soon after the savage suppression of the Scrope rebellion a lucky accident made King Henry IV even more secure. The Scottish king decided to send his heir James to the friendly court of France, where he could be safer than in a Scotland then on the brink of civil war. The young James's ship was unluckily captured by Norfolk pirates off Flamborough Head.[38] The Norfolk men dutifully sent their rich prize to Henry IV at Westminster, and James of Scotland remained an English prisoner for eighteen years. Meanwhile, Northumberland had found Scotland less safe than he had hoped. Early in the year 1406 he sailed to Wales to the help of Glendower and still in defiance of Henry IV. In June he suffered a defeat at the hands of Lord Powys, and as a last resort he retreated to France. In 1407 he again returned to Scotland and in a last raid he finally met his death at the battle of Bramham Moor in February, 1408.

But revolt in Wales was still stubborn. In August 1405 Glendower had boldly staged a second parliament at Harlech, and this time the promised further aid from France gave the Welsh renewed hope.[39] Something approaching a French armada reached Milford Haven carrying a force of 800 men-at-arms, 600 crossbowmen and 1,200 light armed troops to Glendower's help.[40] Glendower met the French reinforcements with his own considerable army and their joint forces reached as far into England as Woodbury Hill in Worcestershire. It was the nearest Glendower ever came to final victory. Henceforth Prince Henry, though still unable to meet him in pitched battle, was now able to contain him and pin him down.

By the spring of 1406 Glendower's French auxiliaries had tired of an expedition which promised them little in either booty or ransoms, and not even Glendower's agreement to transfer his religious obedience from the Roman pope to the French pope at Avignon was able to keep them in Wales – they retreated in their ships and the promised replacements never materialized. On April 5th, 1406, Prince Henry by the petition of parliament[41] was re-appointed to the full-time supreme command of the war in Wales with the title of Lieutenant of Wales – it was a well-earned tribute to the twenty-year-old prince, and Glendower's star was on the wane. The year before, one of Glendower's sons had been captured by Lord Talbot who had won a minor battle at Grosmont near Hereford. Now, in a fight near Usk, Glendower's other son Griffith was captured and his brother Tudor killed by Prince Henry.[42] In 1407 Aberystwyth was again lost to Glendower, but in the same year the English parliament held at Gloucester again recognized the prince's merits by a special vote of thanks. The Welsh war continued with summer victories for the English and winter recoveries by the Welsh.

There is a curious entry in the Rolls of Parliament for October 1407.[43] For long an Englishman of the Welsh Marches had been allowed to escape the death penalty for felonies by transferring his allegiance to another lord and paying an annual fine of fourpence. It was a special dispensation to keep up a body of able and ruthless fighting men in an area where the English badly needed them. This privilege was now rescinded. Where Prince Henry's writ ran he meant it to be obeyed to the letter – it was a first sign of that passion for justice which was soon to impress a wider audience.

In the years 1408 and 1409 the Welsh war saw Glendower on the defensive. At the siege of Harlech Sir Edmund Mortimer's death preceded its final surrender and the loss of most of Glendower's remaining family.[44] The saga of the last native prince of Wales fades into the Welsh mists – Glendower is heard of spasmodically until 1413, but after that he is a legend and not a menace. His decline can be attributed to bad luck and bad communications with powerful allies. He was never decisively defeated, and he never surrendered. He was never a mere rebel – his statesmanship envisaged an archbishopric at St David's and two Welsh universities, and in spite of the sneers of English chroniclers he had held two Welsh parliaments and treated with the kings of Scotland and France on equal terms. No one knows exactly when Glendower died or where he was buried, but he lives in the songs of the Welsh bards and in the traditions of his native land. He probably lived until 1415[45] – a lonely tragic old man who had outlived his large family and who was still too proud to accept the free pardon which Prince Henry was to offer him when he became king. It is no small tribute to the young English prince who thwarted but never defeated him, that with so much in Glendower's favour the cause of Welsh independence had by the end of the reign of Henry IV failed for ever.

Prince Henry had been fighting with underpaid and inadequate forces against an older and experienced national hero who had the advantages of what strategists term 'interior lines' and of a difficult terrain which the rebels knew well. In the early stages of the war the prince had had the friendly advice and guidance of a Hotspur who was an able and seasoned campaigner. In the later stages, especially before the castles of Aberystwyth and Harlech in 1408, he had learned for himself the new craft of siege-work which was to stand him in such good stead in later years. Glendower's significance to a history of Henry V is that his Welsh rebellion converted an inexperienced youth into a fully qualified general steeled in the hardest of guerrilla fighting and skilled in all the stratagems and mechanics of medieval siegecraft.

Chapter 4

PRINCE IN COUNCIL

THE HISTORY of the last five years of the reign of Henry IV is bewildering. The king himself was a sick man leaning on such elder councillors as Arundel, archbishop of Canterbury. The prince, fresh from Welsh successes and supported by the brood of the Beauforts, was eager to play a full part in affairs of state. Henry IV's incapacities were his eldest son's opportunities, and the prince seized them avidly. Whether he went too far and seriously contemplated supplanting his ailing father cannot be proved, but that father and son were frequently at loggerheads cannot be doubted.

Early in the year 1408 Henry IV suffered a severe epileptic fit at Mortlake – it was the first of many, and from then until his death in 1413 he was subject to bouts of illness which frequently left him totally incapacitated. The superstitious alleged that the mysterious disease which finally killed him was a leprosy inflicted upon him by divine justice for beheading an archbishop. Modern medical opinion has doubted this diagnosis and preferred to suggest that some form of venereal disease, either inherited (allegedly) from his father John of Gaunt or contracted during his Baltic campaigns, was responsible.[1] But these are hazardous and prejudiced guesses. By the end of the year 1408 the prince could feel that he had taken the measure of Glendower and that his responsibilities in Wales were less weighty, and earlier in the same year his father had finally disposed of all baronial opposition by the defeat and death of the earl of Northumberland on Bramham Moor. The king was now forty-two years of age and old before his time. The prince was twenty-one, a successful soldier now, without a serious war to wage, eager to prove his prowess further and very conscious of the fact that he was heir to the throne, and, when his father was ill, already head of the state. It was a difficult situation for both. Henry IV was only spasmodically *hors de combat* and had no intention of surrendering any part of his regality.[2] The prince therefore had to reconcile brief periods of authority with longer periods of acquiescence – his father was always a disciplinarian. If the facts of life made the prince now virtual regent and now subservient councillor it is obvious that the suspicion would arise that he might prefer to put an end to such a dual role and supersede his father forthwith. To support this suspicion there is good evidence to show that father and son were in dispute not only in home affairs but in matters of foreign policy, and to clarify these confusing last years of Henry IV it is necessary first to consider the equally confusing affairs of France in some detail . . .

Shortly after Richard of Bordeaux had ascended the English throne as a boy of eleven, Charles VI of Valois had ascended the French throne as a boy of twelve. Both kings suffered from the jealousies of their uncles.[3] Charles VI had three, the most important of whom was Philip the Bold, duke of Burgundy. Charles's minority was closely similar to the minority of Richard II in England. In court circles in both countries there was an uneasy rivalry between the king's uncles, and the English Peasants' Revolt was paralleled by the revolts of La Harelle at Rouen, of the Maillotins in Paris and of Philip van Artevelde in Flanders. The French revolts were mercilessly suppressed, and the Flemish revolt expired on the disastrous field of Roosebeke in 1383. The English revolt was circumvented by the courage of a boy king and the wise mercy of his advisers. But whereas Richard II grew up to an impressive stature which only just failed to overcome baronial opposition, Charles VI was smitten in 1393 by a disastrous stroke of madness which recurred with increasing frequency and left the throne at the mercy of rival factions until his death. When Charles VI was 'in his malady' it was never clear who had the right to take over his royal responsibilities. On the one hand was his brother Louis, duke of Orléans, and on the other was his uncle Philip the Bold, duke of Burgundy – each contending for the headship of the state. Louis was, at the beginning of the reign of Henry IV, a young man of twenty-eight while Philip was a magnificent veteran of fifty-eight. In 1404 Philip the Bold died and handed over to his son John the Fearless an appanage which stretched from the Scheldt and the Ardennes to the Saône and the Jura. Louis of Orléans was suspected of a criminal liaison with Charles VI's queen which, when the king was ill, gave him a certain advantage. John the Fearless, however, had the greater power, although his prestige had never fully recovered from the fact that in 1396 he had been captured by the Turks at the battle of Nicopolis. He was a man of no scruples, and in 1407 he encompassed the sordid murder of his rival Louis near the Porte Barbette in Paris. It was the first tragic chapter in a tale of murderous rivalry which was to ruin France for a generation.

Charles of Orléans, son of the assassinated Louis, had been married at the age of fifteen to Isabella, the young widow of England's Richard II. In 1409 Isabella died and Charles was quickly married to Bonne, the daughter of Bernard VII the great count of Armagnac. The marriage brought the house of Orléans the alliance of one of the greatest lords in France and the support of many Gascon nobles – henceforth the followers of Orléans were to be known as Armagnacs. The internal history of France in the early fifteenth century is the history of the rivalry between Charles, duke of Orléans and leader of the Armagnacs, a worthy prince and an esteemed minor poet, and John the Fearless, duke of Burgundy and leader of the Burgundians, a noble of meaner mould and a master of double-dealing. When the king was sane there was little difficulty – he was able and astute – but when he was not sane the rival appanages were prepared for civil war and anxious to find what support they could from neighbouring powers.

Henry IV of England favoured a diplomacy which supported the Armagnacs. His son favoured the Burgundians. Both were fishing in troubled waters, and seeing in the difficulties of France an opportunity for profitable intervention. Behind the prince of Wales was the formidable phalanx of the Beaufort family. By letters patent in 1407 the legitimization of the Beauforts by Richard II had been confirmed, but Henry IV was careful to add a proviso that they were debarred from any possibility of succeeding to the throne. The Beaufort family therefore owed everything in the first place to Richard II and secondly to Henry IV, but their ambitions though limited were now linked indissolubly with the fortunes of the house of Lancaster. One and all they were loyal to the Henrys. As with so many illegitimate children they were a brilliant progeny. The eldest Beaufort was John, earl of Somerset, who had survived the fall of Richard II to become captain of Calais, lieutenant of South Wales and deputy constable of England under Henry IV. He died in 1410. The second Beaufort, and the most distinguished, was Henry. When only twenty-one he had been made bishop of Lincoln by Richard II, he had been appointed tutor to Prince Henry by Henry IV, in 1404 he had succeeded to the bishopric of Winchester, and he was destined to outlive his royal pupil and to achieve a cardinal's hat in the reign of Henry VI. The third Beaufort was Thomas, duke of Exeter, whose life as admiral and general though less distinguished was not less devoted and loyal to the fortunes of Prince Henry. The family of Beaufort, specifically debarred from the throne, was never a threat to its security, but it was perhaps natural that in any dispute between king and prince they were consistently on the side of the prince who was their contemporary.

Opposed to the Beauforts and the prince was the powerful influence of Thomas Arundel, archbishop of Canterbury. He had accompanied Bolingbroke into exile after the Lists of Coventry, and he had returned to crown him Henry IV of England. But he now represented an older generation. In 1408 he was fifty-five years old – an elder statesman in those days – whereas Henry Beaufort, bishop of Winchester was in his early thirties and therefore in the prime of life. It was only to be expected that, while the Beauforts aligned themselves with the young prince of Wales, Archbishop Arundel sided with the rapidly ageing father.

The troubles of France had tragic consequences not only for France but for England. The diplomacy of Richard II had held the promise of a long and fruitful peace between the two countries, but the intermittent madness of Charles VI, the jealousies of his appanages, and the fact that England was

vitally interested both in the looms of Flanders and the vine-
yards of Bordeaux created a complicated situation which found
France divided and England tempted to aggressions which were
beyond her power. The Burgundian alliance could offer England
the safety and consolidation of the great bridgehead of Calais
and its links with the looms of Flanders. The Armagnacs could
offer the safety and consolidation of Gascony as an English
appanage and the security of its profitable wine trade. Both
could offer an English king a free entry into the heart of France
if ever an English king were disposed to revive the claims of
Edward III and attempt to make the lilies of France in his
escutcheon more than meaningless symbols. Neither Henry IV
nor his son sufficiently realized that both Burgundians and
Armagnacs were bribing England not to conquer France but to
help one or other party to obtain an overlordship of France
which would finally not need English support and might
eventually recapture both the English bridgeheads – at Calais
and at Bordeaux – and leave all France in the undisputed power
of either an Armagnac or a Burgundian.

During the reign of Henry IV the 'way of marriage' and
diplomacy was preferred to the way of invasion and war – the
king of England was too much involved in consolidating his
own position against internal rebellion to afford the luxury of
major expeditions across the Channel. In July 1411, John the
Fearless in asking aid from Henry IV proposed to give his
daughter Anne in marriage to the prince of Wales. The
Armagnacs countered in 1412 with a guarantee that Aquitaine,
Anjou and Angoulême should be for ever English. And as early
as 1406 a sane Charles VI of France had suggested that his
daughter Katherine should be affianced to England's heir.[4]
But the prince of Wales was by now no pawn in the diplomatic
game of chess. On March 18th, 1410, he had been appointed
captain of Calais for twelve years – one of the most important
of crown appointments – and when his father was ill he was to
all intents and purposes regent, and when his father was well
he was still the most powerful influence in the king's council.
In addition he was now warden of the Cinque Ports and constable of Dover, and at his London home named Coldharbour

in Eastcheap, 'a right fair and stately house', he held his own court and even on occasion presided over the royal council.[5]

At the end of the year 1409 the ascendancy of Archbishop Arundel had been abruptly ended. There is an annoying lack of conciliar records for this period but it is clear that the Beaufort faction secured the dismissal of Arundel from the chancery and the appointment of Thomas Beaufort, duke of Exeter in his place. The new council was composed of most of the prince's friends. It soon included the young earl of Arundel, who had quarrelled with the old archbishop over their respective lands in Sussex and was a firm friend of the prince, and Chichele, bishop of St David's, who was to be Henry's friend for life. This Beaufort council, with the prince of Wales as its sponsor, virtually governed England for over a year. It was a hard-working body of young aristocrats, and its attempts to reform and recondition the precarious national finances were sincere.

In September 1411, when the prince was president of the Council on account of his father's illness, an expedition was sanctioned to help the duke of Burgundy in his civil war against the Armagnacs. It was a small excursion of a mere 1,200 men led by the prince's friend the earl of Arundel. It sailed from Dover to Sluys and thence marched to Paris. Among the knights who accompanied the expedition appears the name of Sir John Oldcastle, a close friend of the prince. In its small way this expedition was a great success and a significant portent. Arundel reached Paris, and in a sharp encounter at St Cloud his English force distinguished itself, secured Paris for Burgundy, and drove the Armagnacs beyond the Loire.[6] If a small English force could achieve so much, a more impressive array might achieve much more – it was a lesson the prince was to remember. By the end of the year the prince's first small overseas venture had been crowned with surprising success, and Arundel and his men returned safely to England handsomely rewarded by Burgundy for their help.

Meanwhile the prince's father had recovered from another bout of illness and the brief reign of the prince's Beaufort council was at an end. In October, six knights were arrested by the king on an unnamed charge and one of them was steward to the prince's household. The prince left London on a progress through the country by which he appeared to be seeking wider support, and the quarrel between father and son looked ominous. The old archbishop was recalled to the chancery for the last time, and the prince and the Beauforts were excluded from the council until the end of the reign.[7]

The way of Burgundy was now abandoned for the way of Armagnac, and, when the Armagnacs offered Aquitaine in full sovereignty as part of a bribe, King Henry promptly accepted and sent an expedition of 1,000 men-at-arms and 3,000 archers under the command of his second son Thomas, now duke of Clarence, to Normandy. It won trifling successes in the Cotentin but was in essence a piratical raid rather than a planned invasion. The English harried, slaughtered, and pillaged, but before they could achieve anything of note found themselves in an absurd situation – the Armagnacs had made peace with the Burgundians behind their backs and were only too anxious to get rid of their allies as soon as possible. Clarence and his men were duly paid off.[8]

The Clarence expedition was undoubtedly against the wishes and policy of the prince, and it reflected no credit on his father. There was a large body in the council and all the Beaufort influence in favour of the prince, and the commons were the prince's enthusiastic supporters. On the other hand, the king could reasonably complain that the Arundel expedition should never have been dispatched without his approval. Clearly at this period there was ill-feeling and jealousy between father and son – had the king grounds for graver suspicions?

Fourteen years later Bishop Beaufort was defending himself before parliament, and added the significant passage 'furthermore I am noysed how that I should have stirred the king that last died, the time also that he was prince, to have taken the governance of this realm and the crown upon him, leaving his father the same time being king'.[9] His refutation was accepted, but in a contemporary English chronicle there is evidence that there was indeed a movement which was seriously considering a forced abdication of Henry IV in favour of his eldest son.[10] If the French chronicler Monstrelet is to be believed, Bishop Beaufort had been sent to Paris as early as 1406 to negotiate a treaty with the French which was to be cemented by the marriage of Prince Henry to Isabella, the widow of Richard II, and that Henry IV 'in consideration of this match would instantly after its consummation lay down his crown and invest his son with the government of the kingdom'.[11] The negotiations failed, but even if the French account is wrongly dated it is evidence of what was mooted if not promulgated. In the parliament of November 1411 at Westminster the Rolls reveal that the sick king was unable to function and he appointed Thomas Beaufort as his deputy.[12] Prince Henry's own acts at this time were at least extremely indiscreet. He was busy raising armed support in the northern midlands, and his excuse was that he was raising forces to help his father's expedition to aid the Armagnacs. In June 1412 the prince issued a public statement refuting evil rumours, and marched to London 'with much people of lords and gentles' to take up his residence at the inn of the bishop of London. The capital was in a ferment, and the prince besought his father to punish his slanderers. The king seems to have tempered the warmth of reconciliation with the cold advice that the slanderers could await the judgement of their peers in parliament.[13]

While the Armagnac expedition was away, the prince again acted rashly. On September 25th, he arrived at the council at Westminster 'with a huge people' to face a charge that he had misappropriated the wages of his Calais garrison. His men were left in Westminster Hall while the prince went on alone and, in a curious disguise, forced his way into the royal presence.[14] After an emotional scene father and son embraced in friendship and forgiveness, and at the subsequent inquiry by the council the prince was fully exonerated from the charges of peculation.

If Prince Henry and his father did not see fully eye to eye in matters of diplomacy they were at least at one in matters of religion. Both were anxious to see the Schism ended, and both were entirely orthodox in their attitude to Lollardy. The efforts of Henry IV to end the Schism by way of a great council of the Church were sincere if unsuccessful. They were never opposed by the prince, and, in his turn, he was to try similar methods as king and achieve success. The problem of Lollardy was more obscure. During the reign of Richard II the followers of Wyclif had penetrated deep into the university of Oxford and even into the royal court. Wyclif himself, as master of Balliol, as philosopher in his own right, and as political supporter of John of Gaunt, had laid the foundations of a movement which in its mildest forms demanded the reform of the church and the expropriation of some of its surplus wealth, and in its most zealous forms did not stop short of the full 'Protestant' programme which a century later was to be nailed by Luther to the door of Wittenburg Cathedral, and which was soon to fortify John Hus in his martyrdom and lend ammunition to the batteries of Bohemian Ziska. But the English Wycliffites, or Lollards, were less fanatical than their European followers – they seem for the most part to have had a typically English genius for making the best of several worlds. Philosophy might point out the absurdities of the Catholic doctrine of transsubstantiation, but Wyclif could still die in peace in the bosom of the Church at Lutterworth, and very few of his followers were of the stuff of which martyrs are made. On the other hand, there were some obstinate characters who never compromised, and one of these, Sir John Oldcastle, was a distinguished knight, an experienced campaigner and a personal friend of Prince Henry. And here there is a puzzling discrepancy. Was Prince Henry a bigoted persecutor of the heretic, or was he a tolerant and enlightened prince whose heart was never in persecution save when heresy became treason? To complicate the answer it must be noted that Archbishop Arundel was a fanatic who would have stopped at nothing to root out what he considered abominable heresy, who had prompted Henry IV to sanction the statute *de haeretico comburendo* of 1401,[15] and who, with shrewd logic, determined to attack Lollardy at its source – in the university of Oxford. It was in this last policy that he met with a good deal of opposition. The Oxford heirs of Wyclif combined a discreet sympathy for his beliefs with a flaming resentment against any interference with their internal affairs and that freedom of thought which is the lifeblood of any true university. They were lucky in having in Henry Beaufort a powerful support which was not so much religious as political.

The struggle for political power between the Beauforts and the Arundel faction became interwoven with university politics and religious dogmas. The Beauforts were no Lollards but they were no friends of old Archbishop Arundel, and Prince Henry – even if he was never at The Queen's College, Oxford – was most certainly the friend and contemporary of Henry Beaufort, and never drawn by either affection or self-interest to the side of Archbishop Arundel. The brow beating of the university by Arundel[16] at least achieved the suppression of the Lollard influence, but, thanks to the opposition of Henry Beaufort supported by the prince, it did not permanently injure the university's freedom. Both the Beauforts and the prince were happy to acquiesce in an official policy which kept England orthodox, but it was a curiously English solution which allowed Lollardy to make progress underground, and, although it sanctioned and used the stake, stopped short of the horrors of an inquisition.

There had been one incident of religious persecution which displays the character of Prince Henry and the characters of his biographers – both medieval and modern – in a macabre light. In January 1409 a certain tailor of Evesham named John Badby had been found guilty of Lollard heresy in the bishop's court at Worcester. The sentence had been confirmed by convocation in London. Badby was orthodox in most things save that, as other Lollards always held, he could not accept the orthodox doctrine of trans-substantiation – if it were true, he said, the priest's blessing of the sacrament would make 20,000 gods in England at every Mass. The ecclesiastics having found Badby guilty – as they were bound to do – he was handed over to the secular authority for execution, because the Church could never soil itself with the blood of a human being. By Henry IV's statute Badby was condemned to the stake. The brutal procedure of burning had not yet been codified, and in Badby's case the civil authorities used a cask into which the prisoner was bound. The cask was then set on a pyre and the fire lit in the presence of Prince Henry. As the flames began to scorch him, Badby called out in anguish for mercy. The prince ordered the fire to be raked aside, exhorted Badby to recant, and offered him a pension if he would do so. Badby refused the bribe, and the prince forthwith ordered the fire to be rekindled and watched Badby burned to ashes.[17]

Both contemporary and modern apologists have retold the story to illustrate Prince Henry's abounding mercy. To the author of this book it is a story which reveals a mind which was truly medieval and in that sense shocking to most modern views. There was an admirable instinct for mercy, but there was a hard logic which, when a good bargain was refused, let the law take its course. If Prince Henry could order the flames to be withdrawn once, he could have ordered them to be withdrawn for good. Throughout his adult life he was to show himself a rigid upholder of the law, and in a lawless age that was a virtue. In authorizing the double agony of Badby he tarnished the legend of the *preux chevalier*, but he displayed the truly medieval and orthodox prince – the heretic must be destroyed, and justice is more important than sentimentality. Prince Henry had been born and bred a soldier, he had a veritable passion for justice, and he had that one-sided logic which never flinched from the direst consequences of justice.

At the end of the year 1412 it was clear that it would not be long before Prince Henry succeeded to the throne. In December the king was unconscious for a period, but recovered enough to be able to celebrate Christmas at Eltham palace. On March 20th, 1413, another seizure proved fatal, and Henry IV breathed his last in the Jerusalem chamber of Westminster Abbey.[18]

It only needs a glance at the bloated face of Henry IV's alabaster effigy in Canterbury Cathedral to realize that when he died at the age of forty-six he was a poor relic of the dynamic baron who had captivated the Londoners in the crisis of 1399 and dared to seize a throne. It is not to be wondered at that the usurper who had triumphed over invasion from Scotland, a major rebellion in Wales and three internal revolts led by senior nobility and even an archbishop, should be a tired and exhausted man when he finally surrendered his throne apparently safe and secure to his eldest son. No one has ever suggested that Henry IV was a popular king – although as duke of Hereford he was the darling of the capital – and none of his contemporaries, least of all his children, ever suggested he was lovable. But of the ability of Henry IV there is no doubt, of his bravery and

1a. Prince Henry being presented by Hoccleve (1370–1450) with his 'works', probably 'The Regiment of Princes' which was dedicated to Henry. There is no record that this incident actually took place.

1b. Prince Henry being knighted by Richard II during the second Irish campaign of 1399. This illumination is from the manuscript of Jean Creton's verse description of Richard, written about 1401.

2. Henry IV and his wife Joanna of Navarre.

resourcefulness in the face of adversity and ill health there is no question, and of his ruthless shrewdness both in warfare and in statecraft there is ample witness.

Prince Henry at his father's death was but twenty-five years old. His youth had been spent for the most part in hard campaigning in a warfare never bridled by the niceties of chivalry – the Welsh were beneath any consideration. His early manhood had taught him much of the intrigues of politics, something of the complications of continental diplomacy, and a good deal of the complexities which resulted from a universal Church which was hopelessly divided and an internal religious dispute which had both doctrinal and political implications. He had seen his father surprisingly usurp a throne, and, in spite of appalling difficulties, he had received from him a throne which seemed reasonably secure. Within fourteen years a new dynasty had been established which commanded the allegiance of most of England and the respect of continental powers – Prince Henry owed much to his stricken father.

Chapter 5

INTERVAL FOR
LEGENDS

To the Tudors Henry V was England's hero king, and it is one of the distinctions of a hero that his reputation depends on a mixture of legend and of fact. The legends associated with King Henry V have been immortalized by the pen of Shakespeare, and, as they may therefore outlive the facts of history, and as behind most legends there is often a substratum of truth, they deserve scrutiny.

There are four groups of these legends. First, those associated with the relationship between Prince Henry and his father. Second, those which portray the prince as the friend and comrade-in-vice of the lowest reprobates. Third, those which assert that as prince he was in trouble with the law. Fourth, those which give us the picture of a dissolute prince suddenly converted at his accession to the throne into an almost lily-white prig.

That Prince Henry and his father did not always see eye to eye has been already established, but Shakespeare went further. We are led to believe that Prince Henry and Hotspur were rivals of the same age, that Henry IV frequently had occasion to contrast the virtues of Hotspur with the shortcomings of his own eldest son, and that Prince Henry slew Hotspur in single combat on the field of Shrewsbury. The facts are that Hotspur was at least twenty years older than the prince, that Henry showed nothing but the greatest respect for the seasoned general who was his tutor and governor in the early Welsh campaigns and who taught him so much, and that if the prince of Wales had indeed slain his experienced elder at Shrewsbury it would surely have found a place in contemporary annals

66

which described the battle in great detail. There is no mention of the story before Tudor times. And at the end of Shakespeare's second play of Henry IV there is the great scene when the prince, thinking his father dead, puts the crown on his own head and takes it away. Again, contemporary annals are naturally silent, and the Elizabethan chronicler Hall, from whom Shakespeare borrowed, had improved upon a very similar story which had been told by the Burgundian chronicler Monstrelet but which unfortunately also has no warranty.[1] The 'crown' scene is magnificent fiction but is nevertheless close to the heart of the matter – during the last few years of the reign of Henry IV his eldest son must frequently have considered how the crown of England would fit him.

That Prince Henry kept low company can neither be proved nor disproved, but it can safely be said that Shakespeare's Falstaff and Bardolph are unknown to history. There was a Sir John Fastolf who lived between 1378 and 1459, but he was an able soldier, later a privy councillor, and a wealthy if somewhat miserly country gentleman who carried on a considerable correspondence with his verbose and litigious, neighbours, the Pastons of Norfolk.[2] He bears not the slightest resemblance to the roistering Falstaff. As to the disreputable Bardolph, who in Shakespeare's play of Henry V is hanged for stealing from a church on the march to Agincourt, again there is no warranty in history save that an unnamed soldier was indeed hung for such a crime, and that there was a Sir William Bardolph who was a loyal knight and a Sir Thomas Bardolph, who was not so loyal and died from wounds received when fighting for Northumberland's rebels at Bramham Moor. Shakespeare appears to have borrowed from a previous play by an unknown author which was entitled *The Famous Victories of Henry the Fifth*, and in it the boon companion of the prince was Sir John Oldcastle. This was nearer the truth – Oldcastle was certainly a friend of the prince but his character as a knight, and later as a Lollard martyr, is far removed from the Shakespearian picture of the bawdy reveller at the Boar's Head tavern in Eastcheap.[3]

In 1531 Sir Thomas Elyot first published his famous *Boke named the Gouernour*, and in it is the first reference to the hallowed legend that the prince in defence of one of his servants defied the chief justice and threatened him with violence and that the chief justice admonished the prince and committed him to the prison of the King's Bench. The story was repeated in the chronicle of Robert Redmayne which was written about 1540,[4] and in a chronicle of Coventry which was composed at the end of the seventeenth century it is stated that the prince was arrested by the mayor of Coventry in the year 1412. These stories have been carefully examined in our own day by a distinguished lawyer, who, having inspected the Rolls and Year Books of the time, came to the firm conclusion that there is no record of any such committal of the prince, and it is highly unlikely that so grave a matter would not have been recorded. It is possible that the origin of this particular legend is in a contemporary chronicle of London which describes a riot in Eastcheap in which Prince Henry's brothers Thomas and John were involved in a 'hurling' with the London citizens. The Elizabethan recorder John Stowe – who wrote about 1580 – repeats this story, and the settling of a riot may well have involved a magistrate, and Prince Henry *may* have been involved although the record does not say so. Shakespeare improved on the legend by describing how, when the prince became king, he rewarded the affronted chief justice – Sir William Gascoyne – by continuing him in office. In fact, King Henry V retired him. Once more history spoils a dramatic fiction.[5]

Lastly, we have the much better authenticated story that, as Prince Henry mounted the throne, he turned his back on his disreputable past and became a new man renowned for his purity and piety.

Elmham's life of Henry V was probably written about 1445, and, having known and revered his king, the author says unequivocally that the prince 'fervently followed the service of Venus as well as of Mars; as a young man he burned with her torches, and other insolences accompanied the years of his untamed youth'.[6] Livius, who was an Italian who served in the household of Henry's youngest brother Humphrey, duke of Gloucester, wrote his life of Henry V not earlier but not much later than 1437. He reports that the young prince 'exercised meanly the feats of Venus and of Mars and other pastimes of youth so long as his father lived'.[7] Walsingham, the monk historian of St Albans, was a truly contemporary witness. In both versions of his great chronicle he tells us that on his accession the prince 'was changed into a different man', and we can therefore safely infer that the 'honesty, modesty and seriousness of purpose' which he attributed to the new king were in violent contrast to the failings of the prince.[8] In the chronicle of the Brut there is a significant addition which dates from about 1475. It repeats that Henry as prince had 'intended greatly to ryot' and 'drew to wylde company' but that four members of his household disapproved and were therefore hated by him. At his accession he summoned his whole household to his presence, dismissed his favourites, having 'rewardyd them richely with gold and sylver and othyr jewels' and, having urged them to mend their ways, he only retained in his honourable service the four whom he had previously hated and now 'lovyd aftyrward best'. It adds that he made them great lords, and called in the help of Lady Katherine Swynford – 'a welgoverned woman who kept the most worshipful housold and the best rewlyd that was within the londe' – to reorganize his own household with gentlemen 'of sad governaunce'.[9] Such a wealth of evidence cannot be discounted or ignored. Fighting in Wales during the summer was no easy assignment, and during the winter months, when medieval soldiering at home and abroad was usually abandoned, it is not surprising if an heir to the throne sought relaxation in sowing his wild oats in London. That they were wilder than most can legitimately be inferred from the fact that contemporary evidence takes the trouble to comment. A twentieth century which has studied its ancient history, and known so many monarchs whose private lives as princes have not been conspicuous for their moral orthodoxy, cannot be surprised at the alleged youthful peccadilloes of a medieval Henry of Monmouth. Neither is conversion-on-accession astonishing. Heirs to thrones have opportunities without responsibilities, and when at last responsibilities are thrust upon them they can shoulder them with a seriousness of purpose which is all the more serious because they have already lived through their youthful and natural frivolities.

The legends – part authenticated and part pure fiction – have provided us with some of Shakespeare's greatest speeches and at least one great dramatic scene. For these we must be duly grateful, but it is possible that even Shakespeare misjudged his audiences in repeating a fiction which portrays his hero in his treatment of old friends – however unworthy – as both mean and priggish. It may have been a mistake to assume that poachers turned gamekeepers are admired or that ordinary mortals sympathize with the roisterer who turns his back on boon companions when duty summons him to magistracy. The poet's version of the young Henry V needs much correction, and in considering all the legends which have clustered round the youth of 'Prince Hal' it must in fairness be remembered that as a soldier he was a pattern of devotion to duty and as a counsellor – and sometimes as president of the council – his work was manifestly both serious and diligent.[10]

If the verdict of history on Prince Henry's salad days must be that he was probably not a saint it must also record a devotion to his princely duties which likewise cannot be doubted.

Chapter 6

POLITICS AND
LOLLARDY

O N TUESDAY, MARCH 21st, 1413, Henry of Monmouth
at the age of twenty-five succeeded to his father's throne
as King Henry the Fifth. On the same night he sought
out a recluse of the abbey at Westminster and was closeted with
him in his cell for several hours.[1] It was an immediate sign of
that seriousness of purpose and devotion to strictest religious
observance which to many observers was so strangely contrasted
with the wayward high spirits of his youth.

The death of the old king cancelled all existing royal appointments, and it was the new king's urgent first duty to name new
officials so that the government of the realm might continue
smoothly. It is not surprising that Henry V lost no time in
relegating his father's chancellor, Thomas Arundel, archbishop
of Canterbury, and substituting his own uncle and supporter
Henry Beaufort, bishop of Winchester. But the Arundels were
not all out of favour – the archbishop's nephew Thomas, earl of
Arundel, who had led the expedition to St Cloud, was appointed
to the important office of treasurer. The chief justice, Sir
William Gascoyne, was superseded by Sir William Hankeford,
but he was not disgraced – he was an old man of sixty-three
ready for retirement, and from time to time he was to be recalled by the new king for special commissions and inquiries.
In more personal affairs, Henry obeyed the dying wishes of his
father; he appointed the learned and highly orthodox Carmelite
Stephen Patrington as one of his personal confessors, and was
soon to promote him to the bishopric of St David's.

On April 9th, 1413, the coronation in all its medieval symbolism and splendour took place in Westminster Abbey, and we

are fortunate in having several descriptions of the personal attributes of the new monarch. A Benedictine monk of Westminster who knew him well at this time gives us a detailed record which, even allowing for a forgivable flattery, nevertheless has the stamp of truth. Henry's head was round rather than long, and his forehead was broad – as a good phrenologist the reporter claims that these were signs of wisdom and intelligence. His hair was thick, smooth and brown; his nose straight and his face oblong; his complexion was fresh if not a trifle florid; his eyes were bright and brown, dovelike when unmoved but fierce as a lion when roused; his teeth were good, even and white as snow; his chin was cleft and his neck 'fair and of a becoming thickness'; his cheeks were rosy and his lips healthily red. Of his physical strength there was now no question – the illnesses of his younger days were forgotten in limbs that were well-formed and bones and sinews that were firm and well-knit. Several chroniclers bear witness to his athletic achievements – he excelled in jumping and running and was an excellent shot. A great stag which fell to his crossbow was presented to his friends at Westminster Abbey, and another chronicler – who was even more of a flatterer – tells us that Henry could even start a deer from a thicket and run it to death, and that he wore his heavy armour 'as though it were a light cloak'. Even making due allowances for observers who later worshipped at the shrine of the victor of Agincourt there is no reason to doubt that when King Henry V ascended the throne he was more than normally handsome and athletically well above the average.[2]

Amid the general rejoicing and popular acclaim the serious demeanour of the new king was noticeable, and at the customary gargantuan coronation banquet it was seen that he ate almost nothing and seemed weighted down by the solemnity of the occasion and the sacredness of his new vows. And the elements conspired with his mood – there was an unusually heavy snowstorm to greet the coronation procession and give soothsayers opportunity to interpret omens – it portended peace after storm or stark and rigid governance; the superstitious could take their choice. Gay Prince Hal was now a very serious and dedicated Henry V.[3]

There is no suggestion in the English chroniclers that the accession of Henry V was either disputed or queried. On the other hand, the French chroniclers suggest that there was still an underground movement of loyalty to the previous dynasty. The monk of St Denis reports from an eye-witness at the coronation that there were many there who still maintained that the crown should have been placed on the head of the young earl of March, who, by the laws of strict heredity, certainly had a far better claim to the throne – if he had wished to pursue it – than Henry of Monmouth.[4] March was the grandson of Philippa, the daughter of Lionel, *third* son of Edward III; whereas Henry V was the grandson of John of Gaunt, *fourth* son of Edward III. Moreover, if the chroniclers of England were silent, the Patent Rolls of the crown reveal that just before the death of Henry IV a yeoman named John Whitelock, supported by a Scottish knight and two chaplains, had been publicizing their conviction that Richard II was still alive. They had been hunted down and found sanctuary in the abbey at Westminster. But, while Henry V's first parliament was sitting, a manifesto from White-lock was mysteriously posted on the abbey doors and in other places in London. It proclaimed that Richard II was still 'in the warde and kepying of the duke of Albany' in Scotland. Meanwhile Whitelock had surrendered his sanctuary. He was duly tried and committed to the Tower, but later escaped; it is an obscure but revealing story.[5]

The new king, however, showed no signs of doubting his security. His first act was to declare an amnesty, and this immediately released young March from the strict but comfortable 'house arrest' to which the suspicious Henry IV had confined him. Henry V went further – he restored him to all his hereditary estates, and was rewarded by a loyalty which outlived him: March was to die of the plague as a devoted and energetic Lancastrian governor of Ireland in 1424. A consistent policy of appeasement can also be seen in the restoration to his rightful position of John Mowbray, brother to the earl marshal who had been executed after the Scrope rebellion, and in the fact that the executed Archbishop Scrope received a kind of posthumous pardon in the licence which Henry V now permitted for offerings at his shrine in York Minster.[6]

Meanwhile, the embalmed corpse of Henry's father was still lying in state in Canterbury Cathedral, and on June 18th, 1413, it at last found rest after a solemn funeral ceremony attended by his four mourning sons. Later the tomb was adorned with the alabaster effigy which has survived to afford us a reasonably reliable if unflattering portrait of the founder of the Lancastrian dynasty. The new king's mother – Mary de Bohun, countess of Derby – had been buried in the unfinished church of St Mary's in the Newarke of Leicester, and one of her eldest son's first acts was to order and finance the completion of the church and to commission a metal effigy from a London coppersmith in her honour. The metal effigy has disappeared but an alabaster effigy is still preserved in the Trinity Hospital in Leicester.[7]

In December of this first year of his reign Henry V organized yet another burial which must ever be to his credit, and which also had political implications which illustrate his shrewdness. As the French chroniclers pointed out, and as events were soon to prove, there were still Englishmen who believed that Richard II was alive in Scotland,[8] and the young king had not forgotten the cultured patron of his youth. King Richard II's remains still lay in an inglorious grave at King's Langley, and now Henry V took speedy steps to show that he himself feared nothing from his patron's followers, and to demonstrate his own genuine respect for the king to whose throne he had now succeeded. He translated the corpse of Richard II with lavish ceremony to the glorious tomb in Westminster Abbey which Richard had himself commissioned, and which is still adorned with the superb effigies of Richard and his first queen. It was an admirable act of piety, it was a good political move – Richard was now surely dead – and it was an almost sublime gesture of self-confidence. The son of the usurper lost nothing by doing honour to the man his father had wronged but who had shown to himself nothing but kindness and friendship.[9] Henry V's translation of the body of Richard II was a pious and graceful act in the life of a king whom soldiering compelled often to appear both cruel and hard.

As Henry V surveyed his family circle and his court there seemed no shadow of doubt that his throne was secure. His step-mother, the dowager Queen Joanna, had remained on friendly terms with her husband's children by his first marriage, and she was not concerned with government. Henry had three royal brothers – Thomas, duke of Clarence, who was already an experienced if not very successful soldier, John, soon to be duke of Bedford, who was warden of the Scottish border and already showing signs of qualities which were later to be proved outstanding, Humphrey, soon to be duke of Gloucester, and who was the least able and already the least trusted. In his uncles – the legitimated children of Lady Katherine Swynford – Henry was especially fortunate. The eldest uncle, John Beaufort, first marquis of Dorset, had died three years before Henry's accession. His new chancellor, Henry Beaufort, was an exceptionally brilliant administrator. Thomas Beaufort, soon to be duke of Exeter, was as able and as loyal as his brother, but a soldier and an admiral rather than a politician. Henry V had nothing to fear from his closest relations.

Of the other princes of the blood, Edward, now duke of York, had outlived the shiftiness which had disgraced the 'Aumerle' of Richard II's day, and was now a faithful if corpulent supporter of his cousin. His younger brother Richard, soon to be made earl of Cambridge, was married to a sister of the earl of March, and therefore linked to the family which had a better legal title to the throne than Henry. There was here more likelihood of treason. But of any serious opposition in the senior nobility of England there was as yet no visible sign. Neville, earl of Westmorland, was married to a Beaufort. Richard Beauchamp, earl of Warwick, was a loyal general and already a distinguished crusader. The sons of the lords who had fought and died for Richard II – Thomas Montague, earl of Salisbury, John Holland, earl of Huntingdon and Richard de Vere, earl of Oxford were all of the new king's generation, and all now of unquestioned loyalty.

In Henry's inner circle was a group of lesser lords of whom he could have had no suspicion. Such boon companions were Richard Grey of Codnor, Thomas Lord Camoys, who had married Hotspur's widow, Henry le Scrope of Masham – a specially close friend – and Sir John Oldcastle now Lord Cobham by right of his wife the Baroness Cobham.

In his churchmen, in addition to Henry Beaufort, Henry V

had the enthusiastic support of Chichele, the brilliant bishop of St David's and soon to be the successor to Arundel at Canterbury. Thomas Langley, bishop of Durham, was a supporter of the Beauforts who had already had a distinguished spell as chancellor. Hallam, bishop of Salisbury, had already represented the English Church at the Council of Pisa in 1409 and was to be one of Henry V's most distinguished representatives at the coming and fateful Council of Constance. Only Archbishop Arundel could give Henry any cause for disquiet – and it was not the disquiet of possible disloyalty. Arundel represented the conscience of Henry's father; he was the older generation, fearful of Lollardy and expecting the new king to root out the heretic wherever he found him.

But if Henry V appeared to have no doubts about the strength and solidarity of his own position it is clear that the deeds of his father still weighed heavily on his conscience. It was in keeping with his new-found piety that he speedily took a number of steps to expiate the sins of a father who had been responsible for the death of an anointed king and who had authorized the execution of an archbishop. The abbey of Westminster received his first favours. Henry V undertook the reconstruction and completion of its nave, and, although the work was not finished when he died, he financed it – with the help of the famous Londoner Sir Richard Whittington – and lavished gifts of vestments, psalters, ornaments and sacred vessels on its monks. The royal manor of Sheen, where Queen Anne of Bohemia had died and which Richard II in his grief had razed to the ground, was replaced by a 'curious and costly house', and nearby a Carthusian monastery named Bethlehem was planned, richly endowed, and even remembered in his will, where special prayers were perpetually to be offered for the souls of both father and son. In Twickenham, across the river from Sheen, Henry founded another monastery, this time for Bridgettines. It was named Syon, and when later it moved a short way down-river to Brentford it lent its name and its foundations to the great country house which the eighteenth-century Northumberland family built on its site. There is some irony in its dedication – Henry V founded Syon 'as a true son of the God of Peace who gave peace and taught peace and chose St Bridget as a lover of peace and tranquillity'. Again, the new foundation was richly endowed with royal gifts, and there still exists in the Victoria and Albert Museum a magnificent cope of English fourteenth-century needlework, celebrated as *opus Anglicanum*, which is an indication of the glory that was Henry V's Syon.[10] There were also some negotiations, for the foundation of yet another monastery for the Celestines, but nothing resulted. It is true that modern research has shown that Henry's methods in the financing of these pious works were not over-scrupulous and led to some legal difficulties, but they bear witness to a sincere and almost passionate wish to appease his own conscience and to ensure so far as he could the peace of his father's soul.[11]

There were other and early acts of the new reign which are further witness to the new mood. A brotherhood of St Giles was founded for the relief of the poor outside the Cripplegate in London; the monastery of Llanfaes near the castle of Beaumaris in Anglesey, which had been punished by his father's troops in 1401, was restored and re-established; his old nurse was granted a pension of £20 a year; an old carter, and old servants who had fallen on hard times, were rewarded and taken care of; a special provision was made for the maintenance of the scholars of King's Hall in Cambridge; and there were several grants to hermits and friars who had given the king spiritual comfort. These are all acts which reveal the new king in a gentle and benevolent mood which was soon to be lost in the turmoil of camp and siege and which cannot be dismissed as mere priggishness – Henry V from the very moment of his accession was, as the contemporary Walsingham put it, avowedly and probably sincerely *deo devotus*.[12]

The mood of appeasement was again illustrated in Henry's dealings with his first parliament. It met in the Painted Chamber at Westminster on May 15th, 1413. It was a singularly co-operative occasion. Generous revenues were provided to the new government, and following two precedents in his father's time a sum of £10,000 was earmarked for the upkeep of the king's 'hostel, chamber and wardrobe'. The old theory that the king must 'live of his own' was slowly being superseded, but the king's household expenses were not yet provided for by what in modern times is known as the 'civil list' – the appropriations made to the first two Lancastrians were really a device for ensuring that purveyors to the royal household had a reasonable prospect of having their bills properly met. The commons' speaker was received by the new king without dispute, and their usual petitions of complaints were all received in good part. It was a significantly 'chauvinist' assembly. The commons prayed that all Welshmen and Irishmen should be expelled to their own homelands and that no English trader should be allowed to leave the country without express permission. England for the English was already a recognizable policy, and their new king was soon to become its protagonist.[13]

But there was one group of Englishmen with whom Henry V failed to come to terms – the Lollards.[14] He was in a difficult position. One of his closest friends was a Lollard leader, and there is no doubt that many Lollards assumed therefore that the new reign might bring relief to their persecution. On the other hand, the orthodox churchmen led by Archbishop Arundel hoped for more stringent suppression of heresy under a new king who seemed now to be almost fiercely orthodox. While Walsingham was reporting that Henry was 'changed into another man and studying to be honest, grave and modest', Thomas Netter of Walden, a Carmelite friar, who was later to become Henry's confessor and in whose arms he was to die, was preaching at Paul's Cross a denunciation of Henry's lack of zeal against the Lollards. The crisis was summed up in Henry's relationship with his old comrade-in-arms Sir John Oldcastle, now the leading layman of the Lollard persuasion.

Sir John Oldcastle came from Herefordshire, and in the Welsh wars despite being older he had become a much favoured and trusted leader under Prince Henry.[15] He had been sheriff of his native county in 1406, and in 1409 he had married as his second wife Joan, Lady Cobham and was therefore summoned to parliament as Baron Cobham. In 1411 Oldcastle had distinguished himself in the duke of Arundel's expedition to St Cloud, and some chroniclers go so far as to assert that he was 'of Henry's household'. Even the very anti-Lollard Walsingham, although he describes Oldcastle as a 'most vicious enemy of the Church', goes out of his way to state that he was an excellent soldier 'beloved and accepted' by the king 'on account of his uprightness'.[16] Clearly Oldcastle was no ordinary character, and as a leader of a movement which had followers in all classes by no means to be despised.

During the coronation period, the convocation of Canterbury had been sitting in the chapter house of St Paul's, and one of its spectacular acts against the Lollards had been the public burning of heretical books at Paul's Cross in the churchyard. One of the proscribed books had contained loose sheets of exceptional 'depravity', and on inquiry from their 'limner' (or publisher) it was revealed that the whole compilation belonged to Sir John Oldcastle. As Henry's first parliament was finishing its business, Oldcastle was summoned to Kennington, where, in the presence of the king and most of the ecclesiastics and magnates who had been attending the parliament, the most offending passages of Oldcastle's papers were read aloud. Henry was horrified – *maxime abhorruit* – and asked his old comrade-in-arms whether he did not agree that such work should be condemned. Oldcastle agreed, but maintained that although he owned the papers he had read only a word or two and thought nothing of it. An awkward moment was smoothed over, but later the same convocation urged that Oldcastle should be immediately pursued with all the rigours of ecclesiastical law – it was only the caution of Archbishop Arundel which prevented immediate action.

When the convocation dispersed, however, Arundel and some bishops approached the king privately and urged that Oldcastle's heretical opinions – well-known and widely publicised – deserved condemnation in spite of his loyal services to the crown. It is to Henry's credit that he refused to be rushed – he would himself attempt to persuade his friend to see the error of his ways, and only if Oldcastle persisted in error would he be handed over to justice both ecclesiastical and secular. A few weeks later Oldcastle sent a party of twenty-six wrestlers to perform before the king in Windsor park, and the athletes were well received and generously rewarded – Henry's affection was clearly not quickly withdrawn.[17] But the king's attempts to convert his friend were fruitless. Oldcastle's Lollardy was deep-rooted and well-argued, and, when the king pointed out the

certain consequences of his persistence, Oldcastle merely retired
from court and locked himself inside his Kent castle of Cooling
defying the writs of both Church and state. At this point the
king understandably ceased to help him, and the wheels of
ecclesiastical justice began remorselessly to turn. The writ of
the archbishop was nailed to the door of Rochester Cathedral,
and when Oldcastle failed to answer at Arundel's court at
Leeds Castle he was excommunicated. Meanwhile a royal writ
for Oldcastle's arrest had reached Cooling, and this time Oldcastle quietly obeyed and he was removed to the Tower by the
king's officers as a state prisoner. On September 23rd, 1413,
Oldcastle was taken before the archbishop and a large bench
of bishops and learned theologians in the chapter house of St
Paul's. The proceedings were conducted with surprising de-
corum, and, throughout, the authorities made every effort to be
persuasive rather than condemnatory. Oldcastle refused to ask
for pardon and calmly asked for permission to state his case. He
produced a schedule of his beliefs from under his gown written
in English, and he was given permission to read it in court.

In this apologia there was nothing violently heretical or
revolutionary, but the court was not to be thwarted by liberal
generalities – it wanted precise answers to two crucial questions.
Did the accused believe that in the sacrament of the Mass the
material bread remained after consecration? Did the accused
believe that confession to a priest was necessary in the sacrament
of penance? Oldcastle replied that he had nothing further to
add to what he had already read out. The court, still understanding and patient but still not to be baulked, gave him – in
English 'so that he could understand more readily' – the
official teaching of the Church, a couple of days to consider his
reply, and a clear warning of what the consequences of proved
heresy would be. Oldcastle was again brought before his in-
quisitors on September 25th, and now he boldly and bravely
sealed his doom. If the Church taught, he argued, that no
material bread remained after consecration, the Church was
wrong and had corrupted the scriptures. Confession was not a
necessity for salvation, but contrition was. When asked what
honour he would pay to a crucifix, he said he would wipe it and
keep it clean. When asked of his attitude to the pope, he called

3. Judge Gascoigne and his wife.

4. The coronation of Henry V: from the south side of his Chantry Chapel
in Westminster Abbey. Below is the king's mantled helm with his crest, a
crowned leopard, standing upon a cap of estate with a small shield of his
arms hanging below. . . .

him antichrist. The archbishop, more in sorrow than in anger, had no choice but to declare the king's knight a heretic and hand him over to secular justice – in other words to condemn him to death by burning.[18]

The ecclesiastical authorities were still nervous of the king's reaction, and, during the usual interval of forty days between clerical condemnation and secular execution, both Arundel and Henry made efforts to persuade Oldcastle to recant – they sent learned ambassadors to the prisoner in the Tower. Their efforts were useless, and the proof of the strength of Lollardy is that on the night of October 19th, 1413, Oldcastle escaped from his prison. There were some who suspected that the king or Beaufort, or both, had connived at the escape, but there is no evidence to confirm the suspicion.[19] The king had deeply regretted Oldcastle's stand, but he was pledged to uproot Lollardy, and Oldcastle had now become its leader and chief spokesman. As King Henry, he was now the fountain of justice affronted by a comrade who had forfeited every claim on his friendship. On their side the Lollards rightly considered that this was the moment for open revolt – if Oldcastle died, the priests would destroy them one and all – and rational criticism and reform now became high treason.

At the end of the year 1413 those of the Lollard persuasion were numerous enough to prompt Walsingham in his St Albans scriptorium to write that behind Oldcastle was 'almost the whole of the fatherland'.[20] Bills posted on London's many church doors threatened that a hundred thousand men were ready for action. Messengers, well supplied with money and propaganda, were dispatched all over the country summoning Lollards to a rendezvous in London, and the new king was now condemned as 'the priests' prince'. The rendezvous was to be at Fickett's Field just outside Temple Bar, and rebellion began on the evening of Tuesday, January 9th, 1414.

The only evidence for the motives and objectives of the Lollards in this tragic episode comes from their enemies and persecutors. King, nobles and priests were to be slain. St Paul's was to be razed to the ground, and the wealth of plundered friaries was to be distributed among the rebels. Oldcastle was to be proclaimed regent. But it is doubtful whether there was any plot more definite than to capture the person of the new king, destroy the powers of the priests, and restore a corrupt Church to the simple purity of its founder.[21]

The king was making preparations for his Christmas festivities at Eltham palace when rumours of the Lollard rising began to reach him – partly through traitors from within the Lollard ranks and partly through spies who had been paid to watch their movements and to discover the whereabout of Oldcastle who, so it was believed, was still in hiding in London. By January 8th, Henry knew that he was faced with rebellion, and he knew the rebels' rendezvous. Promptly he, his three brothers, Archbishop Arundel and most of his intimate entourage left for the city of London, took up quarters in the priory at Clerkenwell, ordered the gates of the city to be closed and guarded, and organized patrols of horsemen over the fields which in those days stretched westwards from Temple Bar. The king himself with a considerable armed force stationed himself at St Giles's Fields just north-west of the Lollards' concentration point. From Yorkshire, from the midlands and from the west country the Lollard bands were unsuspectingly making their way to the capital. Without leadership or organization each group was helpless in face of the shut gates of London and the armed forces of the king. As each group arrived it was easily disarmed and promptly marched off to prison. A movement as potentially powerful but as inept as Wat Tyler's fizzled out in humiliating captivity, and speedily a special commission was appointed to destroy rebels whose only strength was in their creed. Four new pairs of gallows were erected near St Giles's Fields, to be known henceforth as the 'Lollers' Gallows', and the grim work of execution began. Probably about a hundred Lollards suffered in London, but there is no record of recantations.[22] The commission extended its work to the country, but the rebellion was so clearly a failure that before the end of January Henry was satisfied, and his clemency granted pardons and in March declared a general amnesty – the bulk of the prisoners were content to buy their lives with fines. Nevertheless, although the conspiracy of St Giles's Fields was a monumental failure, the remaining Lollards could rejoice that their beloved leader Oldcastle was still at large. He had escaped to the west, and, in spite of the king's proclamation of a lavish reward to anyone who could arrest him, he was not betrayed.

In February, Thomas Arundel, archbishop of Canterbury, had died, but he had lived long enough to see the Lollards scattered and the new king hailed as the Champion of Christ, the Pillar of the Faith, a Constantine, a Theodosius, a Maccabaeus come back to life, God's Holy Knight, and the Worthy Bearer of the Sword of the Lord.[23] The death of his father's staunchest and oldest supporter left the field clear for the Beauforts and the younger generation of Henry's friends.

The first year of his reign showed that Henry V was already as efficient as his father in meeting threats to his security, far more confident that he could erase the lingering doubts which dated from the usurpation of 1399, and as expert in grasping the nettles both of religious discontent and parliamentary ambition. Already Henry V was showing signs of greatness.

Chapter 7

PRELUDE TO WAR

THE SECOND PARLIAMENT of the reign was summoned to Leicester on April 30th, 1414. Coming soon after the easy victory at St Giles's Fields, it passed a statute which would have delighted Archbishop Arundel. It was prompted not by the commons but by the king's council, and directed that all officers of the crown should 'exert their entire pains and diligence to oust, cease and destroy all manner of heresies and errors vulgarly called Lollardies'.[1] It gave the Church every weapon it had ever dreamed of in a concerted effort to stamp out the fires of abominable heresy.

Authority has always thought it could abolish and destroy nonconformity, but the blood of martyrs, as churchmen should have known, has a miraculous power of preserving life. Oldcastle was still at large and in correspondence with the Bohemian Hus. And for the few Lollards who braved the stake there were many more who paid for pardons but still kept their beliefs inwardly alive. Heresy was not stamped out, it was only damped down; and in a book of sermons and tracts named *The Lantern of Light* the Lollard preaching achieved widespread circulation. To a modern eye it is simply the pure faith of Protestantism couched in the homely phrases of Wyclif's 'Poor Preachers'.[2] In the days of Henry V it was death to own it or even to admit having read it; yet throughout its pages there is no trace of political treason.

The usual defence of Henry as a bigoted persecutor is to point out that he was attacking the political implications of Lollardy and not its religious beliefs. He has no real need of defence. He was an orthodox son of the Church and a soldier. He therefore shrank neither from the logic of his beliefs nor the grim business of the stake – it would be absurd to expect anything different.

84

It can be said in his favour that in the case of Oldcastle at least he went out of his way to try to save an old friend, but, when that old friend and comrade-in-arms persisted in his beliefs beyond all reason, the law had to take its course. It is witness to the resources of the Lollards, and the popularity of Oldcastle and his beliefs, that it was four years before the stake was able to claim its distinguished victim.

The story of this Leicester parliament is full of interest. It reveals that the piracy on which so many men of Devon and Cornwall depended for their livelihood was worrying both king and commons. English piracy stimulated Breton reprisals, and, as leaders' thoughts were beginning to turn towards foreign adventure, and the wealth of so many citizens now depended so much on the overseas wine, wool and cloth trades, a Channel free of raiders of any nationality was much to be desired. It reveals too that successive statutes of Livery and Maintenance had been of no avail in preventing the lawlessness of baronial retainers especially in the northern Marches – unemployed soldiery were a perpetual menace to civil peace in the Middle Ages and there was a constant temptation to find them work to do abroad. But the Leicester parliament's chief claim to fame is that in it the commons successfully petitioned that statutes should be enacted in the exact terms of the petitions on which they were based.[3] Henry's reply was equivocal – he promised not to change the purport of a successful commons' petition. This was of great significance in many later struggles between king and commons, and it had been unsuccessfully asked for before. At the time of its first conditional acceptance, however, it was a signpost rather than a landmark; it merely demonstrated that the new king was willing to make a guarded concession – which his ancestors had consistently refused – in order to keep the commons quiet. Henry had a realistic appreciation of whence the wherewithal for government and foreign adventure must come, and he was fully prepared to sacrifice what seemed to him an insignificant matter of principle if the commons were in other directions amenable and generous.

In this same parliament, the commons in their petitions referred to the king's 'adversary of France', and although there is no record of public debate it is clear that at this time king, barons, Church and commons were assuming that the renewal of the war with France was probably not far distant. Within just over two years of his accession Henry V was embarking on his first invasion of France. It was to be the beginning of a series of astonishing victories and diplomatic successes which raised England to the leadership of western Europe, and yet which finally left England exhausted, disenchanted, and rent by a cruel civil war in which the Lancastrian dynasty was ultimately ruined. The motives of Henry in such a fateful enterprise need careful assessment.

If so fair a witness as Froissart is consulted it would seem that Henry was merely expressing the sentiments of all Englishmen at that time. Froissart had been at home on both sides of the Channel, and while he had had very little respect for the dynastic claims of England to the throne of France, he was a shrewd judge of what a modern observer would call the national spirit. 'The English,' he wrote, 'will never love or honour their king unless he be victorious and a lover of arms and war against their neighbours and especially against such as are greater and richer than themselves. Their land is more fulfilled of riches and all manner of goods when they are at war than in times of peace. They take delight and solace in battles and slaughter. Covetous and envious are they above measure of other men's wealth.'[4] Froissart's summary may be unpalatable, and it related specifically to the wars of Edward III and the Black Prince, but it was none the less apposite to the wars of Henry V. At least one motive – and to a man of Henry's mettle it was a powerful one – was that in attacking his 'adversary of France' he was obeying the traditions of his forebears as most Englishmen expected him to do, and he had seen what had happened to a Richard II who had gone against that tradition.

If Shakespeare is to be believed, the renewal of what we now call 'The Hundred Years War' was entirely due to the cynical advice of English churchmen. In the previous reign a warning note had been struck – the commons had suggested that the property of alien priories, which in effect were colonies of foreign monasteries, should be confiscated to provide fund, for the crown which otherwise would have had to come from their own pockets. Some of the French priories had actually suffered, and the Leicester parliament, on the petition of the commons, now sanctioned the transfer of the property of all alien priories into the king's hands in perpetuity.[5] It was a significant sign of that nationalistic tendency of which Henry V was to be the embodiment. It was a move which of course had the approval of all Lollards, but it was not initiated by them. Confiscation proposals had been mooted under Edward III, and John of Gaunt in Richard II's day had associated himself with similar proposals. At the end of the fourteenth century there had begun in England a movement which finally ended in the dissolution of the monasteries by Henry VIII, but in its early stages it was not a movement for religious reform but rather a political solution to the problem of national economics. It was the wealth of the Church which attracted the covetous eyes of the commons, whereas it was its laxities and abuses which called forth the strictures and fanaticism of the Lollards.

In the opening scene of Shakespeare's play of Henry V the churchmen, fearful of yet further confiscations, urge the archbishop to divert the king's energies and the commons' greed towards the rewards of foreign war. There is no contemporary evidence to support the story,[6] and, although the English church was nationalist enough not to resent the disendowment of foreigners, it does not seem to have been unduly alarmed at future prospects. On the contrary, throughout the reign of Henry V it was generous and almost lavish in his support – if the Church did not encourage Henry to war it did nothing to discourage him.

Two other political factors weighed heavily in favour of a war policy. Henry's confidence in his own popularity and in the security of his new dynasty had been somewhat shaken by the St Giles's conspiracy, and he was well aware that throughout the realm lawlessness was rife. The statutes of Livery and Maintenance had had little or no effect, and the commons' complaints against lords and their retainers, who made a mockery of the royal writ, had substance.[7] Outside the walled towns unemployed soldiery were a menace to traders and travellers, and the laws of property were defied by the armed robbery of a warlike caste which had had neither ransoms nor booty of any consequence for a generation. There had been precious little booty to be had in the Marches of Wales and Scotland, and marauders' appetites had recently been whetted by the small continental expeditions of Arundel and Clarence. There were thousands of knights and archers, who still ruled England outside the towns and cities, who were more than ready for new and profitable adventure overseas. A war against the hereditary enemy across the Channel might solve both problems – if successful, the Lancastrian dynasty could be established as the head of a victorious and enriched aristocracy, and thwarted belligerence could be assuaged by the material and financial rewards of victory at the foreigners' expense.

Across the Channel, the condition of France was all temptation. England still had its two bridgeheads – at Calais and at Bordeaux. France itself was still hopelessly divided; its monarch was frequently imbecile, its dukes playing their own hands and feckless of the national interest, its citizens divorced from power and its peasants at the mercy of a social system far more brutal and far less enlightened than the English version. The Armagnac party led by Charles of Orléans had control of Charles VI, and it also had temporary control of Paris. John the Fearless, duke of Burgundy, was preparing a powerful riposte, and he therefore had need of any allies he could find or bribe. Here clearly was a richly opportune moment for Henry V to intervene, and, by allying with the winning side, to reacquire not merely the dukedom of William the Norman but the whole Angevin empire of Henry II; or, an even more dazzling prospect, the throne of France itself. Henry V had been a soldier from his earliest years. He was the son of the most redoubtable jouster of his age, his grandfather had won the battle of Crécy, and we are told that his favourite reading was a book on the life of the crusader, Godfrey of Bouillon.[8] His father's ambition had been to lead a united Christendom against the infidel; with England united to France, with schism in the Church finally healed, the son might become the leader of a victorious final crusade . . .

Such ambitions are not to be despised – Henry V was to realize at least some of them before his short life ended.

But Henry V was no mere dreamer of medieval glory. His apparent recklessness of aim was harnessed to a firm respect for legal forms and theoretical justifications. Before he committed himself to a renewal of the war with France he went to considerable pains to publicize what he had convinced himself were his rightful claims to the French throne. His great-grandfather had done the same thing – Edward III had claimed France through his mother Isabella, the daughter of Philip IV of France, but the house of Valois had the better claim and had never surrendered it. If Edward III's claims had any legal validity – and they had not – they had descended not to the son of a usurping Henry IV but to the young earl of March. And yet, throughout his reign and even on his death-bed, Henry V unhesitatingly claimed that he was the rightful king of France.[9] It is difficult for a modern mind to see anything but hypocrisy in Henry's attitude, but in a lawless age it is paradoxically true that legal claims are especially arguable, and Henry undoubtedly convinced himself first that his great-grandfather's claim through a female was correct, and second that when his father deposed Richard II he had inherited unimpaired the rightful claims of Edward III. Perhaps it was a tribute to a new sense of legality – which Henry V was to display in so many different ways – that the naked sword of the new king needed a scabbard at all; and only modern eyes can see how threadbare its gilded velvet was.

At the time of the Leicester parliament Henry was in negotiation with both parties of distracted France. The Armagnacs, as they were temporarily in the ascendant, offered peace; the Burgundians, as they were temporarily in retreat, offered alliance in war. It was now that one of the most colourful incidents of popular English history is said to have taken place. In the chronicle of John Strecche, which dates from the early years of Henry's son, it is written that the Armagnac ambassadors offered to send the young king 'little balls to play with, and soft cushions to rest on, until what time he should grow to man's strength'. Henry in anger replied that he would within a few months play such a game in the streets of France that it would cease to be a joke, and grief would be their only gain. Another version is that Henry replied that he would teach Frenchmen good tennis, and that his big guns would toss a service of balls

FRANCE · 1413–1422

ENGLISH — ARMAGNAC
BURGUNDIAN

Miles
0   100   200

W. Bromage

into their towns which the French would be incapable of returning. And Shakespeare made the most of so picturesque a
legend:

> When we have matched our rackets to these balls,
> We will in France, by God's grace, play a set
> Shall strike his father's crown into the hazard . . .
> And tell the pleasant prince this mock of his
> Hath turn'd his balls to gun-stones.

It is a pleasant but unlikely story. Charles VI when sane could
not have wanted war, and when insane his representatives
were willing to pay a handsome price for peace. There is no
mention of the episode in the contemporary French historians
or in the contemporary English chronicles of Walsingham. It
does appear in a contemporary ballad attributed to Lydgate,
in the metrical but not in the prose version of Elmham and in
the much later chronicle of Otterbourne. So egregious an insult
must certainly have resulted in the disruption of normal diplomatic relations. The contrary is true – negotiations continued;
and when later Henry V in the mood of his chivalrous ancestors
challenged the dauphin to single combat, to avoid the shedding
of much Christian blood on both sides, there was no mention of
so mortal an affront. It is sad that the legend of the tennis balls
is so suspect.[10]

But it was clear that the English king was preparing to break
the twenty-five years' truce which in 1396 Richard II had
sealed with his marriage to the child princess Isabella of France.
Appropriately, Henry's close friends and relatives were now still
further promoted. His brother John became duke of Bedford; his
brother Humphrey became duke of Gloucester; Richard, second
son of Edmund Langley who was the last son of Edward III, was
made earl of Cambridge, while his elder brother continued in
honour as duke of York. Henry's confessor Henry Chichele
became archbishop of Canterbury shortly after the termination
of the Leicester parliament – it was a striking example of the
fact that the best career open to talent in the Middle Ages was
by way of the Church. Chichele had been one of the first poor
scholars whom William of Wykeham's foundations at Winchester and at New College, Oxford, had enabled to emerge from

obscurity into the seats of the high and mighty – he was to hold his archiepiscopal throne for nearly thirty years and throughout was a faithful supporter of the House of Lancaster.

In the parliament summoned in November 1414 to Westminster, and in the great council held just before it, the king was advised to exhaust the power of negotiation but not to shrink from the necessity of war.[11] Both clergy and commons voted generous finance, and national unity was symbolized in measures taken for restoring the son of Hotspur, still a prisoner in Scotland, to his ancestral earldom of Northumberland, in encouraging the young heir to the Ricardian house of Holland to look forward to full reinstatement, and in restoring the young earl of March to full freedom in the closest confidence of the king.

Meanwhile, the game of diplomacy was to be played for all it was worth. In the beginning of the next year, Thomas Beaufort, earl of Dorset and youngest uncle of the king, was sent with a bevy of bishops and earls to make extravagant claims on the court of France. First, they claimed the crown of France, but if this, as they expected, were to be rejected, they claimed Normandy, Anjou, Maine, Touraine and all the territories which had been ceded to Edward III by the treaty of Brétigny in 1360. Second, they claimed half of Provence and the castles and lands of Beaufort and Nogent as part of the rightful Lancastrian inheritance. Third, and this was the most exorbitant of their exorbitant demands, they claimed the payment of all the arrears of the ransom of King John of France who had been captured by the Black Prince at Poitiers in 1356. These arrears were calculated at the enormous sum of 1,600,000 French crowns. In addition, Princess Katherine, daughter of Charles VI, was to marry Henry V and bring with her to England a dowry of 2,000,000 crowns – a demand which takes much of the glamour from the charming love-story of Shakespeare's Henry V.[12]

The French negotiators, led by the duke of Berry, were surprisingly conciliatory. They offered an enlargement of the English duchy of Aquitaine which was very near to the limits of the conquests and inheritances of our Henry II. So far as the ransom of King John was concerned, they considered that their territorial surrenders would be sufficient repayment. So far as the dowry of Katherine was concerned, Charles VI was willing to provide 600,000 gold crowns even though this was more than any king of France had ever considered proper to accompany a daughter into matrimony. The English negotiators were in Paris, and they reduced the proposed dowry to a still unlikely one million crowns. The French replied in the beginning by raising their offer to 800,000 crowns, and later in addition promised to provide a suitable trousseau to accompany the bride. These generous concessions were immediately rejected – the English would seize what they could by force of arms and do better for themselves by war than by the subtle haggling of such diplomacy.[13] The embassy returned to England and preparations for an invasion of France began, although Henry V had no sure warranty for his dynastic claim, no rights which France was not prepared to concede, and no justification beyond his own natural ambitions and the right of any medieval king to seek glory and plunder wherever he thought he might win the day.

Chapter 8

STAFF WORK

HENRY'S PREPARATIONS for war display him as one of the most expert administrators England has ever had. His logic may have been at fault, his philosophy may have been suspect, but his instructions could not have been more precise; his pretensions may have been pretentious, but his planning was prodigiously efficient.

Throughout the early months of 1415 Henry busied himself with his plans for a continental expedition. No sooner had the English ambassadors returned from Paris than two of the king's knights were detailed to go to the Low Countries to make contracts for ships and captains to serve the English.[1] Henry himself spent his time in the south of England organizing his forces.

During the previous century the methods of raising a royal army had changed. By the so-called 'feudal levy' a medieval king could summon to his standard all able-bodied men who held their lands by military tenure. But these feudal tenants were only bound to serve forty days each year, which was of little use when an overseas expedition was in sight. The 'feudal levy' had long been obsolete.

The ancient right of an English king to summon all free men to his cause – a right descended from the Saxon general or great, as distinct from the selective, 'fyrd' – had been systematized by the procedure of 'Commissions of Array'.[2] The king's commissioners were sent into every county to summon the freemen to an 'array' at which they had to present themselves fit and properly accoutred or pay a fine. From this assembly the commissioners could select the men they wanted – but their obligation was only to serve within the realm of England.

94

From the days of Edward I in his wars against the Welsh and Scots, and especially in the French wars of Edward III, the system of 'indenture' had superseded the more haphazard methods of the early Middle Ages. The old 'feudal levy' and the ancient army of freemen had sufficed for the defence of the English throne within English frontiers – they were both useless for a prolonged campaign overseas. The indenture system simply meant recruitment by contract – the indentures were careful legal contracts made between the king and his nobles and knights which fixed the numbers, ranks, pay, conditions and rewards of those willing to serve overseas for a stated period which might be for as long as a year or more. The documentation necessary for the efficiency of this system was formidable. It is clear from the many surviving indentures that the Exchequer took every precaution to register precise obligations and to prevent payment for absentees or other fraudulent claims. The organizing of Henry V's army presupposes a large and expert body of civil servants.[3]

'Men-at-arms' formed the backbone of Henry's army. The phrase is confusing to modern readers; a truer description would be 'knights-at-arms'. They were fully armed and armoured knights with their attendant esquires and pages and a proper supply of armoured horses. In the early fourteenth century indentures, a unit of this force was described as a 'lance', which meant a knight with perhaps three or four esquires and pages and the necessary transport, and usually only the knight was fully armed. Their weapons were the lance, the sword, the dagger and occasionally the mace; their defence was in plate armour for man and horse and a small shield which was frequently discarded before battle – plate armour was in itself an over-all shield. The great 'helm' of the previous generation had been superseded by the much smaller 'bascinet' with its movable 'ventaille' or face-protector hinged to it. It was a significant change because the great helm anchored to the breast-plate, and heavy with chain mail, had made quick turns to the left and right difficult unless the whole torso was turned. The bascinet allowed a man-at-arms the maximum freedom of head movement with reasonable protection and less weight to carry. On the other hand, the weight of a complete sheath of plate armour was already making the man-at-arms less and less mobile. A jupon emblazoned with his heraldry was worn over the armour, and feathers in the bascinet distinguished knights from squires. The horses had housings of mail and a caparison which reproduced the knight's insignia. The men-at-arms and their esquires had learned to fight on foot – before action their horses were led to the rear by the pages. It was a lesson which the Scots had first taught the English at Bannockburn, and it was a lesson which the French had not yet fully learned.

But before men-at-arms could actually cross swords with the enemy, archery[4] was provided to perform the functions performed in modern warfare by rifle-fire – to stop the enemy in his tracks, to disorganize his attack and to kill his horses. In the time of Richard Coeur de Lion the Plantaganets had relied on the cross-bow (usually in the hands of foreign mercenaries) for this function, and it was not until the Assize of Arms of 1252 that the ordinary bow was recognized as a normal weapon for English soldiers.[5] It was in the campaigns of Edward I that the superiority of the long-bow was first demonstrated by the rebel South Welsh, and Edward's men with Welsh help proved its superiority at the battle of Falkirk in 1298. The defeat of Bannockburn (1314) drove home the folly of relying only on armoured knights on heavy horses. At Neville's Cross (1346) the northern militia again proved the worth of the long-bow, and at Crécy (1346) and Poitiers (1356) Edward III and the Black Prince won overwhelming victories which were largely due to the accuracy, speed and fire-power of their long-bowmen. It was in the reign of the pacific Richard II that the first statute for the promotion of English archery was enacted. 'All servants and labourers should have bows and arrows, and practise shooting on Sundays and festivals, and not waste their time with such games as dice, quoits, football and suchlike play.' This statute had been confirmed by Henry IV[6] and was to be re-enacted so late as the time of Henry VIII. It was a petition of the commons in Edward IV's day which summed up a whole era in the memorable words 'the defence of this Land standeth moche by Archers'.

The English archer of Henry V's day could discharge his cloth-yard shafts with deadly accuracy at the rate of six a minute at a range of between 200 and 300 yards.[7] The cross-bow, which had preceded the long-bow and was still favoured on the Continent, was more powerful, but it was also more cumbersome and its bolts could only be discharged at the rate of one or two a minute. Henry V was still to rely on his long-bowmen. They were now frequently mounted. They wore skull-caps of plate armour or a mail cap covered with canvas or leather. They wore a *hauberk* of chain mail or a *brigantine* jacket of leather. As well as their long-bow and arrows they usually carried a sword or a battle-axe or a club. There were also English long-bowmen on foot and such supernumeraries as valets and pages armed with the fearsome bill-hook. Henry's armament was to depend for its distant striking power on the long-bowmen and for its close-quarter impact on men-at-arms, spearmen and pikemen of lesser degree who travelled on horseback but who were trained to fight shoulder to shoulder on foot.

A third force was now effective – artillery.[8] In the wars of Henry V it was primarily a weapon of siege-warfare, although the French at Agincourt were reported to have had some 'guns' which were never used. But the word 'artillery' needs careful definition at this stage in the art of warfare. The Middle Ages had inherited from the ancient world all the weapons of siege-craft which had served the Romans so well. With many variants such weapons can be divided into three classifications in accordance with their method of propulsion. The marngonel was worked by torsion, the balista was worked by tension, and the trébuchet was worked by counterpoise. All three methods were devised for propelling balls of metal or of stone in order to break down gates and fortifications, or for throwing red-hot metals or pots of flaming materials to set fire to the enemy's houses or the wooden towers and palisades which protected his fighting men and miners. But none of these were essentially cannon – their missiles were not projected by explosions. It is true that for centuries western Europe had known of 'Greek Fire'. It is supposed to have been invented by a Syrian and was certainly used by the Saracens as early as A.D. 673. It was a liquid composed of sulphur, pitch, dissolved nitre and petroleum, and it was either spurted from a tube or projected in a container by any of the three methods described above. When used from a tube it must have been very similar to, and as demoralizing as, the German *flammenwerfen* used in the war of 1914–18. When used against a besieged city where timber was the most usual building material, or against a wooden ship, it was a very effective weapon – only sand could subdue its flames. But 'Greek Fire', terrifying as it was, was still not cannon fire.

Cannon proper had had to wait upon the skilled application of gunpowder. The Chinese had used gunpowder for rockets and crackers for a thousand years, but it was an English friar – Roger Bacon – who in 1249 discovered the secret of its manufacture and first suggested its use as a propulsive force in warfare. Gunpowder is a mixture of saltpetre, sulphur and charcoal; and it was not until 1327 that we have evidence of its use for discharging shot by an explosion in the lower end or chamber of a barrel. After the period of Crécy we hear of 'guns' in use, but there is no evidence that they were used in battle – they were the latest weapon for both besieger and besieged. Henry V in preparing his expedition to France certainly had his 'guns' – they were bombards of considerable calibre clamped on to gun-stocks and not on to wheeled carriages. They were to do very effective work at many sieges in his succeeding campaigns but they were far too immobile, and far too difficult to aim, to be of service in open warfare, and disasters from bursting barrels were frequent for a century or more. Meanwhile, Henry's preparations made thoughtful provision for a formidable array of the old-fashioned catapults and rams, and all the timber, ropes and wheels that were necessary for their mountings and mechanisms.

The pay of Henry's army varied not according to military rank but according to social status – although this was frequently the same thing – and the pay was duly written into the indentures. A duke received thirteen shillings and fourpence, an earl five shillings and threepence, a knight baronet four shillings, a knight two shillings, an esquire one shilling a day; and these were the men-at-arms. Archers and 'other ranks' were paid sixpence a day. All forces were to be considered fully mobilized from April 1415, and pay was to date from then and be paid quarterly to senior officers who in turn were to pay their juniors. The first quarter's pay was issued on mustering, and the second and third quarters' pay were to be issued at the end of the second quarter, but by that time Henry's finances were over-strained and it was agreed that pay should be issued at the end of each quarter. To encourage recruitment there was a bonus of 100 marks for every 30 men-at-arms enrolled.

These terms were considered sufficiently generous although no allowance was made for armour, weapons, horses and food – the army was expected to muster fully-equipped and mounted, and to live off the country it conquered either by fair purchase of victuals or if necessary by requisition and confiscation. The king had to provide shipping for transport across the Channel, and the value of any horses lost abroad was to be replaced by the royal exchequer. Horses were of course vital to transport once the Channel was crossed. A duke could bring 50 horses, an earl 24, a baron 16, knights baronet and knights 6, an esquire 4 and an archer 1. Again, it was the king's responsibility to provide the shipping.

Henry's indentures further dealt with the very vital matter of prisoners and booty. Prisoners in medieval warfare were more important than casualties – a corpse might give the victor booty but a live prisoner could more usefully give him ransom money. Every prisoner was to belong to his captor except that anyone capturing the French king or his son or any chief officer must hand him over to the king, and later he would be suitably rewarded. Of booty taken by his men the officer took a third, but a third of this had to be surrendered to the royal exchequer.[9]

Transportation across the Channel was a formidable royal responsibility – there was no royal navy capable of solving the problem. True, there were at least six 'great' royal ships, whose names we know, and the king could also call on the ships and seamen of the Cinque Ports according to the ancient obligations of their charters. But these resources were utterly inadequate to cope with the transportation of Henry's large forces. In addition to ships hired from Holland, Henry instructed royal commissioners to commandeer every ship 'with a capacity of

twenty casks or more' between Newcastle and Bristol, and
sailors were to be pressed to serve in them at a wage of threepence halfpenny a day with a bounty of sixpence a week, and
sail them to the south coast ports facing France. The owners of
these ships received no compensation but they were covered
against total loss.[10]

There has been much learned dispute as to the total numbers
of Henry's forces simply because the supernumeraries were
never enumerated. On the other hand, thanks to a surviving
muster roll, known as the Agincourt Roll but more properly
named the Harfleur Roll, there is general agreement that
Henry's expedition transported over the Channel an army of
2,500 men-at-arms and about 8,000 archers, but with these
combatant front-line troops were a very large number of essential supporting 'other ranks' many of whom could be reckoned
as combatant if need be.[11] On Henry's own staff are listed
miners, master gunners, gunservers, stuffers of bascinets,
armourers, serjeants and yeomen of the king's tents and
pavilions, physicians and surgeons, grooms and surveyors of
stables, clerk of the king's 'avenrie' (oats), purveyors, king's
guides by night, smiths, saddlers, cofferers, servitors, pages,
messengers, yeomen of the poultry and of the bakehouse, clerks
of the kitchen, pantry and buttery, yeomen of napery, clerks of
spicery, scullery and hall, carpenters, labourers, bowgemen,
clerks of the wardrobe, cordwainers, fletchers, bowyers, wheel-
wrights, colliers, almoners, clerks and doctors in law, chaplains,
and fifteen minstrels paid at a shilling a day.[12] The list gives
a clear idea of the complexity of medieval warfare and of
the organization necessary to an efficient overseas expedition –
and from all accounts which have survived it is clear that
Henry himself was his own quartermaster-general and chief of
staff.[13]

When 'owre kynge went forth to Normandye' he was no
Galahad leading a crusade of chivalry, he was an experienced
young general at the head of an army of professional soldiery.
His men were neither conscripts nor mercenaries – they were
either members of a military caste or its retainers, all of whom
had to be paid for their services but none of whom grudged their

services. War was their trade and they had been unemployed for too long; they were English soldiery with a tradition of victory over the king's 'adversary of France', and when called to active service they responded without demur in the expectation of fair pay, tough campaigning and the possibility of rich rewards.

It is not surprising that the ordinary revenues of the crown were quite inadequate to finance so lavish an enterprise. The exchequer was rapidly exhausted, and Henry sent out urgent appeals for cash loans to wherever he was advised money might be available. The private resources of the crown were ransacked to provide security for these loans – crowns, jewels, swords, gold collars, almsdishes, rosaries, relics, and even the royal lying-in gear were placed in pawn to every type of wealthy citizen, to most towns and cities, to rich gentry and to accommodating clergy. Compulsion was only necessary where foreign merchants were concerned, but there is evidence that at least in the rising city of New Sarum (or Salisbury) there was certainly some reluctance to contribute. It was not unusual for a medieval monarch to cash his credit by such means, and Henry seems to have been well satisfied with the results. Many of the loans were repaid with surprising celerity, but some pledges remained unredeemed until well into the succeeding reign.[14]

With men, ships, and money reasonably provided for Henry was still faced with the problem of his commissariat. He had to ensure that his troops arrived in France fighting fit, and that meant the provision of generous basic food supplies until the expedition could feed itself at the enemy's expense. The Orders of the Privy Council for April and May 1415 contain many examples of the strenuous activity which ensured a concentration of wine, beer, cattle, flour and spices (then the usual food preservatives) in the areas nearest to Southampton Water where men and ships were assembling.

In the midst of all these complicated preparations Henry still found time for pilgrimage.[15] In the early days of May he rode from London to Shrewsbury by way of Reading – a distance of some 160 miles – and thence to the shrine of St Winifred at Holywell in Flintshire. It is an astonishing example of a religious devotion which was now characteristic of this soldier king.

By mid-June Henry was back in London and on June 16th, 1415 he made his elaborate farewells to his step-mother Queen Joanna, his household staff and the authorities of the city of London. There was a solemn service in St Paul's whence the mayor, aldermen, and citizens accompanied him through Southwark to the Portsmouth road. On June 20th the royal cavalcade reached Winchester in time to play a last round in that diplomatic game at which Henry was so rapidly becoming an expert. The archbishop of Bourges, the bishop of Lisieux and the count of Vendôme in an embassy of three hundred and fifty horsemen arrived from Dover on June 30th on a mission to try to avert war at the last minute.[16]

The French ambassadors were in England for a fortnight, and the proceedings at Winchester were conducted with elaborate ceremonial. Henry received his visitors in the bishop of Winchester's hall at Wolvesey Castle clad in regal cloth of gold with his brothers, his chancellor Bishop Beaufort, and his full court around him. The wines and spices of official welcome were followed by banquets, Masses and finally the hard bargaining which was left to the ambassadors and the English chancellor. The chief bone of contention was the amount of the dowry which the French were prepared to offer with the Princess Katherine. Henry had demanded two million crowns, the French offered 800,000; Henry reduced his outrageous demand to 900,000 crowns and there the bargaining stuck. Finally both parties appeared to lose their tempers and the negotiations were at an end[17] – but there were still further masses and banquets and finally the ceremonial exchange of presents.

The letters in which Henry re-stated his position have been recorded and they make strange reading – the determination to make war, and take what he had convinced himself was rightfully his own, is cloaked in references to the laws of Deuteronomy, his zeal for peace and his regard for the dictates of his conscience. It was medieval protocol that God should be claimed as ally to both sides – a protocol which has been the prelude to most wars since. The obvious answer to the French ambassadors was in the camp fires which lit up the night twenty miles away round Southampton and Porchester Castle and the ships making their way to assembly points in the harbours close at hand. It was too late for negotiation – on Saturday, July 6th, 1415, Henry V and his courtiers rode out of Winchester to join the greatest fighting force so far assembled on English soil.

Chapter 9

THE SOUTHAMPTON
PLOT

A$^{\text{S HENRY'S PREPARATIONS}}$ neared completion, men and
supplies mustered between Southampton and Portsmouth
and some 1,500 vessels rode at their moorings in Southampton Water and Portsmouth harbour. He himself divided
his time between the bishop of Winchester's manor at Waltham,
the abbey at Titchfield and Porchester Castle. At Titchfield he
was not too busy with surrounding problems of discipline and
mustering to forget the wider scene. He arranged for one
of Archbishop Chichele's clerks to make copies of the documents of the negotiations with the Armagnacs in 1412 and to
circulate them to the Emperor Sigismund, then sitting at the
Council of Constance, and to other continental princes – they
were part of his propaganda to give his claims on France every
appearance of strict legality and moral justification, they were
an example of that passion for legal forms which never left
him.

It was while at Porchester Castle in Portsmouth harbour
that he first heard of what is now known as the Southampton
Plot. Its leader was Richard of Conisborough, the younger
brother of the duke of York. He had received the earldom of
Cambridge from Henry at Leicester only a year before, and he
had already pledged himself and a following of 2 knights, 57
esquires and 160 mounted archers to Henry's French expedition.
By his first marriage to Anne Mortimer he had become brother-
in-law to Edmund, earl of March and was therefore closely
linked to Richard II's legal heir. By his second marriage – Anne
had recently died – he was linked with the Percy opposition;
his second wife was the sister of a Lord Clifford who had

104

married Hotspur's daughter. But for no other reason was there any breath of suspicion as to his loyalty to Henry V.

Henry's plans for appeasing every possible opposition had recently continued to press for the restoration of Hotspur's son Henry Percy who was still an exile in Scotland. He was to be exchanged for Murdoch,[1] son of the Scottish regent the duke of Albany, and a ransom of £10,000 was to be paid by the Scots. The deal was approaching a successful conclusion when French influence in Scotland called a halt. The French were more aware of the dissident elements behind the apparent unity of Henry V's England than the English chroniclers, and their diplomacy was ready to exploit to the full the belief that there was still a person in Scotland who was either Richard II himself or one who could be passed off as Richard II.

Murdoch had been sent north under escort, but in Yorkshire he was captured on May 31st, 1415, by an armed force under one Henry Talbot of Easington who was apparently privy to the designs of the earl of Cambridge.

Meanwhile, Sir Thomas Grey of Heton, a cousin of Hotspur's, arrived at Cambridge's castle at Conisborough near Doncaster. There Cambridge revealed a plan to exchange Murdoch for Henry Percy and the person who was impersonating Richard. With these two aces in their hands the conspirators could raise the north with Percy help. If they could persuade the earl of March to their side, they would proclaim him the rightful king, and with the help of Oldcastle and his Lollards, of Glendower and his Welsh rebels, and of Scots ever ready to discomfort the English they would eject 'Henry of Lancaster, usurper of England'.

The plot now struck two snags. Cambridge thought he had converted Sir Robert Umfraville, warden of Roxburgh, to his side, and it was to be his duty to let in the Scots when the time for action came. The Scots actually invaded, but Umfraville, instead of welcoming them, chased them back over the border inflicting heavy losses. Meanwhile Murdoch had been rescued from Cambridge's men by the daring exploit of one Ralph Pudsey, and was now again safely in Henry's hands. But Cambridge and Grey were not to be so easily deterred. They went south to the great muster near Southampton.

It was at Southampton that the plot finally matured, and the conspirators engineered a major stroke – they suborned the loyalty of Henry, Lord le Scrope of Masham. Scrope was the grandson of one of Edward III's most devoted knights and he was nephew to the Archbishop Scrope whom Henry IV had summarily executed and who was now known in the north of England as Saint Richard. During the reign of Henry IV Scrope had served with distinction as an ambassador with Henry Beaufort, and in 1410 he had been appointed treasurer to the crown and a knight of the Garter. He was on terms of the greatest intimacy with Henry V, sharing his public and private confidences and on occasion even sharing his bed.[2] As recently as July 22nd Henry had added his name to the list of trustees who would administer his private estate if he himself never returned from France.

Cambridge, Grey and Scrope now broached their plans to Edmund Mortimer, earl of March – and the signal for general revolt was to be the assassination of the king and his brothers on August 1st. Conversations began on July 21st and continued at various rendezvous in the neighbourhood of Southampton until the end of the month. On the night of July 31st the earl of March finally made up his mind – he went to Henry and exposed the whole plot.[3]

Henry's reaction was typical of his self-control. It is possible that his spies had already warned him of the conspiracy, but the extent of it as revealed by March would have driven a lesser man to panic action. Instead, Henry quietly summoned his magnates – most of whom were close at hand – to Porchester Castle as though to an ordinary council. There he indicated that he had heard rumours of a plot against his life but that he found it difficult to believe. What did his nobles advise? The conspirators collapsed, and confessed on the spot – they were removed to prison in Southampton, and a commission of ten lords and two judges was at once appointed and a jury of twelve Hampshire men impanelled. The trial was held in Southampton Castle on Friday, August 2nd. By this time the king had the written confessions of Cambridge and his pitiful plea for mercy – and both letters are still extant.[4] Cambridge and Grey admitted the assassination plot, but Scrope pleaded that, although he knew of the conspiracy, he knew nothing of the planned assassination – his excuse was that he had only listened to Cambridge in order to expose him. Grey was immediately condemned to a traitor's death, but Cambridge and Scrope demanded trial by their peers. Twenty peers were easily and quickly assembled – and it is odd that they included the earl of March and Lord Clifford – and on August 5th the duke of Clarence pronounced sentence. The three conspirators were to be drawn, hung and beheaded, but, by the king's mercy, the hanging was remitted and Cambridge and Grey were also excused the drawing. Scrope alone suffered the infamy of the traitor's hurdle and was drawn through the streets of Southampton to the north gate, where all three were beheaded just outside the city wall. Scrope's head was later spiked on one of the gates of York and Grey's on the Tower at Newcastle as grim warnings to their northern friends.

Henry's justice lacked full legal propriety but this had every excuse in the fact that the expedition was ready to sail and time was short. In any event justice was done and seen to be done, the sentences were inevitable, and in November they were formally confirmed in full parliament.[5] Henry deserves credit for the modicum of mercy he extended to all three conspirators.

The position of the earl of March was, however, still in doubt. It was so precarious that it was not until August 9th that he was granted a full pardon and cleared of any imputation on his loyalty.[6] He had undoubtedly toyed with the prospects outlined to him, and the suspicion remains that he had purchased his immunity by the somewhat tardy betrayal of his friends. On the other hand his loyalty was never again in question.

This Southampton Plot is obscure in many of its details but it was a revealing crisis of great significance. There is the evidence of the Brut chronicle that the conspirators 'for lucre of money had made promise to the Frenchmen', and in fact that 'they received of the Frenchmen a million of gold',[7] but there were enough dynastic reasons for conspiracy within England without resort to bribes from overseas. The Brut story appears nowhere else and can be discounted. The Southampton Plot proves that in 1415 not only in the north of England but within the king's most intimate circle there were still powerful interests who had not forgotten 1399. The suggested alliance of the conspirators with Lollards, Welsh, Scots and the northerners who had been crushed at Shrewsbury reveals the internal weakness of the Lancastrian dynasty[8] – it was a plot which with shrewder planning might well have been rewarded with over-whelming success. The king handled a critical situation with decisive speed and without brutality – the young heir of Cambridge was brought up in the royal household and the earl of March was not disgraced. Henry V was never again troubled with treason, but his dynasty was to meet its fate in the person of the grandson of the executed earl of Cambridge who in 1461 was to become Edward IV of England. 'The evil tradition of bloodshed,' as Bishop Stubbs phrased it, had its roots in Ponte-fract Castle, it was fed on the blood of Shrewsbury's field and it was to blossom into what we now know as the Wars of the Roses. In that tradition the Southampton Plot was a tragic early chapter.

Amid these exciting events and all the turmoil of embarkation Henry now found time to put the finishing touches to his will[9] – it had been under consideration for some six months – and to sign it. It contained the most elaborate and detailed instructions for his funeral and tomb, which was to be elevated to the most prominent position in the Confessor's Chapel in Westminster Abbey, for masses and endowments for the welfare of his soul, and for bequests not only to his relatives but to humbler friends and his household servants. A jewelled sword was left to the Emperor Sigismund, but Henry's brother Thomas, duke of Clarence, was not mentioned – from the time when his father had relegated Henry in favour of Clarence there was apparently no love lost between the two elder sons.

A week later, on Sunday, August 11th, 1415, King Henry V in his magnificent ship *La Trinité Royale* and with his armada of 1,500 ships and perhaps 10,000 men sailed from the Solent. As warden of England, Henry left behind him his brother John, duke of Bedford, supported by a regency council of eight which included Chichele, archbishop of Canterbury. But Henry's troubles were not yet over – a mysterious fire broke out which destroyed three of his vessels.[10] There were faint-hearted readers of omens who attempted to dissuade Henry from continuing, but the king was not to be baulked, and the English chroniclers give an ecstatic description of the fleet gay with all the pomp of heraldry making out across the Channel.[11] The expedition took two days to reach the French coast.

Chapter 10

THE HARFLEUR
DISASTER

I F HENRY HAD WANTED to use an easy bridgehead for the invasion of France there was no need to go farther than English Calais. But Calais was a good hundred and fifty miles from Paris with the marshes of Picardy in between. On the other hand the mouth of the river Seine was less than a hundred miles from the capital with a fine river route leading through 'his' duchy of Normandy direct to Paris. Sentiment and a bold strategy steered the English fleet towards the mouth of the Seine, where on the north bank, the town of Harfleur commanded the estuary.

In those days Harfleur was a busy port of great renown for its salt and weaving industries, and it was reputedly impregnable.[1] Its well-fortified moated walls were about two and a half miles in circumference, each of its three gates was protected by drawbridge, portcullis, and barbican, there were twenty-six towers of massive thickness punctuating the crenellated fortifications, and the river Lézarde running through the centre of the town guaranteed a good and sufficient water supply.[2] Harfleur was Henry's first and very difficult objective.

The invaders made landfall in the shelter of the chalk cliffs at Chef de Caux where today the great port of Le Havre sprawls. The fleet anchored in the Seine estuary, and, after a preliminary reconnaissance which revealed no signs of opposition, the men, horses, stores and siege trains were safely and speedily disembarked. The investment of Harfleur began.

The garrison and citizens of Harfleur prepared for stout resistance, promptly flooded the flat lands to the north of the town, and sent for help to the dauphin who was beginning to assemble a considerable French army at Rouen. Before Henry could complete the encirclement of the town the floods forced Clarence to take a circuitous route to close the northern approaches, and in the meantime the besieged received welcome reinforcement. The commander of the garrison was the seigneur d'Estouteville and he was now joined by the seigneur de Gaucourt with three or four hundred men-at-arms.[3] They were to fight bravely and well, and it was not until August 19th that Harfleur was completely ringed. Henry built a trench and rampart round[4] the walls to give protection to his men and to make sallies or attempts at further reinforcement or revictualling extremely hazardous. The king himself lodged in comparative luxury on the neighbouring hill of Graville, and his chief officers' tents were pitched on the low hills to the north and east. The rank and file were not so fortunate – they had to keep watch in the marshy terrain near the walls.

Henry now issued stringent orders to curb the brigandage of his men.[5] The English army was no worse and no better than any other army of the fifteenth century. Its declared tactics were to live on the invaded country – and that was approved and customary. But Henry had all along proclaimed that Normandy was his own duchy, and it was therefore natural and sensible that he should seek to prevent too brutal a harrying of a countryside which he had promised to rescue from foreign bondage. Priests and women were given special protection, prostitutes were not allowed within the camps but were to be collected together some three miles away, and all English soldiers were to wear the large red cross of St George on chest and back so that they could be recognized – it is an early attempt at using uniform as a stimulus to an *esprit de corps* and to general morale.[6] But for the most part such regulations were common to most medieval armies, and the fact that they were issued at all argues as much for their regrettable necessity as for the mercy and loving kindness of those who made them. Six years later Henry's proclamations had to be solemnly re-enacted[7] on account of the 'enormous crimes and excesses' of his soldiery. The ordinances at Harfleur were part of a medieval drill, and Henry, while deserving credit as a strict and efficient soldier, does not therefore earn the title of saint. And there was much excuse for excesses amongst the lower ranks – they were living in appalling conditions in marshy country, and they were soon decimated with dysentery while king and court kept regal state in the safety and comfort of Graville.

The siege lasted until September 22nd. It took five weeks for the best equipped army England had yet sent abroad to take a small town weakly garrisoned but bravely defended and well protected by its fortifications and the lie of the land. Although the river Lézarde ensured Harfleur's water supply there was obviously a limit to food supplies unless the king of France could send help and raise the siege. Meanwhile Henry had to rely on assault and battery, with starvation as his ultimate weapon.

In most of its methods the siege was as old as history – mining and counter-mining, the use of the 'ram' and every kind of stone-slinging engine harnessing all the devices of tension, torsion and counterpoise to increase range and effectiveness. On the defenders' side the age-old methods were still in use – pouring boiling water, oil, and fat on the besiegers, firing blazing arrows to burn the wooden fencing of the rams, throwing quicklime and powdered sulphur into any enemy faces they could see and reach. But both sides now had the help of gunpowder in guns which were beginning to be formidable. The biggest of Henry's guns were some 12 feet long with a calibre of over 2 feet, and all of them could shoot stones of 400 lb. or even 500 lb. weight over the walls into the nearest houses. They were used to great effect to make breaches, and by their blast and thunder to wear down the morale of the besieged whose artillery was far less impressive. An eye-witness has told how the king himself superintended the gunnery, spending whole nights in preparations and inspections, and arranging for the thrice-daily bombardments which followed.[8] But after nightfall the besieged had the time and energy to make good the breaches before the next day's onslaughts began. Food was beginning to run short within the ramparts, but food was also a problem for the besiegers. Marshy air, the hot work of the day followed by the night frosts of an early autumn, too much eating of rotten apples and unripe grapes, too much drinking of young wine and raw cider, inordinate feasts of shell-fish eaten in surroundings poisoned by rotting offal – fever and dysentery were the natural results of such conditions, and they struck both high and low.[9] Bishop Courtenay of Norwich, an especially close friend of Henry, Michael de la Pole earl of Suffolk who had gone into exile with Henry's father and had remained a devoted adherent of Lancaster ever since, many faithful knights and some 2,000 of the rank and file died of disease outside the walls of Harfleur, and many more were rendered *hors de combat* – the king's brother the duke of Clarence, the earl of March, the earl marshal, the earl of Arundel[10] and about 5,000 more had to be sent back to England grievously sick.

On September 18th the citizens of Harfleur sought parley. Henry's first reply was a stern call for unconditional surrender, but his remaining nobles and the health of the surviving soldiery caused him to think again – he would permit a deputation from the besieged to visit the dauphin near Rouen and ask for help. If no aid were forthcoming Harfleur was to be surrendered on September 22nd, and hostages were taken and a solemn oath publicly sworn to ensure the good faith of the besieged. The French army was in no state to be able to offer help, and, as promised, the deputation returned, and Harfleur surrendered.

Henry was a great believer in the propaganda of display. His reception of the town's leaders required throne, crown and every effect of pageantry, and his ceremonial entry into Harfleur was staged with all the brilliant trappings of Church and State. But Henry's sense of drama – or it may have been a sincere and strange humility – was not content with mere spectacle: as the king reached the town gates he dismounted, took off his shoes, and went barefoot to the church of St Martin to return thanks to God for his victory.[11]

It was a victory won at appalling cost, and the citizens of Harfleur now reaped the bitter rewards of their stubbornness. The leaders and chief citizens were taken prisoner and held for ransoms. The lesser inhabitants were divided into two parties – those who were prepared to swear allegiance to Henry would be permitted to stay in Harfleur, some 2,000 others, including many women and children, were to be evicted. 'They put out alle the French people both man woman and chylde and stuffed the town with English men' says the Brut chronicle.[12]

It was a ruthless policy based on the assumption that Normandy was an English possession by right, and Henry offered substantial rewards to London merchants and craftsmen who would settle in Harfleur in place of the departed natives. On the other hand, Harfleur was not sacked – as the French expected it to be – and the deported women were not only allowed to take what possessions they could carry but were even provided with small sums of money to help them on their sad way. They were met farther up the Seine by the French forces and escorted to Rouen. And although Harfleur was to be an English bridgehead the ancient Norman privileges and customs of its citizens were confirmed and preserved – Harfleur was to be a second Bordeaux rather than a second Calais.

While arrangements were being made for the restoration of Harfleur's battered defences and the anglicized reorganization of its civil government, Henry, without consulting his council, commissioned the seigneur de Gaucourt to take a challenge to single combat to the dauphin at Rouen. It was written in Anglo–Norman and dated September 26th, 1415.[13] The throne of France was to go to the better fighter but not until the present king, Charles VI, died, and thus two Christian princes would avoid the shedding of much Christian blood, the desolation of fair countrysides, the lamentations of women and children, and so find favour in the sight of God and approval from all mankind. When it is remembered that Henry was a hardened soldier of twenty-seven years of age, and that the dauphin was not yet nineteen, without experience of war and so sickly in health that he was to die within a twelve-month, the glint of Henry's armour appears somewhat tarnished. On the other hand, the personal challenge of leaders before the clash of armies was part of medieval protocol, and it may be doubted whether Henry even expected an answer – it is certainly not surprising that he never received one.

The siege of Harfleur was reported to London's mayor as a resounding victory[14] – it was in fact a disaster. The considerable armada which had left the south coast in August was now reduced by at least a third to an effective strength of 900 men-at-arms and about 5,000 archers – the rest were dead or invalided home, and to counterbalance the optimism of Henry's dispatches to London there is the eye-witness's report that Henry was enraged to hear of many desertions.[15] There were many in the king's council who were appalled at the prospects and advised, in view of the losses during the siege, the health of the survivors, and the approach of winter, that Henry's wisest course was to return home with all speed from Harfleur. Henry had other views.

Chapter 11

THE AGINCOURT
TREK

ONE OF THE TERMS of the Harfleur surrender was that the seigneur de Gaucourt and the garrison should be granted parole in order that they might make arrangements for obtaining their ransom moneys, providing that they would surrender to Henry at Calais by Martinmas (November 11th).[1] Henry was determined that he at all events would keep the appointment. Yet between his depleted army and Calais were over a hundred and fifty miles of hostile and difficult country with many fortified towns, much forest, marsh and many swollen rivers to bar the way, and at Rouen the French forces were now assembling in formidable numbers. To the consternation of his council at the time, and with the condemnation of every military historian of any consequence since, Henry determined to set out for Calais.

The general opinion of this venture can be summed up in the crushing words of a great modern historian not always unfriendly to Henry – it was 'the most foolhardy and reckless adventure that ever an unreasoning pietist devised'.[2] On the other hand, if Henry had followed the more timid advice of his council he would have returned to England with a shattered army, a broken reputation, and a bankrupt exchequer – his throne might easily have tottered to ruin. If he reached Calais unopposed, he would at least be able to maintain that he had carried out a useful reconnaissance and established an excellent third bridge-head at Harfleur. If he were forced to fight, he had an unshakeable faith in the protection of his God and the memories of Crécy, Poitiers and Nájera to support his optimism. Henry couched his recklessness in terms of a religiosity which jars on modern ears, but in the fifteenth century it was neither unusual nor shocking.[3] He was faced with an excruciating choice – as a soldier he preferred a prospect of glory or death or modest success to the certainty of failure and perhaps disaster if he retreated. The trek to Calais was not mere foolhardiness, it was the lesser of two evils.

It is fortunate that there rode with Henry a certain remarkable monk attached to the king's chapel. His identity is still in dispute and he will be referred to in subsequent pages as 'the chaplain'. He had a competent skill in the composing of Latin elegiacs and we still have both the metrical and the prose version of his description of the march to Calais.[4]

The king's uncle Thomas Beaufort, earl of Dorset, was given 1,200 men to keep Harfleur safe and to guard the heavy artillery and siege impedimenta which had to be left behind. On October 8th the depleted army of a mere 900 lances and 5,000 archers set out on the 200-mile march to Calais with rations for eight days. Henry's baggage included a crown, a precious sword of state, the chancery seals, much of the regalia which was not in pawn in England, and a handsome portion of the 'true cross'. The army rode as usual in three divisions. The vanguard was under the command of Sir John Cornwall and Sir Gilbert Umfraville, the main body under the personal command of the king, and the rear-guard under the duke of York and the earl of Oxford. The basic rations needed supplementing, and the army, as all medieval armies, scoured the countryside for extra supplies. Most of the French chroniclers report the sufferings of their compatriots, but there is no record of excessive atrocity.[5]

There were minor skirmishes at Montivilliers just north of Harfleur and near Fécamp on the coast, but the first major obstacle was the town of Arques on the river Béthune some four miles south-east of Dieppe where they arrived on October 11th. The threat of fire and sword was sufficient to bring the citizens of Arques to terms – they agreed to supply bread and wine and allowed the English to cross the river without hindrance. The walled town of Eu on the river Bresle was the next halt, but Henry's threats again secured supplies and the unmolested crossing of another river.

The English were now approaching their most formidable

obstacle – the river Somme, where the ford of Blanche-Taque at its mouth was reported to be defended by a large force of French cavalry, with its causeways destroyed and the actual ford staked to prevent the passages of horses. It was by this ford that Edward III had crossed the Somme to win the great victory of Crécy in 1346, and Henry, realizing its importance, had ordered the Calais garrison to send out forces to safeguard his own crossing. But the French had not been altogether idle. The dauphin and his Armagnac allies had now a sizeable army within striking distance – they had moved up from Rouen. True, the duke of Burgundy was of no assistance to either side – he had been negotiating with the English right up to the start of the invasion, but at this moment of crisis he preferred to enjoy hunting in his forests in the Côte d'Or.

Under the celebrated Marshal Boucicault the French were mustered in force, and along the direct route from Harfleur to Calais both garrisons and citizens had been warned to resist, harry, and thwart the English invaders. Henry was advised that the ford at Blanche-Taque was now impassable even at low-tide, and, whether rightly or wrongly cannot be determined, he was also informed that strong French forces had beaten back the troops from Calais and were prepared to offer stout resistance if he attempted the crossing.[6] Henry's own men had been on the march for a week, and food was short.[7] His scouts reported nothing but difficulty, his knowledge of French geography was none too accurate, disaster stared him in the face.

There was only one direction in which Henry could go – up stream to find a crossing of the Somme at Amiens or beyond; but it was a perilous undertaking when a large French army was now threatening his every move. There was a possible crossing near Abbeville, but French reinforcements made it too hazardous. The next possibility was at Pont Rémy, but on the opposite bank of the Somme French forces marched in formidable parallel. The great city of Amiens was by-passed, and on October 16th Henry reached Boves where the castle belonged to a partisan of the theoretically friendly duke of Burgundy. It was here that a celebrated incident occurred. The hard-pressed English forces found wine in plenty, and a drunken orgy, which someone excused as brave fellows merely filling their bottles, was met by Henry's furious disgust: 'Their bottles,' he exclaimed, 'they are making big bottles of their bellies and getting very drunk,'[8] and he ordered his marshals to restore strict discipline.

The army toiled on, and now left the great bend of the Somme at Péronne where the main body of the French army stood ready to fight, and on October 18th, nearly sixty miles from the Channel, they at last approached a feasible crossing. Somewhere between Boves and Nesle an English soldier stole a copper-gilt pyx which contained the Host – he had mistaken gilt for gold. The theft was reported to Henry who immediately called a halt until the thief was discovered. Forthwith, the guilty pillager was hung on a tree outside the church he had robbed – Henry's justice was prompt and ruthless.[9] Meanwhile two fords had been revealed to Henry's scouts – at Béthencourt and at Voyennes – but they were both difficult on account of swampy approaches. Henry took personal command of the crossings. A whole day was spent in firming the causeways, and at last on October 19th the vanguard crossed the Somme. Henry supervised the crossing of his fighting men at one ford while Cornwall and Umfraville supervised the crossing of the baggage and horses by the other ford. The way to Calais lay before them, but they were a weary and dispirited force seventy miles from the nearest coast – and the French army barred their road.

At this stage there were divided counsels among the French. The constable of France (d'Albret) and the marshal Boucicault very wisely advised that the English should be allowed to retreat to Calais unmolested – they would take home with them a sorry tale of misery and distress. On the other hand, the dukes of Orléans and Bourbon, rating the English forces diminutive and already broken, urged that a pitched battle would dispose of Henry and his claims for ever.[10] The French king and his heir the dauphin had, for security's sake, been left behind at Rouen, but the duke of Berry with ample forces at his command, which included the pick of the chivalry of France saving only the vacillating duke of Burgundy, now rejected counsels of caution and sent heralds to Henry to announce that before he reached Calais he must be prepared to meet a French army in pitched battle on ground which was favourable to neither side –

the forms of chivalry were still in vogue. Henry received and rewarded the French heralds 'benignly', and, again claiming God as his aid, expressed himself happy to await the conflict.[11]

The reconnaissance of both armies was primitive and inefficient. Neither army was precisely aware of its enemy's whereabouts, and they seem to have marched in parallel from the crossing of the Ancre – which afforded no difficulty – until they both approached the stream of Ternoise. 'The chaplain' gives a vivid account of the mood of the English army at this desperate juncture. The king and his chief officers had donned their coat-armour in expectation of immediate battle. Trampled fields were evidence of the passage of a vast French host. 'The chaplain' could not vouch for the feelings of his superiors, but for himself and most men in the English army there was no hope save in the mercy of God.[12]

For three days the two armies marched almost within sight of each other but still without certain knowledge or contact. On the night of October 23rd, Henry found himself half a league beyond his appointed lodging, and again the customs of chivalry impinged on the new realisms of war. It was impossible for a knight, once having donned his coat-armour, to retreat.[13] Henry therefore slept where he was, close to the village of Blangy on the left bank of the Ternoise stream. On the next day, the armies at last could see each other – the English on the left bank and the French on the right. Slowly and without difficulty or opposition the English made their crossing of the stream to see facing them the French host 'like locusts' barring their way to Calais and home.[14]

The route to Calais lay between the woods of two villages – to the north-west was the village of Agincourt, to the north-east was the village of Tramecourt, and it was here that the French had decided to stand and fight – it was a well-chosen site where a reasonable stretch of unimpeded open country fulfilled the chivalrous condition that the fight must be fair, but apparently no one on the French side had had the sense to consider the lateness of the season and the likely effects of heavy rain.

And now a curious incident occurred which sheds a strange light on the familiar picture of Henry V as the immaculate hero-king. Surveying the coming battlefield, Henry saw the hopelessness of his own position and strength and the banners and overwhelming forces of his foes – he was prepared to make terms. According to French chroniclers and at least one reliable English chronicler – but 'the chaplain' does not mention the incident – Henry sent over to the French such prisoners as he had taken on the march from Harfleur, and offered to restore all that he had captured and repay all the damage he had done, if only he could be granted free passage to his city of Calais.[15] It may be that Henry's offer expected a refusal and was only made in order to give his exhausted troops a night's rest which they sorely needed, but it reveals Henry as more human and less foolhardy than he is frequently made to appear. It was at this juncture, too, that Sir Walter Hungerford dared to phrase in the king's hearing the thought that must have occurred to every sensible man in Henry's army – 'Would that we had ten thousand more good English archers who would gladly be with us today.' It drew forth the celebrated boast, immortalized by Shakespeare, 'Thou speakest as a fool; by the God of heaven, on whose grace I lean, I would not have one more if I could. This people is God's people; he has entrusted them to me today and he can bring down the pride of these Frenchmen who boast of their numbers and their strength.'[16] If military experts must criticize the general, ordinary laymen must admire the courage of the king – such sublime confidence was near to madness, but, when the event was victory, it was also akin to genius.

The English troops were enjoined to rest where they could, to keep silent and to make their final confessions to the priests of the king's chapel – and to add to their miseries it poured with rain. Where all was gloomy silence in the English camp, there was merriment and confidence in the French – they were even betting on who would capture the king.[17] It is said of Henry himself that he spent the night making the rounds of his soldiery in disguise to give them heart and encouragement. There is no contemporary warranty for this hallowed Shakespearian story, but it was not unlikely. We have letters written when Henry was fighting in Wales that show him to have had the first requisite of any great general – a care for his men. Nothing is more to Henry's credit than that, after a fortnight's gruelling march[18] through Normandy and Picardy, after the devastating necessity of a desperate wheel into the heart of France and after a night of horrible weather he was able to lead his men against appalling odds confident in their loyalty and zeal. As a strategist on this occasion Henry V may have been infantile, as a leader he proved himself inspired.

On the morning of Friday, October 25th, 1415, the day of Saints Crispin and Crispinian, the battle was joined. The English were outnumbered by at least three or four to one (and some authorities have said ten to one), and Henry moved his tiny force forward to ensure that any frontal attack was narrowed between the woods of Agincourt on his left and of Tramecourt on his right. The heavy rain of the previous night had left the intervening ground – newly ploughed wheatfield[19] – waterlogged and sodden, but neither side could now call off the battle. Early in the day Henry's baggage train, which was parked to the south near the village of Maisoncelles, had been raided, and his crown, his jewels and his seals had been plundered. Henry summoned what was left of his rear-guard, including his royal chapel, to his centre, and 'the chaplain' was therefore able to give an eye-witness account of the subsequent fighting.

Henry's army was in a line of three divisions. He himself, displaying his surcoat of the three leopards of England and the three golden fleurs-de-lis of France, and with his bascinet encircled with a jewelled gold crown,[20] was in command of the centre. The left wing was under the command of the Lord Camoys, whose handsome brass is still the pride of the village church of Trotton in West Sussex. The right wing was under the command of Edward Plantagenet, second duke of York. Each wing of dismounted men-at-arms was supported by wedge-shaped flanks of the long-bow archers who could pierce an oyster shell at 250 yards with the cloth-yard arrows of their six-foot bows, and, when arrows gave out, could deal speedy death with their leaded clubs.

The French army chose a different formation – they preferred the column to the line, a formation which was partly due to the narrowness of the front and partly to their vast numbers. The vanguard or first line of attack was the post of greatest honour, and here were perhaps 8,000 of France's chivalry dismounted but heavily armoured and carrying long spears. Behind them came a second 'battle' massed about twenty men deep. At the rear was a third 'battle' of fully armed Bretons, Gascons and Poitevins. There were comparatively few archers and they were all cross-bowmen, but on either flank of the first line was a body of heavy mounted cavalry, and there is evidence that a few light guns were included in the French armoury.[21] The French were relying on weight of numbers, the impact of spears and outflanking by cavalry. The English perforce had to rely on the aim of their long-bowmen to break up the cavalry attack before it reached the English line, and also on a new and rude device which was not within the strict rules of western chivalry although it had been used before to some purpose by the Sultan Bayazid when he won his great victory at Nicopolis. It was either the king himself or the duke of York who at the crossing of the Somme had instructed every archer to provide himself with a stout six-foot oak stake sharpened at both ends, which, when stuck into the ground and pointed towards the enemy, could provide a very effective *chevaux de frise* against any onslaught.[22]

For two or three hours neither side began the attack, but at last the patience of the French was exhausted – they launched their cavalry and advanced their first column. The cavalry were immediately hampered by the sodden ground, and those who survived the deadly flights of English arrows were met with the *chevaux de frise* of the archers' stakes. The mounted attack broke up into a confusion which hampered the French vanguard whose men-at-arms were too heavily armoured to make quick progress over the newly tilled soil, and the English archery took a heavy toll as they struggled forward.[23] Even when they reached the English line they were so exhausted by the weight of their heavy armour, and so closely hemmed in, that they could not properly wield their lances. A massacre began. The English archers dropped their bows, and seizing clubs and short swords rushed to slay and maim from on top of an increasing mound of dead, wounded or thwarted Frenchmen. As the French vanguard was halted, the second 'battle' pressed on its rear, and the fighting front became mere butchery – the English climbing over

dead and wounded to slaughter and club the finest fighting men
of France. The third French 'battle' was powerless – they could
not get to grips, and seeing the slaughter in front of them they
fled the field. Meanwhile, the English men-at-arms were already
sorting the piles of the fallen to find prisoners for future profitable ransoms, and, miraculously, the dukes of Bourbon and of
Orléans and the count of Richemont were retrieved from the
gory heaps.

It was at this stage, when the main body of the French army
was stricken beyond hope of recovery, that Henry observed
some movement of French cavalry towards his rear which might
have threatened his tiny force already engaged beyond its
strength.[24] He gave the fateful order to kill all the prisoners,
save only the dukes, earls and other high-placed leaders whose
ransoms would be his own valuable perquisites. Both English
and French were aghast – this was against all the rules of
medieval warfare – and even the threat of Henry that he would
hang any man who disobeyed was ignored; he was compelled to
order 200 of his own archer bodyguard to undertake the bloody
work. The glorious victory which Henry named Agincourt now
became a nightmare. The prisoners were 'sticked with daggers,
brained with poleaxes, slain with malles';[25] their bodies were
'paunched in fell and cruel wise',[26] and, where some of the
wounded had sought shelter in a village shack, the shack was
burned over their heads.

Chroniclers at the time, and historians ever since, have
argued whether Henry was justified or not. It is probably true
that when he gave the order he considered that a new attack
was about to engulf his small force, which was already dissipat-
ing its energies in the search for ransoms. But the attack never
materialized, and it was not the cruelty but the selfishness of
his order which exasperated some contemporary comment.[27]
By medieval standards Henry was obeying his soldier creed –
military necessity justified any butchery – and the fact that his
own rich prisoners were exempted from the general order
tallies with his reputation for shrewd common sense – he simply
could not afford to miss the chance of spectacular ransoms.
Nevertheless, the slaughter of so many of his prisoners reveals
a ruthlessness in Henry which it is easy to excuse but difficult to

admire – it was a trait of his character which did not improve with the years.

The carnage of the day was completed by the corpse-stripping peasants of the neighbourhood during the night.[28] It has been calculated that the English casualties were only between 400 and 500, whereas the French were nearer 7,000.[29] On the English side only two nobles were casualties – the duke of York and the young earl of Suffolk, whose father had died at the siege of Harfleur. It is a fair comment on the increasing absurdity of contemporary armour that the duke of York was not killed in action but died of heart failure due partly to his corpulence and partly to the weight of his armour. On the French side, the casualty list reads like a roll of the whole French nobility – the dukes of Alençon and of Bar, the constable of France, the admiral of France, two brothers of the duke of Burgundy, 90 counts, over 1,560 knights, and probably between 4,000 and 5,000 men-at-arms. The English army was now encumbered with the spoils of a miraculous and overwhelming victory.

Of Henry's deeds during the fighting it is reliably reported that he fought hand-to-hand like a lion – he received many blows on head and armour, and the crown he wore was stripped of one of its jewelled ornaments. When his brother Duke Humphrey of Gloucester was wounded by a dagger thrust, Henry had rushed to his aid and warded off the enemy until Gloucester could be rescued – no one has ever questioned Henry's personal courage or fighting skill.[30]

If Henry attributed his victory to the goodwill of his God a dispassionate analysis can add other reasons. The English army was small, but it was led by one supreme commander whom all obeyed without question. The French army suffered from divided commands, family jealousies and rival allegiances. If the weather was with the English, the French could have chosen their ground more wisely. As it was, they sent their heaviest armour to trudge across soggy ground, which rapidly became a morass, so that they arrived at the point of impact exhausted and helpless before lighter armoured English archers who 'beat upon their armour with mallets as though they were smiths hammering upon anvils'. Agincourt should have been the end of heavy plate-armour; on the contrary, such is the conservatism of the soldier, it became heavier and heavier until powder and shot finally abolished it. For the moment, England had conquered by the strength of the English long-bow and the accuracy of the English archer. If the French had been able to profit from their disasters at Crécy and Poitiers they must have won the battle of Agincourt, and if du Guesclin had still been alive to lead them there would have been no battle of Agincourt, and Henry's trek to Calais would have been a sorry end to his continental adventuring. Fortunately for Henry, his God was on the side of the small battalions.[31]

On the day after the battle, Henry and his victorious army resumed their march to Calais loaded with the spoils of war and taking their distinguished captives with them. There were still 45 miles to go and it was not until October 29th that Henry entered Calais. It was on this same day that a royal messenger arrived in London to give Henry's anxious capital the stupendous news. The mayor and citizens with all the city's bells ringing made pilgrimage on foot to the Confessor's shrine at Westminster to give thanks for victory. They returned to St Paul's where Bishop Beaufort, Queen Joanna and such nobles as were left in England joined in a solemn service of thanksgiving. On November 4th, parliament met at Westminster, and the mood of national rejoicing was translated into the unprecedented grant of tonnage and poundage to King Henry for his lifetime – it was a surrender of the commons' chief tool for holding monarchy in check, and it was gladly made.[32]

Meanwhile, Henry was receiving an ecstatic welcome in Calais. Most of his men were less welcome, and, while encamped outside the city walls, they were compelled to trade many of their prisoners for food and sustenance – it was a sordid end to glorious victory. The king was pledged by his indentures to transport his army free of charge back to England, and it took a fortnight to muster enough ships and to persuade the captains to sail. Before the king himself left Calais there was a pleasant tribute to a dying code – the seigneur de Gaucourt and the other leaders of the Harfleur garrison kept their bond and surrendered their bail to Henry by November 11th as they had promised.[33] On the morning of November 16th, 1415, Henry and his chief captives set sail for Dover – the French nobles were astonished at Henry's capacity for riding stormy seas; the good soldier was also a good sailor.[34] At Dover in the evening, and in spite of a blizzard, the barons of the Cinque Ports waded into the water and carried the victor of Agincourt ashore to the plaudits of an assembled crowd of clergy and citizenry. At Canterbury the next day Henry was greeted by a procession of the cathedral clergy led by Archbishop Chichele, and two days were spent in St Augustine's Abbey outside the city walls for rest and recuperation. On November 20th the royal progress reached Rochester, on the 22nd it had reached the palace of Eltham, and on Saturday, November 23rd, it was welcomed into London.

The mayor and aldermen rode out in their furred scarlet gowns together with a crowd of the city craftsmen and merchants, which some have estimated at between 15,000 and 20,000, carrying the banners and signs of guilds and crafts, and met the royal cavalcade at Blackheath. The king was accompanied by only a small group of his senior officers and a bodyguard to look after the imposing array of noble prisoners who included the duke of Orléans and the marshal Boucicault. The London clergy joined the procession at Southwark, and London Bridge was almost unrecognizable it was so decorated and disguised with arches, flags, banners and sheaves of halberds. Tableaux of English history were mounted in the city streets, and the conduit in Cheapside flowed with wine instead of water. Boys dressed as angels sang welcoming songs, maidens threw flowers and puffed gold leaf towards the king, and the route to St Paul's was beneath a series of triumphal arches and through a madly cheering densely packed crowd of the citizens. The king and his officers gave thanks at the high altar of St Paul's and here they were joined by his step-mother Queen Joanna. The cavalcade, with the mayor and aldermen still in attendance, now rode along the Thames to Westminster, where the abbot and the monks were waiting at the Confessor's shrine. The royal progress took five hours to travel from Blackheath to Westminster, and we are told by eye witnesses that never once did Henry smile. He had urged that no thanks should be given to himself but that all the glory should be given to God and Saint

George – he would not even allow the crown and armour which had been battered at Agincourt to be displayed to the cheering crowds.[35]

On the following day, the mayor and two hundred leading citizens presented Henry with 'a thousand pound in two basins of gold worth five hundred pound',[36] and, now that the revelry and rejoicing had begun to die down, the king and his brothers turned to the mournful duty of remembering the fallen. A specially solemn service was held at St Paul's over the remains of his uncle Edward Plantagenet, duke of York, and the king and his brothers attended both the vigil and the obsequies – 'the false Aumerle' had achieved the semblance of a soldier's death and at last a hero's tomb.[37]

As the year 1415 closed in, Henry and his court relaxed at Westminster and Lambeth, and the Christmas feast was celebrated with much music and great revelry.

But why was Henry so gloomy as he rode through London? His raid into France had ended in a victory without parallel before or since. He and his men had not only won a battle against daunting odds, they had successfully survived a march of about 300 miles in 18 days on short rations in hostile country. Before that, they had successfully besieged under appalling conditions one of the strongest towns in Normandy and had left behind them a new bridgehead for future exploitation. Was Henry remembering that his victory had given him nothing but a few ransoms, and had left him with even the regalia in pawn? Was Henry realizing from his experience of fighting and marching in France that a pitched battle could be won and yet a war be lost if he was not prepared for the long, expensive and deadly business of siege after siege, for there was scarcely a town of consequence in France which was without its castle and its fortified walls? He was soldier enough to know that his trek to Calais had been a gamble from the military point of view, and that his victory at Agincourt had been due as much to the follies and jealousies of his opponents as to his own strategy and tactics. He was now renowned throughout Europe as the king who had revived the glories of Crécy and Poitiers, he was 'a second Hector', a 'king of kings', and even the Pope addressed him as 'the arm of his strength'.[38] It says as much for Henry's intelligence as for his piety that, when everyone else was drunk for joy, he could count the cost and weigh the future. It was neither humble religiosity nor hypocritical mock modesty which rode sternly through the ecstatic crowds – it was the sober realism of a soldier who knew just how much he owed to his astounding good luck.

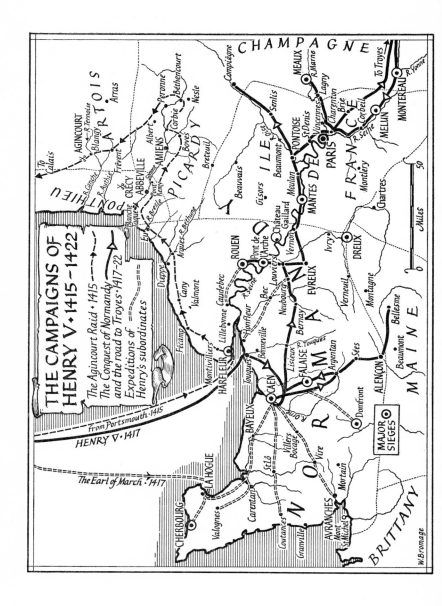

THE CAMPAIGNS OF
HENRY V · 1415 – 1422

The Agincourt Raid · 1415 →
The Conquest of Normandy
and the road to Troyes · 1417–22 →
Expeditions of
Henry's subordinates

From Portsmouth · 1415

HENRY V · 1417

The Earl of March · 1417

MAJOR SIEGES

C H A M P A G N E

A R T O I S

P I C A R D Y

P O N T H I E U

I L E

D E

F R A N C E

N O R M A N D Y

M A I N E

B R I T T A N Y

AGINCOURT
Arras
Bethencourt
Péronne
Corbie
Nesle
Albert
Boves
Breteuil
AMIENS
Frévent
St Riquier
ABBEVILLE
CRÉCY
Blanchetaque
R. Canche
R. Authie
R. Ternoise
Blangy
To Calais
Beauvais
Compiègne
Senlis
MEAUX
R. Marne
Lagny
To Troyes
R. Yonne
MONTEREAU
R. Yonne
MELUN
CORBEIL
Brie
Charenton
Vincennes
PARIS
St Denis
PONTOISE
Beaumont
Meulan
MANTES
R. Seine
Montlhéry
Chartres
Gisors
Château
Gaillard
Pont de
l'Arche
Vernon
Ivry
DREUX
Montagne
Verneuil
Bellesme
Beaumont
ALENÇON
Sées
Argentan
FALAISE
R. Touques
Lisieux
Bernay
Neubourg
EVREUX
Bec
Louviers
ROUEN
R. Seine
Caudebec
Lillebonne
Montivilliers
Fécamp
HARFLEUR
Honfleur
Bonneville
Touques
BAYEUX
CAEN
R. Orne
Vire
Villers
Bocage
St Lô
Carentan
Valognes
CHERBOURG
LA HOGUE
Coutances
Granville
Mont
St Michel
AVRANCHES
Mortain
Domfront
Dieppe
Arques
R. Bethune
R. Eu
R. Bresle
Tancy
Valmont

Miles
0   50

W. B. Bromage

Chapter 12

HARFLEUR AND
DIPLOMACY

THE BATTLE OF AGINCOURT is renowned as perhaps the most overwhelming victory won against fearsome odds that our history has ever known. Its fame has been glamourized by the magic of Shakespeare's muse, and even today it is an unquestioned part of an English myth which believes that our national genius is to snatch victory from the jaws of defeat.

But the defeat of the French at Agincourt did not mean the fall of France. It must be remembered that it was only a portion of the Armagnac forces which Henry had miraculously decimated. The king of France, the dauphin, and that grand old man of France, the duke of Berry, still commanded powerful forces at Rouen while their cousins and brothers were put to the sword or led into expensive captivity. The duke of Burgundy had skilfully, and perhaps traitorously, kept aloof from the fatal field, although two of his brothers – the duke of Brabant and the count of Nevers had fallen there. His main forces were formidable, intact, and committed to neither side. The disaster to French arms was, naturally enough, played down by the contemporary French chroniclers. There was no mention of Agincourt by the clerk to the parlement of Paris until nearly a month later, and even then it was casually referred to as 'the affair that the English had against the king'.[1] In fact it is a telling commentary on the London celebrations that in France after her most spectacular defeat in the field there was no hint of abject national surrender or pessimistic dismay. On the contrary, the formidable Bernard VII, count of Armagnac was immediately summoned to the royal presence at Rouen, and on

November 29th, 1415, Charles VI and his dauphin Louis entered Paris, and Armagnac was appointed constable of France with no signs of defeatism. It was a shrewd move which forestalled the machinations of John the Fearless, duke of Burgundy, who was planning to seize Paris and snatch personal aggrandisement and revenge[2] against the Armagnacs from the national emergency.

By December of 1415 Burgundy's forces had dared to reach as near to Paris as Lagny – a mere 16 miles away – and within the capital itself there were many who preferred Burgundy to Armagnac. On December 18th the dauphin, Louis, not yet nineteen, died in Paris an unlamented and despised libertine. The new dauphin John was married to Jacqueline the daughter of the duke of Burgundy's sister Margaret, and fortunately for the duke the young couple were in his territory and power. John the Fearless surprisingly decided that an immediate attack on Paris was too risky, and that he had everything to gain from waiting in the wings, courting his country's chief enemy and holding on to his own monarch's heir. He retired with his ample forces to his Flemish possessions leaving behind him a trail of brigandage and rapine.[3] Meanwhile, the count of Armagnac was officially installed as constable; he was in effect governor and regent and a man of weight and authority. His first activity was to press forward with plans for the recovery of Harfleur.

In England, Henry V had been recuperating. The Agincourt celebrations had been followed by a Christmas season which the court had had every reason to enjoy to the full, and as spring came round Henry made no secret of his intention to continue the prosecution of his claims on France as soon as he possibly could.[4] On March 16th, 1416, parliament was opened at Westminster, with an address from Bishop Beaufort to the significant text 'He hath opened for you a way', and its purpose was to provide the king with the wherewithal for coming campaigns.[5] The customs and the wool subsidy were already Henry's for life, and the previous parliament had granted a tenth and a fifteenth which were due to be paid in the following November. Henry in some financial embarrassment wished to anticipate that settlement, and a triumphant and subservient parliament found no difficulty in agreeing. The general mood of optimistic goodwill was further signalized by the completion of the negotiations for the exchange of Murdoch, son of the Scottish regent Albany, for Henry Percy the son of Hotspur, who was still held in Edinburgh. The young Percy was immediately restored to all his father's and grandfather's estates, titles and privileges, and was now so far in the king's favour that he was appointed warden of the east March on the Scottish borders.[6] It was an act of confidence which wiped out the bitter memories of Shrewsbury, and which was repaid by an unswerving and notable loyalty.

If there were precious few material gains from the Agincourt victory – ransoms were slow in coming – Henry V had at least won for himself and his country spectacular gains in prestige. The son of a usurper in the off-shore islands of Britain was now hailed as the greatest general in Europe, and he was about to be courted by no less a person than the Holy Roman Emperor. For the next two years Henry could pull the diplomatic strings of Europe while never losing sight of his main objectives. The raid of 1415 into Normandy and Picardy must be followed up by a major invasion which would finally establish himself in Paris. There might, of course, be 'growchings' from some whose loans could not yet be repaid, but, for a while, the victor of Agincourt could rightly feel that he had the bulk of his people – and they were very much a race of fighting men – behind him.[7] He could afford to ignore, even though he genuinely deplored, the appallingly lawless state of the land outside the towns and cities. For a while Henry the soldier could act the diplomat in safety. The Emperor Sigismund landed in England on May 1st, 1416, and remained for four months, but before the story of that significant episode is told it is necessary to refer to events across the Channel.

Henry's only new foothold in France was at Harfleur. Within six months of Agincourt he nearly lost it. On February 14th, 1416, the earl of Dorset was in command of a fresh garrison of 900 men-at-arms and 1,500 archers at the Norman port. The count of Armagnac with very much larger French forces was already threatening to invest the town, supplies were short, and living on the country was becoming more and more difficult. In March, Dorset, supported by Sir John Fastolf, Sir John Blount and a thousand men, foolishly undertook a major raid along the northern coast.[8] At Valmont near Fécamp the English forces were trapped by the Armagnacs. In a brisk action Dorset was severely wounded and his men routed. They retreated in disorder along the coast in a desperate attempt to get back within the walls of Harfleur. Dorset, in spite of his wounds, was able to rally his men near Etretat, and in a long night march of some twenty miles along the shore they reached the marshes near the Chef de Caux within sight of Harfleur and safety. There the French cavalry caught up with them, and, rashly dismounting, rushed down from the cliffs to a straight fight against exhausted infantry in the low-lying land below. The English had the better of the ground and in hand-to-hand fighting quickly established their superiority – the rout at Valmont was luckily retrieved, and the English marched into Harfleur leaving 200 French dead and taking 800 prisoners with them.[9]

The minor battle of Valmont was very nearly a major disaster, and proof that the count of Armagnac and the French powers of recuperation were not to be despised. When the news of its victorious sequel reached England it was hailed as yet another proof that God was indubitably on England's side.[10] In fact, Dorset's sally had been foolhardy, his defeat severe, his victory lucky, and the Harfleur garrison was crippled and still in grave danger.

In May the count of Armagnac, fortunately for the English, was diverted from his investment of Harfleur to Paris, where his ruthlessness quickly crushed a rising in favour of Burgundy. He was soon back in the environs of Harfleur, and with a shrewd sense of naval strategy he set about the encirclement of Henry V's lonely and hard-pressed conquest. The Seine was blockaded not by French ships but by nine large carracks and eight long galleys hired and manned from Genoa, whose shipwrights and seamen were at that time masters of the Mediterranean. In addition, sixty ships of lesser tonnage were hired from the king of Castile and shortly arrived off the Seine estuary from their home ports on the Biscay coast. The Genoese ships were not content with merely passive blockading, they scoured the Channel, raided the peninsula of Portland and the Isle of Wight, and only a severe storm halted an attack on Portsmouth.[11]

By midsummer 1416 the victor of Agincourt was faced with a desperate situation. There was famine in Harfleur, the Genoese allies of France were in command of the Channel, the count of Armagnac and overwhelming forces were poised ready to retake Harfleur – Henry decided on immediate and decisive intervention.

Men and ships were hastily mustered at the Hampshire ports ready to sail to the relief of Harfleur, and Henry at first intended to lead the expedition in person. On June 26th, 1416, he left London for the south coast and with his customary attention to detail busied himself in organizing a relieving force of about 10,000 well-equipped men. At the last moment he had second thoughts – he was heavily involved in diplomatic exchanges with his guest the Holy Roman Emperor, he would let his brother the duke of Bedford take command. At the beginning of August the English fleet was ready to sail but heavy Channel storms delayed its departure, and it was not until the evening of August 14th, 1416, that it reached the mouth of the Seine. The next day saw the rival fleets ready for combat. The English ships outnumbered the Genoese – the Spaniards at the last moment refused action – but the Genoese had the advantage of greater tonnage, loftier 'castles' for the crossbowmen, and a great tradition of success in naval warfare. In the ensuing sea-fight which lasted seven hours the English sailors and fighting men proved that long experience of Channel piracy, expert seaman-ship and an indomitable fighting tradition were more than a match for Mediterranean professionals. The day ended with the duke of Bedford severely wounded but four great Genoese carracks sunk and five more as English prizes.[12] The victorious English fleet relieved Harfleur in the nick of time – once more God had been on Henry's side. The Genoese prizes were absorbed into the English fleet, and king and emperor could share at Canterbury a joint Te Deum for another astonishing victory.

On July 18th, 1415, the Emperor Sigismund had left Constance on a mission to France, Burgundy and England. Sigismund of Luxembourg was the brother of that Wenzel, king of Bohemia, whose daughter Anne had been the beloved first wife of our King Richard II. By a profitable marriage he had become king of Hungary, and there he had spent his time as a great jouster, a keen if unsuccessful soldier, and an incorrigible hunter of every class of woman. Twenty years before his visit to England he had joined John, count of Nevers – who had since become John the Fearless, duke of Burgundy – in a crusade against the Ottoman Turks, who, under their Sultan Bayazid, had conquered the Balkans (leaving Constantinople isolated behind them) and were encroaching on Hungary. At the disastrous battle of Nicopolis in 1396 on the lower Danube John of Nevers had been captured and, he had remained a Turkish prisoner for two years. Sigismund had barely escaped with his life and had been rescued by Venetian war galleys which had sailed up the Danube; but he had survived these early misfortunes. He had the reputation of being savagely cruel but he was also an excellent linguist, a good Latin scholar and an enthusiastic patron of learning and the arts. In 1410 he had first been elected king of the Romans, but the election was irregular and on July 21st, 1411, it was confirmed at a second election. He was crowned king of the Romans at Aachen on November 8th, 1414, and soon declared himself Holy Roman Emperor.[13] Thenceforward he was more interested in Bohemia and the west than in his original kingdom of Hungary. At home in Prague he was faced with the formidable problem of the Hussite movement for religious reform, but in spite of that preoccupation he pursued two further objectives both of which do him credit – to heal the Schism of the western Church and to pacify Christendom so that a united crusade could drive the infidel first from Europe (and his own borders) and finally from the Holy Land. His methods and his manners were considerably less praiseworthy.

The diplomatic stage had other distinguished performers – from the Church, from France and from Burgundy.

The Church was not only being assailed by critics of its servants' shortcomings, laxities, exactions and pretensions, it had suffered the embarrassments of the century-old Babylonish Captivity only to be faced with the appalling disaster of the Schism.[14] Since 1378 there had been two popes – Clement VII at Avignon and Urban VI at Rome. The papacy had become a pawn in the chess-play of cardinals whose allegiances were more national than Catholic. Instead of acknowledging one rightful heir to St Peter and one sole regent of God on earth the European heads of state had taken sides in accordance with political expediency – England had become Urbanist because France was Clementist, just as Flanders, Portugal and the Empire became Urbanist while Scotland and Christian Spain became Clementist. The Schism had not only stimulated heresy it had decided the diplomatic bias of all contemporary European states, and it was not necessary for Henry V to be a Wycliffite, or for the Emperor Sigismund to be a Hussite, when they jointly desired to end the scandal. In 1410 the scandal had become even worse. At one stage there were three popes – Benedict XIII at Avignon, Gregory XII at Rome (he had refused to acknowledge his deposition by the Council of Pisa the year before) and the notorious John XXIII, better known as the condottiere Baldassare Cossa.

On November 16th, 1414, a General Council of the Church had been summoned at Sigismund's invitation to meet in the imperial free city of Constance. Its purposes were to bring the Schism to an end, to organize the reform of the Church and to stamp out heresy. It was not until November 1417 that this council of Constance finally ended the Schism. The tragic episode of Sigismund giving John Hus, the Bohemian Wyclif, a safe conduct to the council and then sanctioning and witnessing his condemnation and martyrdom at the stake in Constance took place while Henry was preparing his Agincourt raid.[15] While Henry was besieging Harfleur, Sigismund was travelling as far as Perpignan to persuade Benedict XIII, one of the three 'popes', to resign. And throughout, the English king was keeping a very high-level embassy at Constance – Henry V even before Agincourt was staking his claim to be a European leader. After the great victory Henry could enjoy the acknowledgement of that claim in the visit of the emperor to England.

It was clearly essential to Sigismund's ultimate objective that France and England should settle their quarrels so that, together with himself, they could show a united front to the infidel. The extent of Sigismund's travels in pursuit of this aim, in the days when even princes had no land transport other than the horse, was remarkable. On his way back from Perpignan he visited Avignon, and, after spending the Christmas of 1415 there, he arrived in Paris in a desperate attempt to bring to his side a unified France in company with France's hereditary enemy across the Channel.

He was met with a disheartening situation. Charles VI of France was still at most times an imbecile. The young Dauphin Louis had lately died. Bernard count of Armagnac was constable of France and held the Ile de France for Charles. Implacably opposed to the Armagnacs was John the Fearless, duke of Burgundy, who had skilfully held aloof from Agincourt, yet who was still intriguing with Henry V of England and prepared to sell France if Henry's bids were high enough. A France licking its wounds was in no mood to welcome talk of an English alliance; on the other hand Sigismund must be prevented from alliance either with Burgundy or England. The Armagnacs in Paris despised Sigismund's coarse manners, but they nevertheless paid handsomely for his board and lodging. They found it difficult to stomach his imperial pretensions,[16] but they were prepared to tolerate him in order to thwart a movement which might encircle France. By April 1416, however, it had become clear to Sigismund, in the intervals of parleying wenching and wining at St Denis, that he had nothing to gain from Paris. He decided to proceed to England, and see what he might do to bring the victor of Agincourt to his way of thinking.

From Henry V's point of view the approach of Sigismund had useful possibilities. If he was to seek 'his' kingdom of France in earnest, it would be a valuable sanction to his claims if the head of the oldest monarchy in Europe could be persuaded to endorse them. He decided to receive the emperor with as impressive a ceremonial as he could muster.[17] On April 27th, 1416, Sigismund and his cavalcade reached Calais, where they were lavishly welcomed in Henry's name by Richard Beauchamp, earl of Warwick, captain of Calais, and already known to Sigismund as the lay head of the English embassy to Constance. On April 30th, 300 English ships provided by Henry brought the imperial party to England. They were not suffered to land at Dover on the following day until they had assured Henry's youngest brother Humphrey, duke of Gloucester and the knights of Kent that they claimed no imperial sovereignty or jurisdiction over England. The ducal reception party even drew their swords, waded into the sea and held up the emperor's ship before it touched the shore until they received suitable assurances from Sigismund himself.[18] England after Agincourt could show the emperor his place.

Sigismund was accompanied by as many as 1,500 knights and also by the archbishop of Rheims as ambassador from the French court. At Canterbury they were received by Archbishop Chichele, at Rochester by the duke of Bedford, at Dartford by the duke of Clarence, at Blackheath by London's mayor and aldermen, and at last, a mile from London by King Henry V in person escorted by 5,000 nobles and knights. Sigismund was lodged in the royal palace of Westminster while Henry politely retired to the manor of the archbishop of Canterbury at Lambeth. Throughout his stay in England the Holy Roman Emperor and his considerable retinue lived at England's expense – the travels of emperors, like the provincial progresses of English kings, were a grievous charge on the exchequers of their gracious hosts.[19]

For the four summer months of 1416 Henry and Sigismund wedded business to pleasure. At an investiture at Windsor Sigismund was made a knight of the Garter, and in exchange he gave Henry the heart of St George. As a personal gift, Henry presented Sigismund with his own Lancastrian collar of S.S. which the emperor is supposed to have worn on every ceremonial occasion afterwards.[20] Diplomatic exchanges did not run quite so smoothly. Henry, it is true, while still maintaining his *right* to the French throne was willing to surrender it, providing France could be persuaded to restore everything she had ceded at the treaty of Brétigny (1360) and to forgo her rights to Harfleur – and Harfleur was the stumbling block. It had cost England dear the year before, in March it had nearly been lost, and the rout at Valmont had been barely balanced by the subsequent action below the cliffs of Chef de Caux. Henry had no intention of surrendering a city into which he had poured so many men and so much money and which he had begun to organize as an English enclave in France. The summer was fully occupied with elaborate negotiations with envoys from the court in Paris, from Burgundy, and from Holland,[21] in which the French prisoners at the English court also played a part. But Sigismund was quite unable to bring England and France to terms – he finally abandoned his original plans and decided to lend his full support to Henry.

On the day of the battle of the Seine, August 15th, 1416, Sigismund and Henry sealed the treaty of Canterbury.[22] It was a complete offensive and defensive alliance between the two sovereigns, and a far more impressive achievement for Henry than the slaughter of Agincourt – he now had the Holy Roman Emperor as his ally and warranty for all his claims on France. A few days later the glad news of Bedford's naval victory and the relief of Harfleur reached Canterbury, and on August 21st the two monarchs joined in a great service of thanksgiving in the cathedral.[23]

It was decided that a last effort to preserve west European peace should be made at Calais where both the Armagnacs and the Burgundians could be represented. Sigismund sailed to Calais on August 23rd and Henry followed on September 4th. Sigismund was lodged, again at English expense, in one of the great English houses in Calais, while Henry took up quarters in the castle. French ambassadors arrived, departed fruitlessly, and finally conversations were begun with John the Fearless, duke of Burgundy. If Henry could now conclude a treaty with Burgundy his projected attack on an encircled France was doubly secure. But Sigismund was still anxious to prevent an open breach, and John the Fearless was not anxious to become too involved – he had everything to gain from allowing Henry and the Armagnacs to fight themselves to mutual exhaustion. There is some obscurity about these Calais negotiations. On the English side, there was much play with the fact that while Armagnacs were talking peace they were still threatening Harfleur. The Armagnacs maintained that during the negotiations Burgundy committed treason by concluding an alliance with Henry, and there is a treaty in the records which, if it was ever sealed, goes far to prove the charge.[24] But in effect the most that Henry achieved was a more or less benevolent neutrality from Burgundy, and it is reported that he was lucky to achieve so much in view of the rudeness which his truculent youngest brother Humphrey, duke of Gloucester, showed to Burgundy's heir.[25]

By the end of October 1416, Henry V had returned to England, John the Fearless was back in Flanders, and Sigismund was on his way back to the final scenes at the Council of Constance.[26] Henry V's two years of strenuous diplomacy left him with a free hand in France, the benevolence of a fickle Burgundy, the avowed support of the Holy Roman Emperor, and the prestige which came from his ambassadors exercising a weighty influence in the Council of Constance. These were no mean achievements.

Chapter 13

MOUNTING INVASION

AFTER THE CONCLUSION of the Calais negotiations Henry returned to face his sixth parliament which sat at Westminster from October 19th to November 18th, 1416. The bishop of Winchester's opening speech combined almost sacrilegious reference to the fact that God had rested after six days' labour with the ancient aphorism that if you wished for peace you must prepare for war.[1] From his parliament Henry expected the means with which he could equip an invasion of France on a scale far greater than the reconnaissance of 1415. The commons for the first time showed signs of a certain reluctance. In granting a reasonably generous two tenths and two fifteenths it was stipulated that three-quarters would be payable at Candlemas, the balance at Martinmas of the following year, and that there was to be no demand for any prepayments and no demands for further subventions before the second instalment became due. The convocation of Canterbury gave Henry two-tenths to be paid within a year, and the convocation of York granted a usual one-tenth. Henry could not have expected more, but he needed more – and very soon he set about obtaining it. Meanwhile, parliament duly ratified the treaty of Canterbury, and on the day of its dissolution Henry's uncle Thomas Beaufort, earl of Dorset, was made duke of Exeter, with a pension of £1,000 a year for himself and his heirs, in recognition of his services at Harfleur. It was a curious appointment. Walsingham noted that there were some who thought the award unworthy of Dorset's deeds and worth, and that John Holland, the son of the last duke of Exeter (who had been executed by Henry IV) had already earned restoration to his father's title – he had distinguished himself at Agincourt and at the sea-battle of the Seine.[2] Henry with a high hand gave

Holland one of his father's titles – the earldom of Huntingdon – and promised him his lands when he came of age in the following year, and it may have been understood that Dorset's new title was only to be for life. At all events the young Holland did finally become duke of Exeter under Henry V's son, and in the meantime there was no sign of discontent on either side; both men served the Lancastrian cause to the death.

It was at this stage that Henry's distinguished prisoners of war made their own bid for peace and freedom. They had been very well treated, they seem to have been given ample opportunities for trying to arrange their ransoms, they shared the court life of their English sureties, they were free to hunt and otherwise enjoy their exile and at least one of them contracted a fruitful liaison with an English lady.[3] There had been some reluctance on the count of Armagnac's part to speed their delivery, and the English victory at the battle of the Seine had stimulated a change of attitude – hitherto the prisoners had refused to agree to Henry's demand that they should recognize him as the lawful king of France but now some of them were inclined to waver. The duke of Bourbon had been assured that, if Henry were granted all that had been offered at the treaty of Brétigny together with Harfleur, he might renounce his claim to the crown of France. He considered this a 'great and reasonable proffer', and had managed to persuade the duke of Orléans, the marshal, Boucicault and the seigneur de Gaucourt to his view. Bourbon proposed that he should go secretly to France on parole to persuade the French court to agree. Henry went to the length of preparing safe-conducts, but at the same time recorded that 'I wol not leve my voyage for any Tretee that they make'.[4] Apparently Bourbon never did cross to France, but de Gaucourt did, only to find the Armagnacs even more strongly opposed to Henry's 'proffer'. Only one of Henry's prisoners – Arthur de Richemont – saw France again before Henry's death. Bourbon's secret *démarche* was near to treason, and in the face of Henry's determined preparations for war a waste of effort.

Having spent Christmas at Kenilworth, Henry returned to London in late January 1417 to find himself in need of ready cash to finance his war efforts. The celebrated Pusan collar which had been redeemed in the previous May was again pawned to the city of London. The sacred royal crown was pledged to Bishop Beaufort for a further loan of 21,000 marks. Up and down the kingdom Henry's demands extracted loans from towns, cities, cathedrals, abbeys, priories, guilds, merchants, bishops, and gentry on the security of future revenues, and it is a remarkable tribute to Henry's popularity at this time that there were so few who demurred.[5] While cash was being amassed for immediate disbursement on munitions and stores, estimates of man-power were being prepared and indentures being drawn up ready for a general muster near Southampton in the spring. Master craftsmen were imported from Normandy to make cross-bows, arrowheads were bought throughout England, and – a picturesque touch – six of the wing feathers were to be plucked from every English goose, save breeders, to dress the shafts of the long-bowmen.[6] Colossal food supplies – mostly of corn and bacon – were stored along the southern coast, and non-combatant branches of the coming expeditionary force were carefully recruited. Carpenters, masons, and engineers were just as important, and appear as frequently in the records, as men-at-arms and archers.

Any continental English expedition demanded as a prerequisite at least temporary command of the Channel, and Henry's appreciation of his need for organized naval transport has led some enthusiasts to name him as the founder of the Royal Navy.[7] For his great invasion he needed many more ships than he needed for the Agincourt raid. He was still dependent on the traditional quotas supplied by the Cinque Ports, and on the requisitioning of merchant ships – native or foreign – which happened to be ready in English ports. A special fleet of eleven vessels, including a sizeable carrack under the command of Sir Thomas Carew, was commissioned to keep the Channel clear, and they successfully fought off and sometimes captured ships from France, Castile, Scotland and Genoa which might otherwise have hampered Henry's main invasion fleet. Even for the Agincourt raid Henry had had the nucleus of a royal fleet. For the 1417 campaign he was to own nearly thirty ships including eight large carracks, four of which were prizes taken from the French, and we have record of his detailed instructions for the building of a large warship as far away as Bayonne and of his

5a. English and French knights in a mêlée. The crowned figures at the centre of the picture are unidentified but are thought to be apocryphal representations of Henry V and the Dauphin, though they in fact never met 'face to face' in this way.

5b. An illumination depicting Charles, duke of Orléans during his imprisonment in the Tower. Charles was captured at Agincourt and was not released from captivity until after 1436 and then only on condition that he would never take up arms against England.

6. Thomas,
Lord Camoys
and his wife.

negotiations with the shipwrights of Barcelona.[8] The whole fleet comprised well over 1,500 vessels, but many were small and of the larger craft at least half were hired from Holland.

It was a well-disciplined fleet. Henry seems to have re-issued and publicized a code of conduct which may not have been original but which, as with his military codes, he meant to be obeyed. The Black Book of the Admiralty lays down detailed procedures for sailing signals, for fleet conferences, the treatment of neutral vessels, the allotment of prizes, and it also contains those prohibitions of sacrilege and the molestation of priests and women which are part of the military disciplinary code which Henry issued two years later before the siege of Mantes. Henry was not the author, but he was certainly the supporter of these idealistic standards.[9]

But Henry's fleet was far from being a Royal Navy. In fact it is doubtful whether at this stage of sea-warfare a royal fleet was necessary. Naval tactics were the tactics of simple sailing, and any ship could quickly become a warship when the chief armaments were the bow and cross-bow. A few of the larger ships had small guns but victory was achieved usually by boarding and hand-to-hand fighting. Henry needed ships to carry his men, his weapons and his commissariat, and merchant tubs, quickly converted by 'castles' fore and aft and equipped with a fighting main-top, sufficed, providing he had enough of them. Nevertheless, the care with which Henry attended to the naval side of his expedition was as creditable as his attention to detailed organization in all other fields, and in the next reign the author of *The Libelle of Englyshe Policye* was to give the fullest credit to Henry V as the protagonist of the theory that the English must be 'maysters of the narowe see'.[10]

In June 1417 a combined Genoese and French fleet was still threatening Henry's Channel crossing. Henry ordered the young earl of Huntingdon to put to sea with part of the fleet and sweep the Channel clear. Off La Hogue the two fleets met on June 29th and for a whole day battle raged. Finally Huntingdon gained an invaluable victory – four large carracks were captured and the French commander – the Bastard of Bourbon – was taken prisoner. The prizes were added to the royal fleet and never again during Henry's reign was he faced with serious opposition in the Channel – the way to invasion was safe thanks to the young Holland who had already more than justified his earldom.[11]

Henry had planned a spring invasion. On April 27th he had left London for the south coast, but it was another three months before his men and ships were ready to sail. The delay is difficult to explain. All over southern Hampshire men had been mustering since early March, and ships had been gathering in the Solent and off the castle of Porchester. There may have been many tardy arrivals, and Henry may have been unwilling to set sail before his Channel crossing was safe. But on June 29th Huntingdon's naval victory at least settled the latter problem. Through June and July the records show that Henry was moving about from Reading to Salisbury to Bishop's Waltham and to Titchfield, and the people of Hampshire must have been very relieved when on July 25th Henry at last boarded his flagship. A few days before, he had made a second will, and again it is remarkable that no mention was made of the duke of Clarence.[12] He had also again appointed his brother John, duke of Bedford, to act as his regent during his absence with a salary of 8,000 marks a year.

On July 30th, 1417, Henry V set sail from Southampton with a well-equipped armada intent on the conquest of France. With him went his brothers Thomas duke of Clarence, and Humphrey duke of Gloucester, and an army which his biographer says amounted to 16,400 combatant troops – including nobles, knights, archers, and artillery men – and in addition 1,000 smiths and carpenters, skilled miners, hordes of servants, and a mass of equipment including 'gonnez, tripgettes, engynes, sowes, bastilles, brygges of lethir, scaling laddres, mallis, spades, schovylles, pykys, pavys, bowes and arowes, bowstrynges, scheftis and pipis fulle of arowes, as nede for such a worthi warriour . . . and whanne tyme come thither come to hym schippes lade with gunepowder'.[13] Modern research has however whittled down these contemporary figures to a more likely outside total of some 10,000 fighting men with perhaps three times that number of non-combatants. It was probably the most formidable army sent overseas up to this time, and it needed well over 1,500 ships for its transportation.[14] As the population of England at the time was under 3,000,000, it was no mean feat to organize a striking force of such calibre and so well equipped – Henry V was an outstanding quartermaster. It was an army of professionals many of whom had seen hard service in the Welsh campaigns and all of whom were attracted by generous pay and the prospects of booty and ransoms, and they were Englishmen. Where the French had to hire Scots, Spaniards, Aragonese and Germans, England had readily available a native populace trained to arms, and, in Henry's day, accustomed to new disciplines of warfare; and, although guns and German gunners[15] were clearly necessary for what promised to be a war of sieges, the backbone of Henry's army was still the expert English longbowmen who outnumbered the men-at-arms by three to one. Some conception of the magnitude of the staff-work involved in such a venture can be obtained from the fact that the king had to find transport and fodder for the horses of his fighting men. It has been calculated that 15,000 horses were needed for the Agincourt raid – the invasion of 1417 needed many more. And although it was hoped finally to live off the invaded territory the forces had to be fed before they sailed, during the crossing, and for some time after their landing in France. It is perhaps not surprising that Henry had needed three months to complete his arrangements.

The destination of the expedition was secret – instead of Harfleur, which was still threatened by the Armagnacs, Henry chose to land on the west side of the Seine at Touque between what are now the plages of Trouville and Deauville. The great invasion of France began on August 1st, 1417.

Chapter 14

LOWER NORMANDY

A STUDY of the physical map of France will reveal what a formidable task Henry had undertaken. Normandy, which with some stretching of legality he could claim as his heritage, was only a fraction of France. Paris, if he were ever to get that far, was still only in the north of France,[1] and beyond it were difficult rivers and the great mountain bastion of the *massif central*. He was invading a country where almost every town was fortified, where even if the town surrendered the invader would still have to subdue its castle, where although the sympathies of citizens and garrisons might be either Armagnac or Burgundian there was a growing realization by all that they were French, and where, when surrender was achieved, it entailed the diversion of men and munitions to the duties of alien garrisons and the risks of sullen revolt.

On the other hand Henry's strategy in this second invasion cannot be faulted. His main objective was Paris. He already held the northern side of the estuary of the Seine at Harfleur, but, the dauphin of France with considerable forces was in Rouen on the north bank barring the way to the capital and on the south bank was the strong castle of Honfleur. Henry's secret choice of Touques as a landing-place had the virtue of surprise, and no sea journey could have brought him nearer to Paris.[2] If he could spend the autumn and winter in subduing lower Normandy he could neutralize Brittany and Anjou, widen his base in rich country where foraging would be fruitful, and then turn on Rouen, first cutting it off from Paris. Once lower Normandy and the Norman capital of Rouen were his, the direct road to the capital of France was open, while he could hope that his allies of Burgundy and the Empire would cover the eastern approaches. It was a masterly plan but it entailed a

148

formidable series of sieges, and unfortunately Henry could not be sure of either of his allies.

After a brief skirmish, the landing at Touques was successfully completed, and Henry celebrated the occasion by dubbing forty-eight new knights. Barely a mile away was the important castle of Bonneville, and Henry sent the earl of Huntingdon to demand its surrender. The garrison was allowed to send for help to Rouen, and if it was not forthcoming within six days surrender was agreed. On August 9th Bonneville was surrendered without a blow – such was the fame of the victor of Agincourt – and Henry could write to the mayor of London a story of his first success which was received with acclamation. The dauphin hanged the garrison's messenger, and later beheaded one of the esquires who had arranged the capitulation.[3] On August 13, 1417, Henry led his army westwards towards Caen, the key to lower Normandy. Instead of a frontal approach he circled south of the town and so cut it off from Paris and Brittany. On August 18th the siege began.

The size and importance of medieval Caen can be gauged from the remark of a chronicler of the time of Edward III – England had no town save London as large as Caen.[4] Its woollen serge had a European reputation, and thirteen parish churches and nearly thirty religious houses ministered to a thriving and prosperous population. In Edward III's day it had been unfortified, but in Henry's day it boasted a wall some seven feet thick with thirty-two towers and deep water-ditches. Just outside the walls were two famous abbeys – St Stephen's on the west where William the Conqueror was buried, and the Trinity on the east where his wife Matilda was buried. Both abbeys were strongly fortified, and within the town walls was the great castle begun by William the Conqueror and completed by his son Henry I. The river Orne in those days allowed ships to reach the town from the sea, and its tributary the Odon was a useful line of defence against attacks from the south.

Henry decided to begin the siege by surprise attacks on the two great abbeys. The duke of Clarence was sent ahead with a thousand picked men. The garrison in Caen Castle, as their forces were too few to hold every point, had ordered the clearance of the suburbs outside the walls and the destruction of both abbeys – no cover was to remain for the besiegers. Clarence was in time to find the Trinity abandoned but not yet destroyed, and he promptly occupied it and set up his headquarters there. Fortunately for posterity, a certain monk of St Stephen's warned Clarence that his beloved abbey was about to be destroyed, and he offered to guide the English to a weak point in its fortified wall.[5] Clarence promptly led a scaling party and captured St Stephen's before the demolition workers could take action. By the time Henry and his main forces reached Caen two excellent fortresses were already in English hands, commanding both the western and eastern approaches, and, as Henry had crossed the river Orne at Eterville on August 17th, Caen was also cut off from the south. On the following day he completed the investment of the town.

Henry's headquarters were set up in the abbey of St Stephen. In those perilous days abbeys frequently needed to be well fortified – Henry therefore needed no justification for using holy ground for military purposes and his heaviest guns were mounted on the abbey walls. Clarence acted likewise in the abbey of the Trinity. On the south the various channels and tributaries of the river Orne made both attack and sortie impossible, but Henry had had the forethought to bring with him a portable bridge of hides which enabled the two main attacking forces to keep contact across the waterways. The bridge had been made at Plymouth to the order of the king's master carpenter and had been shipped to Harfleur in sections in August 1415 and stored there for future use. It was an interesting early experiment in pre-fabrication and a striking example of Henry's planning and resource – it was to be used again several times on the road to Rouen.

The siege of the town of Caen was brought to a successful conclusion in just over a fortnight – a remarkably speedy achievement. It was a victory for the new arm – the artillery. The age-old methods of mining and counter-mining were still used, and we read of 'sheddinge of skaldinge water and boylinge pitch and oil',[6] but it was Henry's heavy guns mounted on the walls of the two great abbeys which made the final assault effective – a primitive kind of iron shell filled with fire-raising materials wrecked the timber houses close to the walls. On the other hand one of Henry's chroniclers admits that the artillery availed 'not by the stroke onelie but by violent noyse of the gunns'.[7] The defenders fought bravely and well but their walls could not withstand Henry's artillery, and on September 4th a final assault was mounted. The duke of Clarence attacked from the east while the king attacked from the west. The burgesses and the French men-at-arms were unequal to the double thrust. Clarence and the earl of Warwick led the victorious English to the centre of the town slaughtering as they went, but, in obedience to the king's express commands, sparing priests and women. It was a bitter struggle, and the streets were piled high with dead and dying when the victors turned to the grim business of sack and plunder.

If Henry's victory had been won 'with right little death of our people', as he boasted, the casualties on the French side were grievous, and in later days a resurgent France never forgot the butchery of Caen. There is no doubt that at first the English ran amok, and only when a semblance of order was restored did Henry arrange for the remaining spoils to be assembled 'in a great and strong house'. He gave the collection to Clarence reserving for himself only 'a goodly French book' of history.[8] When the rioting finally ceased, Henry's orders were strict – 'there was no man, howe hardysoever he was, durst to robb or spoyle any Church or hallowde place for feare of the King's justice which was extreme in such case'.[9]

It is impossible to be certain of Henry's motives in permitting massacre and pillage in one of the greatest towns of 'his' duchy linked so closely with his own Norman ancestry. It was probably intended as a warning to the intransigent and a promise of the fate that awaited them, but it may have been that Henry was at first powerless to control his men infuriated by so stubborn a resistance. On the other hand, the sack of Caen did not strike contemporaries as anything but the normal aftermath of victorious assault. In the light of Henry's own pious professions it would appear as a stain on the escutcheon of a *preux chevalier*, but Henry was now fighting a new kind of war which had little to do with the tenets of chivalry – its morality had greater affinity with the modern doctrines of total war and the necessity for 'frightfulness'.

Within five days of the capture of the town the garrison in Caen Castle sued for terms. If no relief came from the dauphin they would surrender on September 19th, but they were to march out with horses, armour (but not their weapons), clothing, a sum of 2,000 crowns to be shared between them, and a safe-conduct to the town of Falaise. Perhaps the sack of the town was justified – Henry obtained its formidable castle without bombardment or assault.[10] Nevertheless the butchery of citizens whom Henry claimed as his own people is in startling contrast to the graceful terms he conceded to professional soldiery.

It is remarkable testimony to Henry's boldness and originality that he began his invasion in the autumn and continued it throughout the winter. This was contrary to the canons of normal medieval warfare – campaigning was a summer occupation to be followed by a mutual agreement to retire safely to winter quarters. But Henry was not Edward III; he was now not leading a *chevauchée* hoping for another Crécy or Agincourt, he was the skilful generalissimo of an invading army which had also to become an army of occupation, and while he himself was the spearhead of the main advance he had able captains to undertake lesser tasks and protect his flanks. It is one of the earliest examples in medieval Europe of strategic warfare, and it was brilliantly planned and successfully executed.

Before Caen had surrendered, the earl of March had landed reinforcements at La Hogue and plundered the Cotentin. The earl of Huntingdon had captured Creully and Villers-Bocage, and, the day before the fall of Caen, Henry's youngest brother the earl of Gloucester had occupied Bayeux without serious resistance. From devastated Caen Henry himself led his main forces not towards Paris or Rouen but due south. Within a month the strong fortresses of Argentan and Alençon were his without a blow struck in their defence – such was the fear inspired by the massacre at Caen. The reputedly impregnable fortress of Falaise had been by-passed, lower Normandy was cut in half, Brittany was isolated and Maine and Anjou were within striking distance if Henry wished.

On November 16th at Alençon, Henry was able to make a truce with the duke of Brittany,[11] who was the son of his step-mother, Queen Joanna – it ensured that his right flank was, reasonably safe, and enabled him to undertake the conquest of the east of Normandy without fear of attack from his rear. Only one major fortress in lower Normandy remained to be taken before Henry turned his attention to Rouen – the capital of Normandy – and to the opening up of the river road to Paris. He turned back to undertake the formidable task of besieging Falaise.

The siege began on December 1st. Henry had his main army and the useful help of his brothers the duke of Clarence and the duke of Gloucester. It was at Falaise that William the Conqueror had been born a bastard – his mother Arlette was the daughter of a tanner who had lived in the valley below the town. Falaise was even more of a challenge than Caen. Its cliff castle was reputed to be impregnable, and Henry was beginning his attack in the middle of a more than usually severe winter. Lesser men would have cautiously awaited the spring; Henry of Monmouth refused to wait.

His camp was no canvas city; he erected huts of timber roofed with turf and fenced with ample palisades.[12] He decided to eschew frontal attack and to rely on gunstones of some two feet in calibre, and the even deadlier work of starvation, as his main armaments. The town was well defended by Olivier de Mauny, but, without help from elsewhere, ultimate surrender was inevitable. Henry spent the Christmas feast of 1417 in the camp before the walls knowing that within a few days impregnable Falaise would be his. On January 2nd, 1418, he entered the town, but the cliff castle was still to be won. His guns could not reach to the towering castle walls and mining was impossible – the castle was built on solid rock. Henry was not to be thwarted. His engineers built sheltered approaches over the moat on the town side, and with pick and shovel began to breach the walls. To smoke out the pioneers, de Mauny's men lowered lighted faggots, but these were quickly extinguished and a breach was slowly widened. Again, unless help could come from outside, the castle was doomed. De Mauny recognized the inevitable, and on February 16th, 1418, Falaise Castle was surrendered to Henry. There was no massacre.[13] The gallant de Mauny was taken prisoner but given his liberty six months later.

Within a few months all the ancient privileges of the town were restored, and its defences were repaired by the labour of those who had so stoutly defended it.

By the spring of the year 1418 nearly all lower Normandy acknowledged Henry as its duke. The policy of 'frightfulness' exemplified at Caen had been skilfully wedded to an able strategy and a brilliant tactical victory at Falaise. Henry could now organize his conquest not as a savage and foreign invader but as the rightful and just duke of Normandy which he claimed to be.

It was Henry's deliberate policy to leave civil government as undisturbed as possible. By the spring of 1418 his Norman conquests had been organized under four 'baillages'. The 'baillis' were English – Sir John Popham at Caen, Sir Roland Lenthall at Alençon, Sir John Ashton in the Cotentin, and Sir John Radcliffe at Evreux. Under these 'baillages' were fourteen 'vicomtes' and the great majority of these were left in native Norman hands. At Caen, centralized administration was provided by the clerical Philip Morgan as chancellor and Sir John Tiptoft as treasurer or president of the Norman *chambre des comptes*. Every encouragement was given to the local population to submit to the change of overlordship – for a fee of 10d anyone might receive a certificate to his new allegiance and continue his normal life without disturbance.[14] Ecclesiastical authorities were quick to appreciate that under Henry of Monmouth they could find greater security than under Charles of Valois – many of them acknowledged the new rule immediately and received back their estates and privileges without let or forfeit. On the other hand, there were many Norman knights who could not bring themselves to swear an oath of allegiance which was coupled with Henry's claim to the throne of France. Churchmen and lay citizens could salve their consciences with expediency; Norman chivalry as a whole refused to acknowledge the invader.[15]

There was one reform which Henry initiated which eased the way to winning over the civil population – the reform of the hated 'gabelle' or salt-tax. The taxation of salt – essential to all medieval economy[16] – was concentrated in the hands of the central government. Instead of an exorbitant 50 or even 75 per cent the tax was reduced to a reasonable 25 per cent, and once the tax had been paid the salt could be freely sold in the open market. An even more welcome concession was that there was no obligation – as there had been – to buy a fixed quantity of salt every three months regardless of whether it was wanted or not.[17] The English chroniclers make great play with the benevolence of Henry as contrasted with the tyranny of Charles – but to modern eyes the reform of the 'gabelle' appears no more than a simple bribe. But it was a bribe which worked – Henry had little trouble from the conquered civilian population.

While Henry went to great pains to disturb native civil government as little as possible, he nevertheless bestowed Norman estates on Englishmen. It was no crude expropriation, it was a skilful policy of planting a few loyal captains in hostile territory, where the reward of land and privilege was balanced by the obligation to keep the populace quiet, and, if needs be, to provide the king with stipulated men, arms, and services. Henry's 'plantation' of Normandy was designed to provide him with an army of occupation, and sometimes with reinforcements to his army of conquest, at no charge to the English exchequer. It was a shrewd if cynical insurance policy.

There is one remarkable incident which occurred in the spring of 1418 just before Henry entered on the next stage of his conquest. Henry, while busy with administration at Caen, was visited by the celebrated Vincent Ferrer, preacher, reformer, and later a saint. It is said by one English authority that Ferrer was specially invited by Henry. On arrival he preached before the king with 'marvelous audacité' and denounced him as a slaughterer of Christians who had done him no wrong. Henry heard him without objection, and then summoned him to a private audience of two or three hours. No one knows exactly what took place, but apparently on leaving the court Ferrer spoke to several of Henry's captains and urged them to serve Henry well. He was not the tyrant he had imagined; he was, as he had said, the scourge of God, but his cause was just.[18] The story may have been rewritten for propaganda's sake but it at least pays tribute to Henry's tolerance, and is in keeping with much other evidence which vouches for Henry's enthusiasm for private colloquy with religious zealots and hermits.

Chapter 15

THE ROAD TO
ROUEN

'WHILST HENRY WAS WORKING out his comparatively easy task in Normandy, his work elsewhere was being done for him by the French themselves' – that is a somewhat disparaging summary by Henry's most distinguished modern historian.[1] It is a fair summary except that the conquest of lower Normandy had been easy only because its conqueror had displayed a consummate skill in what today would be termed strategic generalship. That the French were engineering their own discomfiture is nevertheless lamentably true.

The state of France in the spring of 1418 was more than usually chaotic. King Charles VI was seldom in a fit state to rule, although in his rare lucid intervals he seems to have been both kindly and able. His queen, Isabella, was a woman who played politics with all the ruthless shrewdness of a Borgia. There seems to be no doubt that she had carried on a shameless, if understandable, liaison with Louis duke of Orléans, and yet now she was leagued with a duke of Burgundy who was never sure of her ultimate support. Her second son John had been a hostage of the Burgundian faction. After his death in April 1417, his young brother Charles, who had been married as a mere boy to Marie of Anjou, became a treasured hostage in the Armagnac camp – and the Armagnacs ruled the bulk of France including Paris. Isabella was at the centre of a very complicated web.

Just prior to Henry's landing at Touques the Armagnacs had finally quarrelled with Queen Isabella. Her profligacy shocked even a profligate court and her zest for power – while her husband sank deeper into imbecility – was insatiable. In May

1417, the Armagnacs were strong enough to banish Isabella to Blois and later to Tours,[2] and a tortuous situation became worse when the duke of Burgundy was invited by Isabella to come to her aid and free her from her Armagnac exile. John the Fearless eagerly seized his opportunity.[3] Isabella was rescued from her guards and joined the Burgundian duke at Chartres where he was debating a final attack on the capital. There, Queen Isabella pronounced herself regent, and, when Burgundy felt unsure of support within the capital, she openly allied herself with him and at Troyes announced that she had appointed him governor of France.[4]

While Henry of England was completing his conquest of lower Normandy, Burgundy, in alliance with Isabella, was intriguing to capture Paris – not for his nominal ally Henry but for himself. He was prepared to use the Parisian mob – who really ruled the capital – not to install Henry but to oust the Armagnacs. On May 29th, 1418, his intrigues succeeded, and the Armagnacs in Paris suffered the first phase of what became known as the Burgundian Terror.[5] On June 12th the count of Armagnac himself was murdered by the mob, and on July 14th the victorious duke of Burgundy entered Paris with Queen Isabella and was gracefully received there by the imbecile king. The only drawback to Burgundy's triumph was that the dauphin Charles escaped him and found sanctuary with the Armagnacs at Melun. The duke of Brittany attempted at this stage to reconcile the two factions.[6] He was unsuccessful, and when Henry V began the siege of Rouen he found the defenders were Burgundians with the rival Armagnacs under the dauphin holding a separate 'parlement' at Poitiers. The French were their own executioners.

Meanwhile, Falaise Castle had fallen to Henry on February 16th, 1418. With his main army he himself thence marched steadily towards Rouen while his captains covered his flanks and rear. The earl of Warwick invested Domfront and, after a costly siege, by July 10th both town and castle were taken. The duke of Gloucester and the earl of March had accounted for Vire, St Lô, Carentan and Avranches and had now invested the strong fortress of Cherbourg. It needed a five months' siege before it capitulated. The duke of Clarence was capturing the remaining castles on Henry's left flank, and the duke of Exeter was storming Evreux to Henry's right. By May 27th the king was at Lisieux. He advanced eastwards through Bernay, Bec and Le Neuberg and reached the strong and recently fortified town of Louviers by June 8th. It held out for three weeks, and it was here that Henry nearly lost his life. He was visiting the tent of the earl of Salisbury for a conference when a gunner sent a stone-shot from the walls which narrowly missed the king. When Louviers fell on June 20th, Henry took petulant and savage revenge – nine of the gunners were condemned to death. One of them escaped death, thanks to the intervention of Cardinal Orsini who was present in the town; the rest were hung, or, as Henry's biographer insists, were crucified.[7]

By the end of June, Henry was at Pont de l'Arche at the main crossing of the river Seine south of Rouen. Rouen was therefore cut off from the river route to Paris, and the mouth of the Seine was already in Henry's power – Honfleur on the west bank had been taken by the earl of Salisbury in the preceding February.

Pont de l'Arche was a formidable obstacle. The town itself was well fortified on the southern bank of the Seine. At the northern end of the famous bridge was an island fortress to ward off attacks from the north. Henry's army had to cross the river if they were to invest the town. Henry, however, had foreseen the difficulties – his men were provided with pontoons and engineers rapidly constructed boats of wicker covered with hides.[8] The details of the crossing are obscure but by July 14th, 1418, the English had crossed the Seine without the loss of a man. Bridges were rapidly constructed both above and below the town, and by July 20th Pont de l'Arche had fallen.[9] It was a skilful and notable victory.

Henry immediately dispatched the duke of Exeter and a small force of knights to Rouen to demand its surrender. They met with an unpleasant surprise. A sally of the garrison slew many of the English, and only Exeter's cool generalship prevented disaster.[10] To add to the king's fury, he was informed that the garrison was now Burgundian. He swore to be at Rouen's gates within three days, and, as good as his word, on the night of July

29th, 1418, the English army encamped on the eastern approach to the city.

Before the tragic story of the siege of Rouen is told it is necessary briefly to record events in England. It was said that Henry's old enemy Owen Glendower was dead at last.[11] He had never been defeated, he had never surrendered, and the place and manner of his death are shrouded in mystery. On the other hand, Henry's old friend Sir John Oldcastle, who was still at large when Henry left for France, had at last been captured in December, 1417. For Oldcastle's trial before parliament and his brutal execution – he was hung as a traitor and roasted alive as a heretic[12] – no blame can be attached to Henry: his brother, John, duke of Bedford, must carry that weighty load.

One parliament had sat during Henry's absence[13] – it had authorized the execution of Oldcastle, and it had granted the usual monies to the crown without demur in view of the encouraging news from France and the recent successful repulse of a raid – known as 'the Foul Raid'[14] – from Scotland. The raid had been led by the duke of Albany and the earl of Douglas and was repulsed by the duke of Exeter and a surprisingly well-equipped army – England had not exhausted all her resources in her attempt to ruin France. Henry the Conqueror, as he began the siege of the capital of Normandy, had the comfort of knowing that England was safe and comparatively undisturbed behind him.

Chapter 16

THE SIEGE OF
ROUEN

Rouen was described by one of Henry's earliest biographers as 'the Master Cittie of all Normandie'.[1] Its walls were about five miles in circumference on the north bank of the Seine some fifty miles as the crow flies up river from Harfleur. They were high, and the six gates were well protected by flanking towers and outworks. There were over sixty towers between the gates, and outside the walls was a deep and wide fosse except on the south side where the river Seine was a more than sufficient natural moat. At the north-west corner was the great castle, first built two hundred years before by Philip Augustus after he had retaken Normandy from King John, with its elaborate defences quite independent of the city. At the centre of the river front was a stone bridge which had been built by the Empress Matilda, with its northernmost arches made of wood so that in an emergency it could quickly be put out of action – it linked the main city with suburbs on the south bank. For nearly three hundred years Rouen had jealously maintained its privileges as a commune against the attempted encroachments of archbishops, dukes and kings. Its cloth industry was famous. It received rich revenues from the river trade which linked Paris with the Channel and, apart from its great cathedral, there were thirty-five parish churches and thirty-four religious houses including three great abbeys. In the quarrel between Armagnac and Burgundian the citizens of Rouen had lately shown where their preference lay. In the autumn of 1417 the citizens had expelled the Armagnacs and declared for the Burgundians, and by the end of that year they had invited Guy le Bouteiller, the commander of the Burgundian garrison at

7. John the Fearless, duke of Burgundy.

8. Charles VI of France.

Dieppe, to become their captain. He occupied the city and speedily drove out the Armagnacs from the castle – Rouen, as Henry found it, was staunchly Burgundian.

The city had had ample warning of Henry's approach, and its defences were well prepared. Beyond the walls, demolitions[2] had spared neither lay nor clerical properties, and military operations were in the hands of able soldiers. Guy le Bouteiller was supported by Guillaume Houdetot the 'bailli', Alain Blanchard who had ousted the Armagnacs and was now captain of the cross-bowmen, and Jean Jourdain who commanded the artillery.[3] The archbishop was an Armagnac; he had therefore discreetly withdrawn leaving the clergy under a Burgundian canon who had the boldness to pronounce Henry's excommunication. Rouen awaited Henry's armies with complete confidence – it was well stocked with food, its water supplies could not be completely cut off, there was 'marvelous plentie of gunns of everie quantitee, bowes and arbelesters' and 'they wanted no arms quarrells nor stones'.[4] Its confidence had even permitted asylum, rashly as it turned out, to thousands of refugees from the English invasion of lower Normandy.

It is ironical that Henry's second invasion of France was to find that its most fanatical opponents were Normans led and reinforced by some of the best soldiers of the duke of Burgundy. That Henry was merely coming to claim his own was now but threadbare fiction, and, as he inspected the scorched earth outside the capital of his Normandy, it looked as though a tricky diplomacy which had kept Burgundy from Agincourt was foundering on the fact that if Burgundians hated Armagnacs they were not yet prepared to surrender France to Englishmen without a struggle.

There is no contemporary record of the siege from the defenders' point of view but there are two descriptions from English sources. One is from the pen of Titus Livius who was present at the siege and closely in touch with the English leaders and especially with the duke of Gloucester. The other was written by a soldier named John Page of whom nothing is known but whose verse tale reveals him as a quite exceptional character – his eye-witness story was used by later chroniclers and was soon well publicized in London. His first rhymes he lived to polish in a second version as he had promised, but it is his first version which is invaluable for its plain and vivid picture of the horrors of medieval siege warfare and for its evidence of how Henry V commanded the loyalty and affection of his men[5]. Henry's justice – severe but impartial – and his attention to detail are the qualities which most impressed the rank and file of both sides.

As usual, Henry made no attempt to take the city by direct assault – his plan was to invest it and starve it into surrender. The siege began on July 31st, 1418. Henry's forces were not large, and several days had to be spent and many lives lost in first clearing away the nailed boards which trapped the approach roads, and the 'caltrops' and other entanglements with which the citizens had skilfully mined the besiegers' approach.[6] Great camps were built round the walls – Henry's on the east, the duke of Clarence's on the west, the duke of Exeter's on the north, the earl marshal's by the castle, and the earl of Huntingdon's to the south of the river. The only gap in the ring was to the south-east where the fortified abbey of St Catherine commanded the Paris road along which the besieged might hope to see help arrive. The great camps were soon linked by deep communication trenches sheltered from the artillery on the city walls, and the first major action was entrusted to the earl of Salisbury – he was given the task of capturing St Catherine's and so closing the road from Paris. It took Salisbury a month to isolate the abbey and to force its surrender, but by the beginning of September Rouen was encircled and both besiegers and besieged faced the stern prospects of a long winter siege.[7]

Henry had only one real worry – his army's food supplies. The surrounding countryside had already been denuded to fill the larders of Rouen, and then razed to thwart the invader. The bulk of Henry's commissariat therefore had to come from England. It was at this stage that Henry's ally the king of Portugal performed an invaluable service in stationing a friendly fleet at the mouth of the Seine estuary to keep the river route open to the English, and Harfleur became the safe base for cross-channel supplies.[8] On the other hand, half-way between Harfleur and Rouen was the Burgundian fortress of

Caudebec in a position to harass Henry's main line of supply by river. The reduction of Caudebec was essential, and the earl of Warwick made short work of it – by September 9th its garrison had capitulated[9] and the Seine route was safe for Henry.

But the broad river could still give the men of Rouen a possible if difficult way of escape, and Henry was quick to close it to them. Above the city he built a new wooden bridge supported by chain booms from bank to bank; he even had ships dragged overland out of range of the besieged to take up positions in midstream beyond St Catherine's Abbey and close the river way to and from Paris – Henry's resourcefulness in siege warfare was remarkable.[10]

With the city completely cut off, with food and munitions from England flowing freely to him up the Seine, Henry could afford to wait. He now received two welcome reinforcements. The first was the arrival of 3,000 seasoned troops under the duke of Gloucester from Cherbourg; they were posted to a position of great danger close to the eastern walls. The second was equally welcome but more bizarre. 1,500 kernes arrived from Ireland under the command of Thomas Butler, the militant prior of the Knights Hospitallers at Kilmainham near Dublin. They wore no breeches and had one foot bare; their weapons were a great knife, a bundle of small darts and a small shield. Some of them were mounted on small but hardy Irish nags. They were an undisciplined body, but they were useful as savage foragers, so savage indeed that Henry had to remonstrate with Butler and to emphasize his protests with floggings for some of the wilder offenders.[11]

The siege now settled down to a war of attrition. There is ample evidence of Henry's customary attention to detail – he was constantly going the rounds of his forces, rearranging their tents, organizing their food supplies, issuing a code of rules of behaviour which he enforced with stern severity, and taking his share of the hand-to-hand fighting when the frequent sorties had to be repulsed. He 'passed menie a long wynter night without sleepe or repose' and 'he diligentlie visited the watches and stacions of every companie'. The rank and file were forbidden to wander from their allotted stations, and, when two stragglers were found outside the set limits of their corps, they were hung as warning to the rest – 'by whose punishment the rest of the armie, fearinge the king's justice, in everie thinge after this obeyed his commandement'.[12] A siege which began with some respect for the old codes of chivalry soon degenerated into savagery. At the beginning we read of personal challenges fought out according to a dying protocol with both sides pausing to cheer on their champions; but soon it was a different story. The English would hang their prisoners in full view of the walls; the Burgundians would reply with gibbets by the fosse or English bodies in sacks flung into the Seine.[13] And within the city, famine was soon at work.

The defence of the city was ably conducted – John Page pays tribute to the bravery of both citizens and soldiery. Sorties from several gates were synchronized and the resultant hand to hand fighting inflicted grievous losses on both sides.[14] But the sorties never broke Henry's ring.

The main Burgundian forces were concentrated at Pontoise, and the Roueners for long expected relief and rescue from this quarter. But the Burgundians were paralysed by disaffection – there were counsellors who said that winter campaigning was foolhardy, and there were traitors who were secretly Armagnacs. In Soissons and Compiègne there were Armagnac garrisons who were only too anxious to see the duke of Burgundy discomfited, and the dauphin with the main Armagnac forces was quite content to watch a Burgundian defeat from the safety of Poitiers and Bourges. Once again a divided France meant disaster.

Messengers from time to time had stolen through the English lines and reached Paris to seek help from their king, and Pontoise to seek help from Burgundy. In November some of the messengers were able to get back to Rouen with the heartening tidings that a huge army was on its way to raise the siege. Within the walls there was bell-ringing and rejoicing; outside there was the prospect of another Agincourt to cheer the besiegers. Henry was fully prepared and even eager to meet any relieving forces, and John Page tells how the king summoned his captains and told them 'Fellows, be merry' because another and perhaps a last decisive victory would soon be theirs.[15] The Irish were posted to the point of danger where the relieving force might be expected – and whether this was due to their fighting qualities or to a belief that they were in modern terms 'expendable' it is impossible to say. In the event, both Henry and the defenders of Rouen were sadly disappointed – there was no relief and no victory. The Burgundian relief forces disintegrated for lack of pay and enthusiasm, and King Charles retired to the protection of Paris. It was at this point that Henry attempted a *ruse de guerre*. He disguised some of his men with the St Andrew's cross of Burgundy and staged a mock relief attack hoping that the men of Rouen would sally forth to join their supposed rescuers only to find themselves surrounded by the English. The ruse failed, but the havoc of famine continued.[16]

Now the tale of horror mounted. Twelve thousand of the non-combatant and unfit refugees who had thronged into Rouen were ejected from the city so that the remaining rations might support the able bodied citizenry. Henry gave orders that they were not to be allowed through the English lines. They were refused re-entry into the city. They were left to rot in pitiless winter weather within the confines of the great fosse. Within the walls, a slice of bread now cost a franc or a young girl's honour, docks were eaten as avidly as cabbages, water and vinegar had to substitute for wine, cats, rats, dogs and mice were butchers' luxuries, and even water supplies were seriously reduced when Henry was able to cut off one of the Seine's tributaries before it reached the city – only the fierce staunchness of the garrison was able to restrain the citizens from surrender. At Christmas the misery of the refugees made even Henry relent – for twenty-four hours he offered food enough for them to celebrate the greatest Christian festival, and although the captain of Rouen rejected the offer, he did allow two priests to take meagre sustenance to the wretched inhabitants of the fosse.[17] By New Year 1419 the end was in sight. The stern heroism of the Burgundian soldiery could no longer command the loyalty of the citizens. A final mass sortie failed, and the Rouen burghers opened negotiations for surrender. There are varying accounts of the fortnight's bargaining which followed – the king's anger at men who had thwarted him so long and who dared to expect mercy from the rightful lord of Rouen; the threat of the desperate citizens that they would fire their homes and offer Henry smoking ashes unless he offered reasonable terms.

The most revealing account is that of the English soldier, John Page. His admiration for his king is reiterated throughout his narrative poem – Henry was 'manful when war doth last, and merciful when it is past', but Henry's mercy was not easily obtained. Sir Gilbert Umfraville had first received the citizens' deputation, and it was with great difficulty that he had at last reached the king's presence and persuaded him to receive it. He gave the Roueners sound advice before they spoke to a king whom Page describes as 'a child of God'. 'Think with heart before your tongue, lest your tongues be too long' he advised, 'for a word wrang out of ward, might make you fare full hard'.[18] On January 2nd, 1419, the deputation of twelve – four knights, four clerics and four burgesses – was permitted to reach the king. Henry was at Mass, kept them waiting and at last listened to their pleas for mercy as they knelt before him. They told of the sufferings of the refugees in the fosse, and the king scornfully replied that *he* had not put them there, that the men of Rouen were keeping him from a city that was rightfully his, and that it was to him that they owed allegiance. In reply the Roueners reminded Henry that their allegiance was to the duke of Burgundy and to the king of France, and they dared to ask that one last appeal might go to them for help and succour. The king at this point lost his temper – he saw no point in further appeals for help, and in any event 'my city I will not go without'. He would take Rouen, and if they continued to oppose him they must suffer the dire consequences. He did, however, grant them time to go back to the city and try to persuade their fellows to see reason.

Preparations for a full-dress parley were hurried on – two tents were pitched just outside the walls, one for the French and the other for the English, so that the negotiators might have shelter from the stormy weather. Twelve Roueners were faced by the earls of Warwick and Salisbury and other knights in solemn colloquy with all the appurtenances of heraldry and anxiously watched both by those on the walls and by the besieging soldiers.[19] Page contrasts the rich costumes of the English 'goodly with gold' and the French with scarcely a clout between them, and he paints a lurid picture of the dead, dying and starving in the fosse near by. Their sufferings would melt the heart of any king, but he reminds his readers that the Roueners themselves had shown no mercy. The astonishing fact is that negotiations lasted for a fortnight and were even then broken off with no result. 'We challenged and accused, they answered and excused; we asked much and they proferred small'. The tents were taken down and at the last moment the English lords granted a brief respite so that the Roueners could return to the city and report. Their reception was stormy – the citizens demanded surrender on any terms, and threatened to turn on their leaders. Once again a deputation issued from the gates, once again tents of parley were pitched, and discussions went on day and night. At last it was agreed that if help was not forthcoming within eight days Rouen would surrender. There is a story from the French chroniclers that the Roueners threatened to set fire to their city, make a final sortie and leave Henry nothing but smoking ruins. There is no warranty for this from Page or the English chroniclers,[20] but it is not unlikely that fear of such an event somewhat tempered Henry's first harshness, and at the final parley Archbishop Chichele was called in to bring both sides to a reasonable outcome. A settlement was finally agreed on January 13th, 1419.[21] The terms were severe but not brutal. If no relief was received by January 19th the city was to submit, pay a fine of 300,000 crowns, and surrender all its horses, armour and munitions of war. Normans in the garrison were to be taken prisoner – other Frenchmen might leave but without their arms or possessions. Citizens who swore allegiance to the English king could keep their property, and the town would enjoy all the privileges it had held before the reign of Philip VI. The forlorn inhabitants of the fosse were to be readmitted within the walls, and food and supplies were to be made available to all from the ample stocks of the invaders. Meanwhile the duke of Burgundy had advised the Roueners to get the best terms they could – he had admired their brave stand but the treachery of the Armagnacs and his own lack of funds to keep his forces in action had prevented his coming to their aid.

On January 19th Henry sat in state in the Charterhouse and the captain of Rouen, Guy le Bouteiller, with a body of representative citizens knelt before him and delivered up the keys. The king handed the keys to the duke of Exeter and commanded him to enter the city and prepare for his own arrival on the next day. Henry's ceremonial entry was similar to his entry into Caen – in his hour of glory he preferred understatement to lavish display. He was welcomed by the city clergy and blessed by Archbishop Chichele. He 'passed in without pride without pomp or bombast' says Page, and the citizenry welcomed him. Henry rode a brown horse with gold breast-cloth and housings of black damask, and he seemed to ride sadly.[22] A page followed him bearing a lance with the fox's brush which was one of the badges of his father. The procession went straight to the cathedral and a thanksgiving Mass was sung by the clerks of his chapel. The sad conqueror of the second city of France spent the night in Rouen Castle.

It was the climax to a half-year of exhausting complexity. Henry's opponents had been the Burgundians whom he had counted as allies. A king who had come to claim his own had found himself faced with the most stubborn opposition from Normans whose allegiance was to their city rather than to any king or duke. The dauphin of France was still with the Armagnacs holding court at Poitiers and still commanding well-armed forces and powerful castles well within striking distance of the invader. The king and queen of France were in the power of Burgundy, who likewise still had huge forces and great castles at his command. The taking of Rouen had taxed all Henry's strength and had only succeeded with the help of a neutralized Brittany, a friendly king of Portugal, and a timely reinforcement of wild Irish. Throughout the siege, embassies from Burgundians, Armagnacs and the Emperor Sigismund had been coming and going. In spite of so many complications and throughout that long six months of a bitter winter Henry had held unflinchingly to his purpose, and he had carried his men with him. No detail was too small for his personal attention, no major decision was taken without his express approval. The military burdens of the siege alone would have frightened a lesser man, but if the taking of Rouen was no glamorous victory, its successful conclusion in the midst of so many distracting dangers was witness to a commander of more than ordinary quality.

Chapter 17

ENDING THE SCHISM

IN SPITE OF HENRY'S preoccupation with his war in France
he had never relaxed his interest in the great Council of
Constance. Although a meeting of the cardinals of the
Church, its political implications made it the nearest thing to an
international conference which the Middle Ages achieved. Its
actual constitution was based on representation by 'nations'.
At first, four 'nations' were recognized – the Italian, the French,
the German and the English. At a later stage, a Spanish
'nation' was also recognized, and it is a fascinating sidelight on
the growth of the idea of nationality that, when the English
delegation was challenged to justify its presence, Henry's representatives claimed that, apart from 110 dioceses and 52,000
parish churches, England comprised eight kingdoms – England,
Scotland, Wales, the Sea and four Irish kingships: Britannia's
claim to rule the waves is of such long standing.

Throughout the three years of the Council's activities, Henry
took pains to see that England was represented by distinguished
and able men who knew his own views. Robert Hallam bishop
of Salisbury was Henry's excellent chief ambassador until his
death towards the end of the proceedings, Richard Beauchamp
earl of Warwick was frequently in attendance, and during the
final stages Henry's famous uncle Henry Beaufort, bishop of
Winchester, played a leading role.

Henry had two important objectives. First, he had sealed a
treaty of alliance with the Emperor Sigismund, and he expected
Sigismund to keep his promises of help in the war with France.
While Sigismund was involved in the complexities of the
Council it was too easy for him to find alibis which prevented
him from fulfilling his promises. Henry was anxious to see an
end of the Schism in order that Sigismund could be free to

implement the treaty of Canterbury. Second, he was a loyal son of the Church who realized that papal pretensions, papal abuses and church laxity were grist to the mills of Lollardy. While standing firm on the rights of the English church he was hoping for a unified papacy and a reformed clergy in order that he might cope more effectively with a religious discontent which smouldered on in England and so easily might be sparked into political upheaval. Henry was anxious to see an end of the Schism in order that at home he could finally stamp out heresy. There was probably a third objective – the hope of a united front against the Ottoman invaders, and, when France was his and a single pope and the Holy Roman Emperor were at his side, the possibility of a last and victorious crusade against the infidel was a not unworthy dream – it was serious enough to occupy his mind even at the point of death.[1]

The detailed story of the Council of Constance is not within the purview of this book, but its outlines must be recorded.[2] The infamous John XXIII was imprisoned and deposed while Henry was getting ready to sail for Harfleur. In July of the same year Gregory XII was persuaded to abdicate. Then followed Sigismund's journey to Perpignan to persuade the third 'pope', Benedict XIII, to resign. His mission was unsuccessful and was followed by his visit to Henry after Agincourt and the treaty of Canterbury. At the beginning of the year 1417 Sigismund at last returned to Constance wearing Henry's collar of S.S. and the ribbon of the Garter.[3] It was a diplomatic accolade to Henry but it produced no reinforcements for Henry's armies on his second invasion of France. In July of the same year Benedict XIII was removed, and it remained for the five 'nations' to produce at last one pope acknowledged by all. It is significant that at this period, just before Henry V was setting sail for Touques, Henry Beaufort, bishop of Winchester and chancellor of England, resigned his chancellorship. He was succeeded by Thomas Langley, bishop of Durham, an able ecclesiastic who was to hold his appointment for seven years. Beaufort announced that he was bent on a pilgrimage to Jerusalem. He set out, and, either by chance or design, had reached Ulm when he was summoned to represent England in the tricky final stages of electing a new pope at Constance.[4] He and bishop Catrick of

Lichfield are credited with the negotiations which finally resulted in the election in November 1417 of Cardinal Oddo Colonna as Pope Martin V and the end of the Schism. It was no small feather in the jewelled cap of Henry's uncle that it was his nominee who at last prevailed, but it was also a triumph for King Henry himself. The 'nation' which Spaniards and Frenchmen had wished to exclude as negligible had, with the help of the Holy Roman Empire, reunified Western Christendom – that was no small triumph for Henry's diplomacy. Beaufort's reward was the offer of a cardinal's hat, and a proposal by Martin V that he should be *legatus a latere* of the Holy See in England. It was at this point that Henry's appreciation of the independent traditions of the English Church stood him in good stead. On the urgent advice of Archbishop Chichele he forbade Beaufort to accept either appointment – 'he had as lief sette his couroune besyde him, as to see hym were a Cardinal's hatte'.[5] It was not until 1426 that Beaufort was at last able to accept his cardinalate. Meanwhile, he continued his pilgrimage and actually reached Jerusalem via Venice and safely returned to England in September 1418.

The Council of Constance had achieved the reunification of the western Church, but its objective of Church reform had been shelved. During its discussions the 'nations' had divided significantly between the Latins and the Teutons, and in the end an Italian pope was left to rebuild a papacy with none of its medieval pretensions clipped and all the forces of reaction reinstalled to thwart the rising remonstrances whose sources for the most part were outside Italy. It is in this sense that the Council of Constance was a failure – it made the Reformation inevitable, and, when that explosion came, the 'nations' were divided very much as they were when Henry Beaufort earned his cardinal's hat.

Henry of England could take pride in the fact that he had played an almost spectacular part in ending the Schism through his able representatives. But practical aid from Sigismund was as far off as before, and in the meantime Henry was in no mood to accede to the pretensions of a newly elected pope who was anxious to reduce the English church to its ancient subservience.[6] Henry was a faithful son of the Church but in ecclesiastical politics he was, as in so many other directions, a staunch upholder of England's unique authority. Meanwhile, the roots of Lollardy were spreading underground, and the established Church was turning its back on reform and providing martyrs for the coming Reformation.

Chapter 18

ROUEN TO MEULAN

WHEN ROUEN FELL, there was no repetition of the massacre and looting which had followed Henry's victory at Caen. On the contrary, Henry quietly occupied the castle 'tylle the toun were sette yn rewle and governawnce',[1] and his first care was to halt the toll of starvation and restore normal prosperity to his Norman capital. In return, the citizens of Rouen seem to have accepted him as duke of Normandy without much demur – they were in any event more loyal to their city than to their king or their duke, and could complain with justice that the duke of Burgundy had heartlessly let them down.

By the surrender terms nine persons had been excluded from Henry's mercy. Only one of the nine was executed – Alain Blanchard the captain of the cross-bowmen, and there is not enough evidence to determine whether he deserved his fate or not. He had fought ably and bravely but in later years French nationalists failed to establish him as a martyr.[2] The captain of Rouen – Guy le Bouteiller – was undoubtedly bought off. Three days after Henry's entry into Rouen he was awarded a safe-conduct, and within a few weeks he was swearing the oath of allegiance. He was the first of the very few distinguished Frenchmen named as having gone over to the invader's side, and naturally he earned the reproachful blame of the French chroniclers.[3] Three of the nine exceptions to Henry's mercy were unnamed, and one of them is referred to as 'that person who spoke the foul words'.[4] It is not known whether he was surrendered or what was his fate, nor is it known what he spoke. It is an incident which reveals a certain priggish pettiness in Henry which was perhaps the unpleasant counterpart to his admirable passion for detail.

One further detail of the surrender terms deserves notice. Henry had secured the right and the land to build a fortified palace at the south-west corner of the city with a covered way connecting it to the old castle. He commissioned Rouen's cathedral architect to carry out the work which was begun in the early summer, and the resulting structure survived until the revolution of 1789. Henry promised that any citizen who was dispossessed of his property by works for the new palace would receive prompt and just compensation.[5]

The fine of 300,000 crowns was a formidable burden for a city just recovering from a six months' siege. The terms stated that half this immense sum was to be paid when the English entered the city and the remainder within a month. They were impossible terms. But Henry had the sense to mitigate them – he appointed the earl of Warwick to negotiate with the citizens for payment by instalments. After much haggling as to the value of a 'crown', it was agreed that the fine should be settled at the rate of 80,000 crowns a year. Hostages were taken to ensure payments, but even twelve years later 40,000 crowns were still unpaid.[6] It seems that some of the richest citizens left Rouen in order to avoid their liabilities, and that there was much evasion of finding the hard cash;[7] on the other hand, the citizens as a whole respected a king whose justice though severe was fair, and whose victory was unsullied by rapine and immediately followed up by sensible reforms. Within a month of the surrender, a meeting of the Norman 'estates' was summoned to Rouen and a uniform system of weights and measures established for all Normandy in place of the previous diversity. It was proclaimed that for grain the Rouen standard should prevail, for liquids the Arques standard, for cloth the ell of Paris, and for all weights the mark of Troyes.[8] This was the kind of mercantile efficiency which a great trading city could appreciate.

There is conflicting evidence as to the reactions of the Norman nobility, but there is no doubt that the clergy, both high and low, and the bulk of the citizenry were reasonably content with their new overlord. Many minor Norman gentry took official appointments under English governance, and a few even joined Henry's armed forces. The clergy were naturally in favour of a conqueror who was a loyal son of the Church and a strict defender of law and order, and who in all his campaigns gave special instructions for the safety of the clergy and their properties and ruthlessly punished anyone who disobeyed.[9]

Henry spent two months at Rouen reorganizing the capital city of his duchy. Meanwhile his captains were completing his Norman conquest. The duke of Clarence, the duke of Exeter and the earls of Salisbury and Warwick rapidly enforced the surrenders of Caudebec, Lillebonne, Fécamp, Vernon, Mantes, Dieppe, Honfleur, La Roche Guyon and Ivry. By the summer of 1419 only the fortresses of Mont St Michel, Gisors and Château Gaillard still held out. Henry could feel that his duchy was now a safe base from which he could mount the next stage of his approach to the French capital.

During the six months' siege of Rouen, Henry's diplomacy had been busy at the Council of Constance, but it had also been busy closer at hand. It has been summed up by a great historian as 'an astute diplomacy which kept the French divided whilst Rouen perished'.[10] It is a complicated story which must be un-ravelled if a true assessment of Henry's abilities is to be made.

In the previous November the earl of Salisbury and Master Philip Morgan had led an embassy of seven to meet the Armag-nacs, or, as they were now called, the Dauphinists. The Dauphin Charles was holding his court at Poitiers and the two sides met at Alençon on the Norman border.

A long and fascinating account of this conference has been preserved in the English records.[11] Bargaining was prefaced by a significant dispute over language. The Dauphinists opened the proceedings in French and the English promptly demanded Latin as the correct diplomatic language – and the English prevailed. Henry had given his delegates strict instructions to wait for 'proffers', and their objective was the surrender of Anjou, Maine and Touraine in full sovereignty and the county and earldom of Flanders as a fief of France, all in addition to England's possessions in Aquitaine and Guienne and Henry's recent acquisitions in his Norman duchy. Henry's objectives now appeared to be not the conquest of the whole of France, but rather the terms secured by the Great Peace – the treaty of

Brétigny – together with the duchy of Normandy. Henry's projected marriage to Katherine the daughter of Charles VI would suitably celebrate the peace which would follow, and English and Dauphinists could unite to drive out the duke of Burgundy and restore the dauphin to Paris. The negotiations lasted over a fortnight with many hours wasted in discussions over protocol and much jockeying for position; they petered out in mutual frustration.

It is questionable how seriously Henry regarded these proceedings – he had good reason to doubt the power of the Dauphinists to implement any promises. Meanwhile he could negotiate with both French parties and see which offered the better bargain. Within a few days of the Alençon parleying Henry was in negotiation with the duke of Burgundy, and a conference with the other half of France was arranged to meet at Pont de l'Arche at the beginning of December.[12]

The English delegation was led by Archbishop Chichele, the earl of Warwick, and Master Philip Morgan. The Burgundians were represented by the bishop of Beauvais and Cardinal Orsini. Once again business was held up while the language question was debated. The Burgundians wanted to use French and the English insisted that proceedings should be in Latin – French was a language which neither Henry nor his council nor his envoys 'could write properly understand or speak'[13] – the new duke of Normandy was now very much the Englishman. Cardinal Orsini, however, managed to persuade Henry to moderate his nationalism – it was agreed that each side should speak its own native language but that all proposals should be accompanied with a Latin translation. This Burgundian *démarche* was notable for the fact that Orsini brought to Henry a portrait of the Princess Katherine painted from life, and he 'liked it well'.[14] But his appreciation was accompanied by the demand for a million gold crowns as her dowry together with Normandy, Aquitaine, Ponthieu and the rest of the lordships named in the treaty of Brétigny. It is small wonder that once again negotiations petered out, but meanwhile neither dauphinists nor Burgundians interfered with Henry's operations round Rouen.

The fall of Rouen and the completion of Henry's Norman

conquests greatly increased his bargaining power – he was now playing from strength, and had the advantage of a central position thrusting between the two rival French parties and driving towards the national capital. With lesser powers Henry was content to prolong existing truces – the duke of Brittany, the duchess of Anjou, and such Gascon lords as the count of Armagnac and Charles d'Albret were quickly satisfied and neutralized, but Henry was still ready to consider any reasonable offers of greater consequence from the dauphin or from Burgundy.

Elaborate preparations were made for a personal meeting between King Henry and the dauphin at a place midway between Evreux and Dreux. It was to begin on March 26th, 1419, and last for a month. Henry moved to Evreux, but the dauphin failed to arrive. The English chroniclers expatiate on the faithlessness of the French, and we still have the letter of an ordinary homesick English warrior who couples his contempt for the French with the heartfelt words 'I pray ye, pray for us that we may come out of this unlusty soldier's life into the life of England'.[15] But peace was still a long way off; and the French chroniclers could as easily claim that Henry's diplomacy was a chronicle of duplicity. Even while arrangements were being made for the Evreux meeting Henry's representatives were discussing with Burgundy, represented by the duke of Brittany, a further meeting at some place between Mantes, held by the English, and Pontoise, where the Burgundians were in force.

In May 1419 all the forces disrupting a forlorn France were concentrated within striking distance of Paris. The sick King Charles VI with his Queen Isabella were in the duke of Burgundy's power in Paris with a large army at Pontoise. The dauphin Charles held court at Poitiers, but his forces under Tanneguy du Chatel were strong enough to make successful raids north and east of the capital, and there were beginning to gather round him some of the young patriots such as La Hire and Pothon de Saintrailles who were one day to be the spearheads of national revival. The invading King Henry, now with the whole of Normandy at his back and flushed with the military victories of Caen and Rouen and the diplomatic success at Constance, was at Mantes. Dauphinists and Burgundians were carrying on a ceaseless struggle of raid and counter-raid with major forces still held in reserve for a possible final blow, and both were negotiating with the national enemy. It is not a pretty picture.

The negotiations with Burgundy were elaborately prepared. At the pourparlers the earl of Warwick represented Henry, while the duke of Brittany represented Burgundy and the king of France. The English indicated that Henry, in return for all the lands ceded by the treaty of Brétigny in addition to everything he himself had conquered since landing at Touques, might be prepared to modify his claim to the French crown, and marry Katherine, the daughter of Charles VI, as part of the bargain. The Burgundian delegates indicated that these general proposals might well be acceptable, and preparations for a definitive conference went on apace.

It was decided that the meeting-place should be in a field called 'le champ de la Chat' close to the west gate of the fortress city of Meulan on the Seine a mere twenty miles from Paris, and the most careful arrangements were made to prevent any possibility of either side breaking the truce and staging massacre and murder.[16] On May 29th, 1419, King Henry and his court moved out from Mantes and took up their allotted positions. At the same time Queen Isabella accompanied by the duke of Burgundy took their places, and all was ready for private negotiations between the principals. The unfortunate Charles VI had had to be left at Pontoise – he was suffering from one of his periodic fits of insanity. The actual conference took place in an elaborately decorated pavilion equidistant from the tents of both sides. The earl of Warwick, speaking in French in spite of Henry's previous objections, initiated the proceedings, and the first meeting concluded with elaborate feastings. Two days later business began, and at this juncture at last Henry came face to face with the Princess Katherine. She was at this time a tall girl of eighteen, and it was reported that her beauty more than justified the life-portrait of her which Henry had already admired. The Burgundians had lavished three thousand florins on her apparel, and Henry's biographer noted her sweetness and her maidenly blushes as Henry kissed her in welcome.[17] When medieval chroniclers of both sides tell a tale of love at first sight when all concerned were organizing what everyone knew to be a diplomatic marriage, it can safely be assumed that there was some truth in their romanticism. Katherine did not grace the proceedings again, and they lasted throughout the month of June 1419.

It was a month of complicated haggling. It is clear that Henry was prepared to give up his claim to the throne of France in return for sovereignty over his recent conquests and the lands that had been promised to his great-grandfather, and that he was more than anxious to seal the bargain by marrying the Princess Katherine. Both Queen Isabella and Burgundy were disposed to accept these terms, but they had to consider whether the rest of France would agree with them. They offered 800,000 crowns as Katherine's dowry but argued that 600,000 crowns should be deducted as the amount which should have been returned to France when Richard II was deposed and his young Queen Isabella had been returned to her French fatherland. There was acrimonious dispute as to the value of Isabella's jewels, which also should have been returned to France and which were therefore deductable from the suggested dowry of Katherine. The conferences near Meulan ended in stalemate.[18] Both sides were overplaying their hands: Henry had a victorious army and a central position to add weight to his claims, Burgundy could let it be understood that in the last resort he could come to terms with the Dauphinists and unite with them to drive out the invader. Towards the end of the month Henry and the duke of Burgundy met in private conclave at Meulan. Henry was aware that Burgundy was already in negotiation with the Dauphinist Tanneguy du Chatel, and the talks broke up with hot words. Henry proclaimed that if his claims were refused and his offer to marry Katherine were rejected 'we will drive the king and you out of his kingdom'. 'Sire', replied the duke of Burgundy 'you are pleased to say so; but before you can drive my lord and me out of his kingdom I make no doubt but that you will be heartily tired'.[19] The conference of Meulan was from Henry's point of view one of his few diplomatic failures – its only substantial result was a *rapprochement* between the dauphin and Burgundy.

On July 11th, 1419, the duke of Burgundy and the Dauphin

Charles signed a formal treaty which appeared to settle their quarrels and leave the way open for the organization of a united front against the invader. On July 19th a royal ordinance confirmed the treaty, the 'parlement' at Poitiers was recognized as the supreme court, and the citizens of Paris and of other French towns 'shouted for joy'.[20] France appeared to have come to its senses, and Henry the Conqueror seemed as far from the realization of his dreams as when he had landed at Touques nearly two years before.

Chapter 19

THE BRIDGE OF
MONTEREAU

URING THE CONFERENCE at Meulan it was quite clear
that Burgundy was also negotiating with the dauphin,
but Henry also was playing other cards. His diplomacy
was attempting to ring France with marriage alliances in his
favour. Attempts were made to have his brother the duke of
Bedford declared heir to the childless queen of Naples, and to
marry him off either to the daughter of the duke of Lorraine or to
the daughter of Frederick of Hohenzollern, margrave of Brand-
enburg. These negotiations failed,[1] but Henry was nevertheless
firmly allied with Sigismund, he had the great elector arch-
bishoprics of Cologne, Mainz and Trier in his pay, and there
was a hope that his brother Humphrey, duke of Gloucester,
might be married to the daughter of Charles III of Navarre.

But Henry was not relying on diplomacy alone. The conference at Meulan had taken place under a truce between Henry
and Burgundy which was to last until July 29th, 1419. During
the conference there had been much coming and going of
English knights between Henry's headquarters at Mantes and
the duke of Burgundy's at Pontoise, and the English on their
frequent visits were not slow to size up the defences of this key
stronghold. The moment the truce was ended, a surprise expedition set out from Mantes for Pontoise in two divisions – one
under Gaston de Foix, count of Longueville[2], and the other
under the earl of Huntingdon. An early morning attack completely surprised the garrison – a formidable 1,000 men-at-arms
and 2,000 cross-bowmen under de l'Isle Adam. Pontoise,
the gateway to Paris from the north, was captured before its
defenders were awake. The town was sacked and enormous

181

stores – valued by the French chroniclers at two million crowns – were added to Henry's resources. It was Henry's first, but not very creditable, victory outside his duchy of Normandy.[3] He wrote boastfully to the mayor of London to announce it, and on August 6th he moved his court to the newly conquered city.[4]

At Pontoise, Henry the Conqueror was only twenty miles from Paris; but the nearer he approached to the capital the farther he was from his comparatively safe bases at Caen and Rouen. His surprise capture of Pontoise was a mortal affront to Burgundy, there was a serious attempt by Dauphinists to re-capture the Cotentin, there were anti-English conspiracies at Dieppe and Rouen,[5] brigandage was rife within his new duchy, and the dauphin had succeeded in gaining substantial help from Scotland. In May 1419 the dauphin already had the help of Sir William Douglas with 150 men-at-arms and 300 archers, and by September a Castilian fleet had brought 6,000 Scots under the earls of Buchan and of Wigtown to the dauphin's court at Bourges.[6]

Henry's position was now precarious, but his reaction to it was typical of the man – he sent his brother the duke of Clarence with a large force to raid within sight of the walls of Paris.[7] Burgundy promptly withdrew himself and the king and queen of France from St Denis and retreated to the safety of his fortified towns on the Ourcq and the upper Seine. The future of France once again depended on Burgundians and Dauphinists settling their differences and joining forces to expel so impudent an invader. The July treaty between Burgundy and the Dauphin Charles was now to be implemented.

After some negotiation the crucial meeting between the dauphin and the duke of Burgundy was arranged for September 10th, 1419, on the bridge of Montereau at the junction of the Yonne and the Seine some forty miles south-east of Paris. Neither side fully trusted the other, and barricades were built at either end of the Seine bridge with a special enclosure in its centre for the protagonists. September 10th was a Sunday, and each principal approached the fateful meeting accompanied by ten counsellors all wearing their swords. The conference in the central enclosure of the bridge began with all due courtesies but the exact details of what followed will never be known. Within minutes the duke of Burgundy was felled by a blow from an axe – probably the battle-axe of Tanneguy du Chatel – the duke's attendants were captured by a rush of Dauphinists, and history had to record the fateful murder of John the Fearless duke of Burgundy on the bridge of Montereau.[8]

No one knows whether the murder was premeditated, although this is more than likely, and no one knows for certain who was the actual murderer. The dauphin Charles – then but a boy of sixteen – was probably not privy to the deed.[9] But what is certain is that the Carthusian prior of Dijon was right when he said, a century later, that the English entered France through the hole in the duke of Burgundy's skull. The vacillations of John the Fearless were over. The new duke Philip, later known as 'the Good', could call on his king and queen, on all good Burgundians, on the parlement and citizens of Paris, and on his ally the king of England to help him to a fitting revenge on the Dauphinists – and Henry of England knew precisely the price he would exact for his help. The advisers of the young dauphin had rashly miscalculated – their crude murder wrecked the last chance of a national effort to drive out the invader, it put the French crown once more within Henry's reach. But he was wise enough not to press his advantage too quickly; he preferred to await events.

Meanwhile, there was work to be done in completing several tiresome sieges, and in settling the detailed administration of Henry's Norman conquests. Gisors yielded by the end of September, Meulan surrendered on November 6th, and at the beginning of December at last the 'impregnable' Château Gaillard fell.[10] Henry spent the next three months at Rouen, and in January, 1420, the duke of Bedford was called from his regency in England, replaced by Humphrey, duke of Gloucester, and was at hand to help the king in his civil affairs in the Norman capital. A sensible policy of reconciliation was continued. While the major administrative offices were left in English hands, minor posts were freely offered to native Normans, and commerce quickly revived – Breton, Flemish and Parisian merchants were encouraged to renew their Norman contacts. Henry and Bedford's efforts were successful enough to make possible the levying of taxes, which helped to pay for the war, and at the same time to promote English long-term interests by encouraging colonization from England. At Harfleur, Caen, Cherbourg and Rouen, English traders and craftsmen were 'planted' successfully. And in the Calendar of the Norman Rolls it is quite clear that the comparative good order and renewed prosperity in Normandy owed a great deal to the initiative of King Henry himself.[11]

While Henry was busying himself in Rouen the rest of France was in a ferment. The Dauphinists were by no means abashed by the horror which the murder at Montereau had roused throughout western Europe. Their forces were still powerful, the sixteen-year-old dauphin was still in their hands, and they had recently received the welcome reinforcements from Scotland. Wisely they took the young dauphin on a progress of the south where their leaders had family connections – in general the Burgundians were northerners while the Dauphinists were Gascons, Provençals and Bretons. The count of Foix, brother of the Gaston de Foix who had surprised Pontoise for Henry, secured Languedoc for the dauphin, and successful overtures took place for help from the king of Castile. The Dauphinists had so far played their hand badly – but they were not yet out of the game.

When the corpse of John the Fearless was given hasty and simple burial in the parish church of Montereau, the dukedom of Burgundy had devolved on the twenty-three year old Philip, count of Charolais. He had all the advantages of youth and high spirits, and his call for vengeance obtained a ready hearing at the royal court at Troyes. In fact, the French queen and the parlement of Paris did not even wait for Philip to declare his intentions – they immediately opened negotiations with Henry for a firm alliance which would complete the work broken off at the conference at Meulan. But Henry was in no easy mood. He received a deputation from the new duke of Burgundy, led by the governor of Paris, in his haughtiest manner. If the new duke of Burgundy did not hurry Henry would march on Paris, and the price of his alliance was to be the hand of Princess Katherine and the crown of France for himself and his heirs the moment King Charles VI died. Meanwhile a sick monarchy should be replaced by firm government with himself as regent of France.

Henry's plain speaking produced speedy results – his terms were accepted by Isabella's envoys and by representatives of the new duke.[12] On December 24th, 1419, a truce was concluded between England and France, and an alliance agreed between Henry and Burgundy which promised Henry his bride and in due course the kingdom of France, while Burgundy received a promise that Henry would help him to his revenge and that one of Henry's brothers would marry one of Burgundy's sisters. At the great Christmas feast on the following day Henry was very merry.[13]

The murder at Montereau had so blinded Burgundian Frenchmen that in pursuit of a personal vendetta they were now prepared to sell France to the invader.

Chapter 20

THE TREATY OF
TROYES

ALTHOUGH HENRY and Burgundy were now bound in a
formal alliance there was not yet a formal treaty between
Henry and Charles VI. The spring of the year 1420 was
occupied by joint military actions of English and Burgundians
against Dauphinist garrisons, and by the diplomatic pourparlers
which had to precede the sealing of a treaty between sovereign
states. The joint warfare was neither very successful nor very
cordial – the soldiers of both allies found the new alliance
strange and difficult. There was joint fighting at Roye and
Compiègne on the road to St Quentin which proved that the
Dauphinists were by no means discouraged and that the new
alliance was uneasy,[1] and in January the Castillian allies of the
dauphin won a galling naval victory over an English naval force
off La Rochelle.[2]

Meanwhile, the new duke of Burgundy marched south from
Arras and joined Charles VI and Queen Isabella in Troyes on
March 23rd, 1420. But Troyes itself was in a precarious position
– Dauphinist forces were harrying the surrounding countryside.
Nevertheless deputations from Henry carried on negotiations
with the French court and representatives of the university of
Paris, and by the beginning of April the outlines of a formal
treaty were agreed.[3] Henry V was to marry the princess
Katherine and her dower was to be 40,000 crowns a year paid
from the English exchequer. Charles VI and Isabella were
to remain king and queen of France for the rest of Charles's
life, but on Charles's death the crown of France was to belong to
Henry V and his heirs for ever. The French king's sickness
rendered it imperative that Henry should be appointed regent

of France forthwith, aided by the counsel of the nobles and wise men of France. The dauphin was to be disinherited and fought to the death. All Henry's conquests, including Normandy, should be subject to the French crown when Henry became king of France, and Henry would rule his new kingdom according to French laws and customs and confirm the parliement in its ancient authority and all churches and universities in their established privileges.

By the end of April, 1420, final arrangements were begun for a meeting between Henry, the king and queen of France, and the duke of Burgundy at Troyes. On May 8th, 1420, Henry set out on a memorable journey.

The great market city of Troyes was about a hundred miles east and south of Paris, and the intervening terrain was a no man's land where Dauphinists held many castles, and where their forces were foraging and raiding with impunity. It has puzzled both contemporary chroniclers and subsequent historians why Henry took such risks in agreeing to go so far into hostile territory. It is yet another example of Henry's unshakeable belief in his destiny. With almost sublime arrogance he marched his men to St Denis and worshipped in its great abbey. The following day the citizens of Paris could watch him and his men as they proudly paraded past their battlements without deigning to enter.[4] In spite of famine and distress the Parisians even sent him four cartloads of their best wine to cheer him on his way. At Charenton he left a small force to keep safe the crossing of the Marne, at Brie he ruthlessly suppressed some show of opposition, at Nogent he crossed the Seine, and as he neared Troyes he was met by the duke of Burgundy and an enthusiastic cavalcade of bishops and citizens who escorted him to a hostel within the city regally appointed for his welcome. Henry's army was carefully quartered in sections of the city and in surrounding villages wisely separated from the Burgundian quarters, and Henry, ever mindful of discipline, issued the celebrated order that his men were to be sure to mix the famous strong wine of Champagne with water.[5]

The reception of Henry V at the court of Charles VI makes a pathetic picture. The king of France was once more 'in his malady'. The young duke of Burgundy escorted Henry to the presence, and Charles seemed not to have noticed. Henry bowed, and the sad king of France roused himself enough to say 'Ah, it's you. You are most welcome since it is so. Greet the ladies.' A tragic scene was relieved by Henry kneeling before Queen Isabella, and then, turning to the Princess Katherine, he bowed low and kissed her 'with great joy'. The formal greetings over, Henry returned to his quarters for the night.[6]

On the next day, May 21st, 1420, the representatives of the two kings and the duke of Burgundy met for the final scene, and the treaty of Troyes was sealed in the cathedral in strict accordance with the terms already agreed.[7] There was one additional clause. Henry pledged himself that he would secure from the 'three estates' of both England and France an ordinance which would ensure that, when he became king of France, each realm, although united under his kingship, would retain its own laws 'neither being subject to the other'.[8] The king of France was not present at this solemn ceremony, but his queen and the duke of Burgundy made oath on his behalf, and a large number of French bishops, lords and notables swore likewise. The treaty was immediately proclaimed in both French and English throughout the city and announced to the English troops, and a copy was dispatched to duke Humphrey, Henry's regent in England, announcing that 'perpetual peace' had been achieved and requiring that Henry's new title of 'King of England, Heir and Regent of France and Lord of Ireland' should be engraved on his seals.[9] On May 24th an embassy from Henry was dispatched to Paris to announce the treaty's terms, and on May 30th the treaty was read, registered and sworn to by the officers of the French parlement, by the university of Paris and by representatives of the city. Once again the English representatives insisted that, as they were unsure of their French, the proceedings should be translated into English. The treaty was proclaimed in London on June 14th and celebrated by a solemn service in St Paul's and a special sermon at Paul's Cross outside.[10]

On the day the treaty of Troyes was sealed, Henry was officially betrothed to the Princess Katherine, but it was another twelve days before the marriage was celebrated. In the meantime there was an elaborate exchange of banquets and present-giving. At last, on June 2nd, 1420, Henry V was married by the archbishop of Sens to the Princess Katherine of France in the Troyes parish church of St Jean, and the only sombre note in an otherwise magnificent ceremonial was the black mourning dress of the new duke of Burgundy.[11]

If anything is more remarkable than the terms of the treaty of Troyes – and they were the high-water mark of the English invasions of France – it is the fact that it was sealed in a city over a hundred miles south-east of Paris with so much of France still in Dauphinist hands and with hostile Dauphinist forces still active north and east of Paris and fully capable of cutting off Henry from his Norman bases. It was the second time that Henry's customary caution had been abandoned for rash adventure, and again his rashness was rewarded – the Dauphinists missed a unique opportunity of bringing Henry's house of cards tumbling into ruin. Henry himself was well aware of the appalling risks he was running. The feastings and entertainments associated with the treaty-making and his wedding were abruptly terminated, and, when some of his courtiers expected more tourneys and joustings, they were promptly told that there was more worthy and more serious business still to be undertaken.[12] The English and Burgundian forces left Troyes for Paris on June 4th. The two kings and the duke of Burgundy rode side by side, and accompanying them were the queen of France and the Lady Katherine now of England. At Sens there was a week's delay before the Dauphinist garrison surrendered, and as the joint armies approached Montereau the ladies were left in the rear – the castle was well fortified and well manned and the Burgundians' thirst for vengeance promised an unladylike sequel.

On June 24th the town of Montereau was carried by assault, and the body of the murdered duke of Burgundy was exhumed from its humble grave in the parish church to be given honourable burial later in the Burgundian Charterhouse at Dijon. But the castle of Montereau still held out in spite of Henry's big guns. And here another revealing incident illustrates the temper of the times and the ruthlessness of Henry the Conqueror. Some eleven gentlemen had been taken prisoner in the assault on the town. Henry swore that he would hang them all if they did not persuade the garrison to surrender. They were allowed to make their supplications from the edge of the castle ditch; and, when the captain of the Dauphinist garrison – the lord of Guitry – refused their pleas, they begged for a last sight of their families. A truce was sounded as the relatives mounted the battlements and waved a last farewell. The next morning the prisoners were one and all hanged in full view of the castle walls. Contemporaries blamed not Henry but the captain of the garrison for so pitiless a deed – the lord of Guitry should have realized that his position was untenable, as was proved by the fact that a few days later he surrendered.[13] The knighthood of Henry V's day had moved a long way from the graceful lists of chivalry; now warfare had no panoply of graceful mercy to hide its naked brutality.

Henry and Burgundy were marching down the Seine towards Paris. Their next obstacle was the formidable fortress of Melun. The siege began on July 13th, 1420, and entailed four and a half months of savage fighting. The joint forces[14] of Henry and Burgundy mustered as many as 20,000 men, and the captive King James of Scotland was brought over from England in order that he might prevail upon the Scots, who were helping the Melun garrison, to surrender. The Dauphinist Scots refused to recognize the authority of a captive king, and, to his credit, James of Scotland did not attempt to assert it. The garrison of Melun was under the command of an able Gascon leader named Arnaud Guillaume, lord of Barbazan, with a force of a mere six or seven hundred men who happened to include a brother of a contemporary chronicler who was credited with the death of sixty lances from his own cross-bow.[15]

At the beginning of the siege, Henry received the welcome reinforcement of 800 men-at-arms and 2,000 archers who had accompanied the duke of Bedford when he had arrived in Normandy in May. In addition, Henry's brother-in-law Lewis, count Palatine of the Rhine, had arrived from Germany with 700 men who became Henry's mercenaries. The king of France and the ladies were accommodated at Corbeil, where Henry visited them until he found it more convenient to see Katherine in quarters specially built near his tent – at sunrise and sunset

English minstrels entertained their new queen there with an hour of sweet music.[16]

Mining and counter-mining produced extraordinary results. Epic fighting took place in subterranean gloom when mine met counter-mine, and King Henry, the duke of Burgundy and the rest of the English dukes took their share of hand-to-hand duels by the light of flares and torches beneath the ground. Above ground Henry's largest calibre guns wrought havoc which was promptly repaired by a garrison who were prepared to sell their lives dearly. The siege dragged on, and, when Henry brought up Charles VI to demand the loyalty of the garrison, he received the nettling reply that Frenchmen would acknowledge their French liege-lord but never an English king.[17] There was even a danger that the Burgundian alliance would fail – the count of Conversen deserted, the prince of Orange with many other knights abruptly rode away, and disease, the accompaniment of all lengthy sieges, began to take toll.[18] Burgundy remained faithful, and summoned reinforcements from his castle of Beaurevoir to replace the grievous losses of the besiegers. At last, hunger accomplished what massive artillery had failed to do – on November 18th, 1420, the heroic garrison of Melun surrendered.

The terms of surrender were harsh. All in the town – whether soldiers or civilians – were to give up their arms and to be held as prisoners until their ransoms were paid. Two groups, however, were excepted; any English or Scots who had fought against Henry were to be at his mercy, and anyone implicated in the murder at Montereau was to be put on trial. Among the prisoners were twenty Scottish mercenaries with their captain who had contributed greatly to the defence and had refused the request that they should surrender to their captive liege-lord King James of Scotland. The discreditable reason why Henry had taken the trouble to bring the captive king to Melun was now apparent – he had no scruple in hanging the Scots for alleged disobedience to their liege lord.[19] It is a blot on Henry's escutcheon which neither contemporary legalistic quibbling nor subsequent advocacy could ever erase. And another incident reveals that Henry at this time was showing signs of a pointless ruthlessness which may have been the beginning of physical deterioration.

One of his favourite captains, Bertrand de Chaumont, who had fought on the English side at Agincourt, was suspected of having been bribed to allow some of those who were implicated in the Montereau murder to escape. He was arraigned before Henry, and, although the duke of Burgundy and Henry's brother the duke of Clarence begged for mercy, the king was adamant. 'By St George, fair brother', he proclaimed, 'Had it been yourself we should have done the same', and de Chaumont's head paid the penalty.[20] About 600 prisoners were sent in boat-loads to Paris where many who could not find their ransom money died, and their commander, the lord of Barbazan, was imprisoned in the recently captured castle of Château Gaillard – he owed his life to the fact that he had crossed swords with Henry himself in the subterranean fighting, and therefore by the old laws of chivalry he could not be put to death by his 'brother-in-arms'.[21] He was not released until Château Gaillard was recaptured by the French in 1430. The story of the siege of Melun reflects little credit on the character of Henry the Conqueror.

The way to Paris was now open. On December 1st, 1420, King Charles VI and King Henry V rode side by side into the capital of France. A little behind them and on the other side of the street rode the young duke of Burgundy in full mourning, and each party was accompanied by a great cavalcade of nobles and knights.[22] Next day the two queens arrived, and while Charles and Isabella were accommodated at the Hôtel St Pol, Henry and Katherine and Henry's brothers occupied the great palace of the Louvre. The citizens of Paris – regaled with fountains of wine and rose-water – gave them all a glad welcome in the fond hope that war and famine were soon to end.[23] They were to be sadly disillusioned; by Christmas the price of bread had doubled, and the capital's dunghills were being searched by children dying of hunger and cold.[24]

But for the king of England December 1st, 1420, was a memorable day. Henry V was the first and last of our kings to be welcomed in Paris as a victorious conqueror, as regent of France and as heir to the French throne – it was a prodigious achievement.

Chapter 21

HEIR AND REGENT
OF FRANCE

O
N DECEMBER 6TH, 1420, the States-General of France
met in the Hôtel St Pol where Charles VI and Isabella
kept their humble court. Henry V sat side by side with
Charles VI, but the men who sat in front of them represented
only a fraction of geographical France. Naturally no Dauphinists
were present. Normandy was a separate duchy entirely under
the English yoke, and was therefore not represented. Most of
France south of the Loire was unquestionably Dauphinist save
only the English enclave in Guienne. East of Paris was a spread-
eagled Burgundy with one foot in Dijon and the other in
Flanders. In Picardy and even in the Ile de France there were
many stout castles still in Dauphinist hands and a countryside
which was a dangerous no-man's-land of raid and counter-raid
and international brigandage.

The main business of the States-General was the ratification
of the treaty of Troyes and this was accomplished without
difficulty,[1] but the members were warned that good governance
depended on an efficient system of taxation and a better
standard of coinage. Plans were made for the re-imposition of
taxes on wine and the 'gabelle' or salt-tax together with a sales-
tax on all merchandise except food, and in order that new
coinage could be minted of high standard there was to be a
general levy of silver (in any form) assessed according to every
man's wealth and only excepting the very poor.[2] On December
23rd a spectacular trial (the *lit de justice*) was staged of absent
Dauphinists alleged to have been responsible for the murder at
Montereau. Among those named and condemned were the
Dauphin Charles, Tanneguy du Chatel, Guillaume le Bouteiller

N   193

and Louvet, president of Provence. Henry sat with Charles on the judge's bench, and the duke of Burgundy and Henry's two brothers were in the body of the hall. The trial made no pretence of judging, or even offering, evidence, but it went into elaborate detail in defining how the guilty should be punished when caught.[3]

The Christmas festival of 1420 revealed the true state of affairs in Paris. While Charles was 'poorly and meanly served' at the Hôtel St Pol 'which must have been very disgusting to all true and loyal Frenchmen', says Monstrelet, it was impossible to detail the magnificence with which Henry and Katherine were surrounded at the Louvre.[4] The States-General could see the force of the new dispensation's measures of reform and sanction their price, but Parisians could only see the bitter contrast between the Hôtel St Pol and the Louvre, and bemoan further rises in the price of bread and a desperate scarcity of vegetables.[5] There was trouble too with the cathedral chapter of Notre Dame. The duke of Burgundy wished for the appointment of one of his council as the new bishop of Paris and Henry supported him. Boldly, the canons defied this pressure and elected the man they themselves had chosen – Jean Courtecuisse, the king of France's almoner. It was at this moment that Henry received an urgent and perhaps welcome plea from the English parliament that he should soon return home with the Princess Katherine[6] – he had been absent from England for over three years. On December 27th, Henry, Katherine, and his brothers left Paris for Rouen and home; and shortly afterwards the duke of Burgundy retired to his Flemish estates.

The treaty of Troyes had stipulated that on the death of Charles VI, Normandy should be re-united to the French crown, but in the meantime it was Henry's by right of conquest – his hereditary pretensions had been ignored but the responsibility for organizing his conquest remained. Therefore, after Henry and Katherine had been officially welcomed to Rouen on December 31st, 1420, for three short weeks Henry busied himself with the internal affairs of 'Normandy and our conquest', which was a loose way of referring to the fact that his armies commanded a territory which reached beyond the old borders of Normandy proper to within fifteen miles of Paris.

The three 'estates' of Normandy met in Rouen in mid-January, and again the treaty of Troyes was ratified, currency reforms were initiated and the machinery of government overhauled.[7]

Both at Paris and at Rouen Henry wisely forbore to disturb local customs and laws – he merely superimposed on existing native institutions the iron rule of his military government. His personal representative in Normandy, when he himself left for England, was to be his brother the duke of Clarence – an ambitious soldier and never a statesman. As military lieutenant Clarence was lucky in the support of Thomas Montague, earl of Salisbury, one of the ablest of Henry's generals. But these two nobles did not govern Normandy. Central government was left in the hands of the 'Great Council' at Rouen, and its president was the chancellor of Normandy at this time, John Kemp, bishop of Rochester, an able diplomat who was later to become successively bishop of London and archbishop of York and later of Canterbury. Financial affairs were centred at Caen where William Alyngton was the able treasurer-general answerable to a *chambre des comptes* whose head was a Norman knight, Louis Burgeys, one of the very few who had gone over to the conqueror's side. Judicial affairs were looked after by a scaccarium which since 1417 had been presided over by John Tiptoft. Henry made one interesting innovation – he revived the power and authority of the Norman seneschal, who, under the Angevin empire of our King Henry II, had been the duchy's senior official. Hugh Luttrell was appointed seneschal in 1417 and he was followed by Richard Woodville. The seneschal seems to have been the civil administrative head of state under whom local government was organized in eight 'bailliages', whose 'baillis' were invariably English, with their thirty or more *vicomtés* or *prévôtés* who were invariably Norman. This organization controlled all civil affairs save finance, which was controlled by the treasury officials at Caen.[8]

It is clear that Henry had no intention of ruling Normandy as an English colony. On the other hand the 'planting' of English trading families at the Norman ports of entry shows that he planned bridgeheads on the coast which might one day have converted Harfleur, Honfleur, Caen and Cherbourg into something approaching the 'Englishness' of Calais – but he did not live long enough to carry such plans to fruition. Neither was there any attempt to anglicize the Norman church, and he had no need to – churchmen wherever he conquered were usually ready to welcome his zeal for order and his care for the safety and welfare of clerics.

Of his financial arrangements it need only be said that, though his currency reforms were sound and well-intentioned, they had little success – bad money was too common and coinage counterfeited by Dauphinists defeated sensible reforms. It is possible that Henry hoped so to organize the finances of his conquests that they would not only pay their own way but even contribute usefully to projects farther afield. Careful analysis of the Norman and English accounts for the period have established that it was a vain hope. Some of the burden of warfare was set off by revenues from Normandy and France, but the English exchequer still carried the heaviest load, and when Henry reached England his first concern was to tour the country in search of funds.

As Henry made ready for his journey home he could be satisfied that he was leaving behind him an efficient governmental and economic machinery, but there were signs that behind the scaffolding of his occupation arrangements there were ominous cracks in the fabric of his achievement. The collection of revenues had to be enforced with the help of troops. Even round Rouen the roads were unsafe owing to 'brigands', who might be free-booting Dauphinists or even deserting Burgundians and Englishmen. None of the greater Norman lords had accepted allegiance to Henry, and many lesser gentry had left their wives to run their estates while they themselves departed to Dauphinist territory. Not all the bishops of Normandy had accepted the new dispensation, and the abbot of Bec had complained bitterly that in his area agriculture was impossible for lack of labour. In 1422 it was officially stated that since Henry's occupation of Normandy, wolves had greatly increased their attacks in the rural areas.[9] It is always easy for the conqueror to promise reform and prosperity, it is not so easy to fulfil such promise when the conquered have to suffer not only an army of occupation but persistent raiding from the conqueror's enemies. It is to

Henry's credit that his Norman intentions and plans were good; they never fully fructified because his war had to be continued.

Towards the end of January 1421, Henry and Katherine left Rouen for Calais accompanied by the king of Scots, the duke of Bedford, and a bevy of earls. At Amiens they received a royal welcome, and, as they approached Calais, the merchants of the Staple and the citizenry came out to meet them with handsome presents for the princess. After a few days in Calais waiting for a favourable wind, the royal party arrived at Dover on February 1st, and some of the barons of the Cinque Ports even waded into the breakers to carry the regent of France and his new wife safely to shore where great crowds were waiting to greet them.[10]

Chapter 22

WELCOME HOME

THE ROYAL PROGRESS from Dover to Canterbury and London repeated the emotional scenes after Henry's return from Agincourt. After a short stay at Canterbury Henry went ahead to prepare London's welcome to Katherine. At Eltham, husband and wife were reunited, and on February 21st, 1421, they were welcomed by the city of London. Henry's biographers give an enthusiastic account of a fantastic scene.[1] All the devices of medieval pageantry – and they are not to be despised – were employed to mark the occasion. Giants guarded the gates and bowed to the princess, heraldic lions rolled their eyes, choruses of minstrels and maidens sang songs of welcome, the conduits supplied free wine to the populace, the streets were strewn with greenery, the houses were hung with gay and costly bunting. The princess was escorted through the cheering citizens to spend the night in the royal palace of the Tower. Next day she was driven to the palace at Westminster in a magnificent coach escorted by nobles, city gentry and the heads of the city's guilds. On Sunday, February 23rd, Princess Katherine of France was crowned queen of England in Westminster Abbey by Archbishop Chichele. The religious ceremony was followed by a gargantuan banquet in Westminster Hall from which by protocol her husband was absent – all honour was to be given exclusively to the new queen. It was Lent, and the menu was a list of fish and shell-fish – including whelks, porpoises and sturgeons – which reads like a detailed Billingsgate inventory. On Katherine's right hand were the archbishop of Canterbury, and Henry Beaufort, bishop of Winchester. On her left was King James of Scotland. Before her were the bareheaded duke of Gloucester, the duke of Bedford and every available noble and prince of the Church with the highest ladies in the land. There were three huge courses to the banquet, and after each there was a 'subtletie', or pastrycook's tableau, each of which surpassed a long tradition of splendour and ingenuity. Queen Katherine can never have forgotten her coronation banquet.[2]

For two months after London's fabulous welcome, Henry and his queen made a royal progress through the kingdom. The itinerary covered St Albans, Bristol, Shrewsbury, Kenilworth, Coventry, Leicester, Nottingham, Pontefract, York, Beverley, Lincoln, Lynn and Norwich, and it included visits to many sacred shrines including the most famous at Bridlington and Walsingham – Henry's devotion to saints and hermits was constant and enthusiastic.[3]

The undoubted purpose of the royal tour was twofold. The people of England outside London had had little opportunity of seeing their victorious king in person; he would now, in the company of his queen, give them the chance to see him and at the same time to demonstrate their loyalty. The cheers of acclamation and the gracious reception of lavish gifts were followed by peremptory requests for hard cash and reinforcements for his armies. Behind the royal progress went royal commissioners for the receipt of loans from both lay and clerical contributors, and their activities were not only confined to those counties which Henry visited – they covered the whole country.[4] It has been estimated that Henry received as much by these methods as he could have received from parliament: the money came in speedily and cost little to collect. Although there was considerable pressure on likely lenders the loans were properly secured, and contributions came from high and low – of the £38,000 which was received by May 18th Bishop Beaufort contributed about £18,000 and Queen Katherine contributed £1,333, but there were many small subscriptions from humble knights and esquires. Henry's general popularity and his overseas successes sanctioned somewhat unorthodox measures which under a less popular and less successful monarch would have roused universal protest against 'forced loans'.

While Henry was on progress near Beverley he was met by a messenger who brought him news of his first major set-back in France – his brother, the duke of Clarence, had been killed in the disastrous battle of Baugé.[5] With characteristic self-control Henry kept the news to himself until the following day. Before leaving France he had promised Charles VI to be back with reinforcements at least by midsummer; in spite of the news of Baugé he saw no reason to change his plans. Henry showed the same sangfroid in adversity as in triumph – he completed his programme.

The last parliament at which Henry was present in person was opened in the Painted Chamber of Westminster palace on May 2nd, 1421. Its main business was to ratify the treaty of Troyes, and it is curious that the chancellor's opening address made no mention of it. The previous parliament had had some doubts about its terms – it had therefore obtained a solemn assurance that the treaty was not to involve the ultimate absorption of England into France.[6] But the parliament of 1421 ratified the treaty without further question. The rest of its work was concerned with currency reform and with a very large number of petitions which demonstrate the growing power of the commons and conditions of much civil disorder in the north. It sanctioned a loan, and the convocation of Canterbury also contributed its quota to Henry's needy exchequer.[7]

There is no evidence in the official records that Henry's recruiting and financial round-ups were resented, but in the contemporary chronicle of Adam of Usk there is a different picture. He writes of 'our lord the king rending every man throughout the realm who had money, be he rich or poor' and of the 'grievous taxation of the people being unbearable, accompanied with murmurs and with smothered curses among them from hatred of the burden'.[8] In the previous year there had been rumours of attempts on Henry's life by witchcraft, and a witch-hunt had been inspired by a circular from Archbishop Chichele. It is of little significance except that it involved Henry's step-mother Queen Joanna. Henry IV had married her as his second wife in 1403 – it had been a diplomatic marriage in that it forged a link in a chain designed to encircle France, and it had economic advantages based on the valuable Breton salt trade. Joanna was the daughter of Charles of Navarre and the widow of John IV, duke of Brittany, and although she left her Breton children in the care of Burgundy she had brought with her to

England a fair number of Breton courtiers. These Bretons were no more welcome at the English court than the Bohemians of Richard II's Queen Anne of Bohemia. To most Englishmen of the day a Breton was simply a pirate, and to most men of Devon and Cornwall a rival pirate. Henry V's feelings for his step-mother seem to have been no more than correct – in April 1415, when arranging affairs at home before departing for Agincourt, he had granted her a pension of 1,000 marks a year for life, but this was in exchange for the revenues of many alien priories which his father had vested in her and which Henry had been eager to seize. Undoubtedly Henry had the better of the bargain. When Henry returned from Agincourt, Joanna had shared in the tumultuous welcome, and later, in 1417, her influence had been useful in securing the neutralization of Brittany. Religious panic in 1419 had allied heresy-hunting and witch-hunting to hatred of the foreigner,[9] and Henry had done nothing to save his step-mother from persecution. On September 27th, 1419, her dowry and other belongings had been confiscated, and she had been arrested and detained in the royal manorhouse of Rotherhithe. She was granted an allowance for reasonable expenses but she had to dismiss her personal household; she was in effect a house-prisoner for the rest of the reign.[10] It is true that the king's Portuguese physician, one Pedro de Alcobaça, had been appointed to attend to her ailments, and that his costly medicines had been bought for her from the royal exchequer, but Henry's treatment of his step-mother scarcely did him honour – he seems to have regarded her as royal property which could be converted into welcome cash, and the suspicion of necromancy had been his useful justification.

But the stories of attempted murder by necromancy and the gloomy grumbles of Adam of Usk do not wholly vitiate the general impression that, although the hindsight of history may query the worth of Henry's continental adventuring, his con-temporaries were for the most part solidly behind him. Never-theless, there was one ominous petition in Henry's last parlia-ment – the commons petitioned that owing to pestilence and war there was a dearth of suitable candidates for the offices of sheriff and escheator and asked that the one year term of these officers should be extended. Henry agreed a term of four years.[11]

Although preoccupied with both civil affairs and arrangements for his next campaign, Henry still found time to give his personal attention to a great assembly of the Benedictine Order which was to meet in Westminster Abbey. He personally submitted to this extraordinary conference a document which in thirteen articles pilloried the Order and laid down proposals for its reform. It is an astonishing illustration of Henry's zest for action, and, even if his proposals resulted in but trifling corrections, they reveal the seriousness of his attitude to clerical affairs and a praiseworthy awareness that while the Church must be saved from the heresies of Lollardy it certainly stood in need of reform.[12]

Henry's typically busy three months in England had weightier matters also in hand. The Scots, whose king was still Henry's honoured prisoner, were constantly lending aid and arms to the Dauphinists, and the victory of Baugé had been largely a victory of Scots over English. Henry made serious efforts to settle the Scottish border and prevent further aid to the dauphin. He used his royal prisoner as a bargaining counter, and to some effect. At the end of May arrangements were agreed with the earl of Douglas that 200 Scottish knights and 200 mounted archers would be furnished to Henry's forces in France, and within three months of Henry's return from his next French expedition James I would be restored to Scotland providing hostages were given for his loyalty, and providing that he married Joan Beaufort the niece of the bishop of Winchester.[13] It was a sensible effort at settling a thorny and perennial problem, but it came too late in Henry's short life to make any appreciable difference.

With the duke of Bourbon, who had been taken prisoner at Agincourt, Henry made an excellent bargain. In return for Bourbon's treacherous acceptance of the treaty of Troyes, a ransom of 100,000 crowns, and the promise of six notable places in Bourbon territory together with their upkeep and defence at Bourbon's expense until November 1422, Henry was prepared to release him. The duke was unable to find the necessary ransom money, but Henry at least had persuaded a notable Frenchman other than a Burgundian to recognize the treaty of Troyes.[14]

With Genoa a treaty was signed which precluded Genoese aid to the dauphin.[15] Attempts were made to obtain similar agreements with the king of Aragon. An embassy was received from Henry's ally of Portugal. In these affairs Henry's diplomacy was moderately successful – he was not so happy in his diplomatic relations with Brittany. Before the battle of Baugé, the duke of Brittany had been effectively neutralized. After Baugé the duke, calculating that the tide had turned at last, entered into secret negotiations with the dauphin, and on May 8th, 1421, the treaty of Sablé[16] bound the duke of Brittany to the dauphin and actually resulted in a considerable force of Bretons under the duke's younger brother fighting against Henry in the next French campaign. There were also difficulties with the duke of Burgundy. His niece Jacqueline of Hainault had fled from her Burgundian husband to England and obtained Henry's protection – the duke was naturally affronted. Henry's motives in this affair are difficult to understand, but not only was Jacqueline honourably welcomed in England she was generously provided with house and housekeeping at the royal exchequer's expense. It was a curious move which in the next reign led his youngest brother Humphrey of Gloucester into folly and disaster. For the moment, relations with Burgundy, although not broken, were seriously strained.[17]

When Henry after his short stay in England again embarked for Calais he left behind him an England sated with victory but perhaps fearful of its cost. In France he faced a task which would have kept a less determined man from ever setting sail. His duchy of Normandy was a wedge that pierced France almost to Paris, but Paris was not France; on his right flank was now a hostile Brittany, on his left flank was an unreliable Burgundy and many a Dauphinist castle, and on and beyond the Loire were two-thirds of France under a dauphin resurgent since the victory of Baugé.

Chapter 23

BAUGE TO MEAUX

WHEN HENRY HAD LEFT France after the treaty of Troyes he had unwisely left his younger brother Thomas duke of Clarence as his deputy. Clarence had missed the glorious victory of Agincourt, and, judging by the absence of his name in Henry's Wills, there was perhaps some antipathy between them and possibly some jealousy. Clarence, however, had fought well in Henry's second campaign and had achieved considerable fame as a dashing and successful horseman, and he had shared in the triumphal march into Paris.

After Henry's departure, Clarence had been irritated by some Dauphinist success to the north-east of Paris and had decided on a thrust into the heart of Dauphinist territory to the west and south, where he hoped to force a pitched battle and perhaps rival the glory won by his brother at Agincourt.

The dauphin's main forces were concentrated round Tours, and they were in good heart as the result of the arrival of considerable Scottish reinforcements under the earls of Buchan and of Wigtown,[1] some minor successes in the raiding warfare which had continued after Henry's departure, and the fact that they were no longer faced with the redoubtable Henry in person. Clarence had mustered a force of some 4,000 men[2] at Bernay, and in March 1421 he marched south to find and if possible annihilate the Dauphinist forces. It was a formidable under-taking – he was looking for an army some 130 miles south and west of Paris. After rapid marching he reached the large town of Angers on the Loire 60 miles down-stream from Tours. He made preparations for siege but found the town too strongly defended by a garrison who refused to fight him in the open. He retired to Beaufort to the east, and sent his men foraging. Meanwhile, the dauphin's army had advanced to Baugé, north of Beaufort, and were therefore blocking Clarence's line of retreat to Normandy. Apparently the dauphin was prepared to offer decisive battle after the Easter festival.

On Easter Saturday, March 22nd, 1421, Clarence was at dinner when his scouts brought in some Scottish prisoners who informed him that French forces were at Baugé. Clarence decided, against the advice of Huntingdon and Sir Gilbert Umfraville, to seek immediate battle, and even refused to await his archers who were out foraging. In rash self-confidence he spurred his mounted men-at-arms against superior forces recently reinforced by fresh Scottish troops and well protected by archers. Clarence wore a glistening jewelled coronet round his helmet, and in the disaster which followed he was one of the first to fall. The details of the action are obscure,[3] but its results were crystal clear. The brother of Henry the Conqueror had been defeated and killed in a straight fight, and the remnants of an English army were in full flight back to the protection of their Norman strongholds. Fortunately for the English, the earl of Salisbury was now in command, and his generalship skilfully extricated his men from a desperate position – if the Scottish scouts had kept themselves better informed not an Englishman could have escaped. As it was, the English losses were grievous – Clarence, Lord Roos, and Sir Gilbert Umfraville were dead, and the earls of Huntingdon and of Somerset were prisoners. The Scots lost not one man of note. Salisbury's men were lucky to be able to salvage the body of Clarence, and it was eventually shipped to England and buried in Canterbury Cathedral.

The battle of Baugé was a rout. It was fought by comparatively small forces, and, if the English had won, it would have gained them nothing, but in losing it they lost more than their dead – the myth of English invincibility had been exploded.[4]

It was with this disaster in mind that on June 10th, 1421, Henry V set sail from Dover for Calais on what was to be his last campaign. He took with him about 4,000 fresh combatant troops – a much smaller expedition than hitherto; but his armies were already garrisoning Normandy, and the earl of Salisbury, in spite of Baugé, still had a sizeable force under his command. During the three months that had elapsed since Baugé the dauphin had unaccountably failed to follow up his advantage, and Salisbury in a series of ably conducted raids as far as Angers and Alençon had considerably restored English prestige. In early June, a bold raid of Dauphinists from Dreux had penetrated as far into Normandy as the famous abbey of Bec – it had once fathered archbishops Lanfranc and Anselm – half-way between Dreux and Honfleur. By a combination of internal treachery and bold assault they had seized its fortifications. An English force quickly overcame the raiders and pillaged the abbey, including the tomb of the Empress Matilda, and Salisbury was justified in reporting to Henry when he landed in France that Normandy 'stood in good plit and neure so well as now'.[5] But the raid on Bec illustrates the precariousness of Henry's hold even on the centre of Normandy.

But why did Henry land at Calais? The main Dauphinist threat was from the Loire south-west of Paris, and it was a long and dangerous march from Calais to the capital. In Picardy, Jacques d'Harcourt, count of Tancarville, who since the treaty of Troyes had abandoned the Burgundian cause, was raiding by land and sea and even recapturing castles for the dauphin. Henry's own explanation is contained in a letter he wrote to the mayor and aldermen of London – he was anxious to put Picardy 'in better governance';[6] but it explains little. The probability is that Henry, knowing that Normandy was again secure in the charge of Salisbury, was anxious to refurbish his relations with his ally of Burgundy. The episode of Jacqueline of Hainault was not forgotten, and Henry was anxious to persuade Burgundy to lend him active help. The Calais route took him close to Burgundy's Flemish headquarters.

Shortly after Henry's landing, news arrived that the Dauphinnists were besieging Chartres, and therefore threatening both Normandy and Paris. Henry's strategy was negatived – if he had advanced via Rouen he would have been better placed. At Montreuil there was a brief meeting with the duke of Burgundy who went ahead to ensure Henry and his new army a peaceful journey through Abbeville. The duke had some difficulty in doing this – Henry's prestige was not so high since Baugé[7] – but all went well. Once across the Somme, Henry marched straight to Paris, while the duke of Burgundy went back to Artois to muster reinforcements for the relief of Chartres.

After an anxious four days in Paris,[8] Henry left to join a concentration of his own forces and Burgundian reinforcements somewhere between Meulan and Mantes, lower down the Seine. The duke had kept his word, and a joint advance to the relief of Chartres was about to start when news came that the dauphin had raised the siege for lack of supplies to press it to a successful conclusion. Paris was safe for the time being, and Henry agreed that the Burgundians should depart and attempt to suppress the irritating Jacques d'Harcourt in Picardy while he himself would deal with the Dauphinists threatening the capital.

The strategic situation at this point was critical. The Dauphinists held a chain of formidable fortresses from the Loire as far north as Dreux, they had an army large enough to threaten Chartres, they held another chain of fortresses from Joigny on the Yonne due south of Paris to Meaux on the Marne due east of Paris. In fact Paris was almost blockaded on three sides, and Henry's wedge from Normandy towards Paris was now threatened by the disaffection of Brittany on his right flank. Henry was on the defensive, and, if the Dauphinists had been bold enough to drive into Normandy after their victory at Baugé, Henry's position would have been even more precarious than it undoubtedly was. The only strategy possible to Henry was to attempt to ward off the triple threat by attacking each strong point in turn; it was bound to be a costly and wearisome business.

Henry began his defence by besieging Dreux where the castle stood high above the town. By August 12th both town and castle had surrendered, and Henry with renewed optimism decided to march straight to the Loire and attempt to crush the Dauphinists in open battle. At Beaugency on the Loire a fortnight's siege successfully took the town but failed to take the castle. Famine and dysentery took heavy toll of Henry's men, and the dauphin wisely avoided any possibility of open fighting and left Henry's army a countryside stripped of supplies.[9] Henry was forced to wheel up the Loire. He was not strong enough to attempt a siege of Orléans although his men raided close to its walls, and he therefore kept on in an easterly direction towards

Joigny. *En route* he captured the castle of Rougemont where bands of raiding Dauphinists had taken refuge. Henry in a display of savagery which was the first definite sign of failing powers burnt the castle, hanged the garrison, and drowned every fugitive he could capture.[10]

Henry now swung due north to subdue the great Dauphinist fortress of Meaux which, some forty miles east of Paris, commanded the valley of the Marne and the eastern approaches to the capital.

The siege of Meaux has been proclaimed as Henry's masterpiece. The river Marne split the town into two, and Henry had to divide his forces. With his customary resource he organized a bridge of boats which secured proper liaison between his men. The defenders were aided by heavy rains which flooded the river, but famine threatened both besiegers and besieged. The siege was to drag on for seven weary months, and for the first time there was evidence of concern about Henry's health – an English physician was specially summoned, but we know of no further details.[11] Nevertheless, Henry was indefatigable in arranging food supplies from Paris, in superintending the construction of elaborate siege engines and personally supervising the mining operations.[12] Food was distributed to his troops from his own headquarters' supplies, but even so disease and hunger began to destroy English morale. Both English and French chroniclers report that desertions were numerous, and that there was murmuring that, although the English people had agreed to the conquest of Normandy, they had never contemplated the conquest of the whole of France.[13] Towards Christmas of 1421 one piece of good news arrived to cheer the besiegers – on December 6th a son, the future King Henry VI, had been born at Windsor to Queen Katherine and 'King Henry's heart was filled with, great gladness'.[14] But the siege of Meaux continued, and there was a threatening attack on Normandy by Dauphinists attacking with Breton help from the west. Avranches was lost and regained, and although the earl of Suffolk gained a victory over the raiders near Mont St Michel the enterprise had been bold enough to cause Henry to detach troops from the siege of Meaux to help. If the dauphin had at this time dared a full-scale invasion of Normandy Henry's position at Meaux would have

9. Thomas Plantagenet, duke of Clarence – Henry's brother who was killed at Baugé in 1421.

10. Henry Beaufort, bishop of Winchester, Henry's half-uncle.

been perilous, but, if the Dauphinists had again missed a great opportunity, they were at least logical in a strategy which avoided pitched battles and left the invaders to exhaust themselves.

Throughout the spring of 1422 the defenders of Meaux more than held their own – they were able and desperate men. On March 9th the Sire d' Offement mounted a brilliant night-manœuvre which succeeded in reinforcing the garrison although he himself fell into a ditch and was captured – he remained a wounded but honoured prisoner in Henry's hands.[15] This contretemps so disheartened the besieged that they decided to abandon the town and concentrate all their forces within the heavily fortified market protected by one arm of the Marne.

It was in the final capture of the market that Henry's genius for siege warfare was displayed at its best. Heavy artillery was skilfully mounted, huge movable structures protected the attackers and gave them footholds first on the bridge and then on the walls, and, at the end of the usual Easter truce, Henry was busy devising an even more ambitious engine – two large barges were lashed together as a platform for a huge tower which when floated down the river could make possible an attack over the wall by drawbridge from its top. The device was never used in action, but it is typical of Henry that nevertheless he tried it out after the surrender of the market and apparently proved its effectiveness.[16]

Towards the end of April the defenders, despairing of further relief, asked for terms. By May 2nd an agreement was signed, and on May 10th the garrison of Meaux surrendered. The whole of the garrison were to be at Henry's mercy but with twelve exceptions they would escape execution, and all stores and equipment in the market were to be the property of the victors. The chief leader of the defence had been the Bastard of Vaurus, and the chroniclers of all sides are agreed that his record justified his immediate hanging on the tree which he had so often used for his own savageries. But no one sought to excuse the brutal execution in Paris of an unknown horn-blower or Henry's treatment of others of the garrison who had displayed an ass on the ramparts, beaten it till it brayed, and then called on the English to come and rescue their king.[17] The prisoners were sent 'like pigs' to various prisons in Normandy and England.[18] Munitions and valuables captured were retained by the king but grain was distributed to the poor, and a library of over a hundred books of canon law and theology was also reserved to Henry and duly passed on to his son.

The siege of Meaux had cost Henry valuable lives – the earl of Worcester and Lord Clifford had been killed, and dysentery had taken heavy toll of the rank and file. A stubborn defence had pinned Henry down for over seven months. It is perhaps not to be wondered at that Henry's treatment of the vanquished was so severe. During the siege he had proved himself as able as ever, and he had exhibited not only his usual pertinacity and passion for detail but also an astonishing ingenuity. It is therefore sad that in his treatment of the horn-blower and the practical jokers he also displayed his conspicuous lack of a sense of humour.

The taking of Meaux not only flushed out a nest of Dauphinists uncomfortably near to Paris, it re-established Henry's authority, and brought with it the surrender of numerous other Dauphinist strongholds which had threatened communications between Paris and Burgundian Flanders. Burgundy himself had had some small successes against Jacques d'Harcourt and had also visited Henry during the siege.

The summer of 1422 saw Henry V again in pride of place. The disaster of Baugé had been counterbalanced by the victory at Meaux in the east and by the able help of Suffolk and Salisbury in the west. But two-thirds of France still remained unconquered, and Henry's health had begun to deteriorate.

Chapter 24

VINCENNES TO
WESTMINSTER

AFTER THE SUCCESSFUL siege of Meaux it was some time
before Henry decided to move his court to the royal
palace at Bois de Vincennes about three miles to the east
of the centre of Paris. He arrived there on the same day (May
26th, 1422) as his young queen who, having left her infant son at
Windsor, had made a leisurely progress south via Rouen. A few
days later Henry and Katherine moved in to Paris, and, after a
visit to Notre Dame, occupied Henry's old quarters in the
Louvre, while Charles VI and Isabella, who had arrived on
the same day, were again in the Hôtel St Pol – and again the
Parisians noted the disparity of accommodation with disapproval. Even the English chroniclers reported the contrast –
Henry and Katherine 'held gret Astate and satte at Dyner at a
gret feste in Parys crowned and ye Queen also... And all peple
resorted unto his court. But as for ye Kyng of Fraunce he held
none Astate nor reule, but was left almost Allone'.[1] But it must
be remembered that at this time Charles VI was a hopeless
invalid pathetically incapable of playing any part in public
affairs.

Two projects were now discussed. Henry and Burgundy were
to make a decisive attempt to dispose of Jacques d'Harcourt
once and for all – he was making a considerable nuisance of himself in his strongholds at the mouth of the Somme. Perhaps on
the way there was talk of another 'cleaning-up' operation
against the Dauphinists who were in the valley of the Oise
north-east of Paris and therefore interfering with one of Burgundy's routes to the capital. On June 11th the two courts
moved to St Denis and thence to Senlis, but Henry had no

sooner pushed on to the newly surrendered fortress of Compiègne when bad news from the south called him back.

There was apparently a small conspiracy in Paris organized by an armourer, his wife and a baker, which was quickly and ruthlessly suppressed – the woman was drowned[2] – when the plans of Henry and Burgundy were completely upset by a very serious threat from the main Dauphinist forces operating from Sancerre on the Loire some seventy miles up river from Orléans. The dauphin Charles had laid siege to Cosne and from there could plan a major thrust through the Nivernais towards the Burgundian capital of Dijon. The duke of Burgundy appreciated the seriousness of this threat, summoned all his available forces, asked Henry for archers, and hurried south to relieve Cosne. Henry promised to join the relieving force in person with the whole of his army.

But Henry was now a sick man. After returning to Senlis from Compiègne it was obvious that he was seriously ill, and a new doctor was summoned from England.[3] On July 7th he moved to the castle of Vincennes and the university of Paris staged processions to pray for his recovery. Henry was not the man to give in easily – he was still determined to lead the combined armies to the relief of Cosne. He found himself too ill to ride, and it took several days for his horse-litter to reach Corbeil – it was the farthest south he ever reached. He remained at Corbeil for over a fortnight and a hopeful improvement was quickly followed by a sad relapse. Henry, who seems to have had a great attachment to Vincennes, asked to be rowed down the Seine to Charenton from where he intended to ride as a king should to Vincennes. He tried bravely to keep on his horse but it was impossible, and he was reduced once again to the ignominy of a horse-litter which carried him to the castle where he arrived about August 10th – and 'there, alas, he entered his bed of pain'. For three weeks he lingered and on August 31st, 1422, he died.[4]

When Henry had said farewell to his queen and to Charles and Isabella at Senlis he could not have realized that he would never see them again. It is a mark of his astonishing determination that, in face of the Dauphinist threat, he was ready to march over fifty miles south into hostile territory far from his bases.

There were all the signs that a major battle was to be fought outside Cosnes – Burgundy and the Dauphinists had even agreed the proposed battlefield – and that he should be forced to turn back at Corbeil by sickness must have been gall and wormwood to the victor of Agincourt.

In fact the pitched battle never took place. In face of the threat from English and Burgundians the Dauphinists ingloriously but wisely raised the siege. From Corbeil Henry had sent on his brother Bedford and the duke of Exeter at the head of the English forces – they were now summoned back to Henry's death-bed.

It is impossible to know for certain the precise nature of Henry's fatal illness. It could have been dysentery, an internal ulcer, an 'inflammation of the fundament', ague brought on by hardships outside Meaux, or smallpox – an epidemic during his last visit to Paris may have explained the move to Senlis. The theory that he had physically exhausted himself in his crowded years of campaigning is now discounted. His troops suffered appalling hardships, but wherever Henry went he was accompanied by the comforts of a generous household, and, although he was always mindful of the sufferings of his men, there is no evidence that he himself went short of anything and no evidence that after Agincourt he had himself seen too much active fighting. For some reason we shall never know, Henry's strength was unequal to his incredible determination.[5]

Henry's last three weeks, when he knew he was dying, are a revelation of the man. Calmly and with cool deliberation he spent his time making thoughtful provision for the future of his country and his conquests, and for the welfare of the infant son he was never to see, and who, thanks to Henry, was to be the only English king ever to be crowned king of France. At his bedside were his brother John duke of Bedford, his uncle the duke of Exeter, the earl of Warwick and others of his council. Bedford was to be regent of France, governor of Normandy and guardian of Henry VI. Humphrey, duke of Gloucester, was to remain regent of England but to be subordinate to Bedford. Henry Beaufort, bishop of Winchester, was to join Bedford, Exeter and Warwick as governors and tutors to Henry VI. Above all,

Henry charged his council to maintain the alliance with Burgundy. Even at the point of death Henry once again proclaimed that he had fought his French wars not from any desire for wordly dominion but simply and solely because of a title which was just and a cause which would bring lasting peace.[6] He did, however, admit that he might unwittingly have done wrong to some, and he begged forgiveness for this, and specifically mentioned his treatment of his step-mother Queen Joanna and the heirs of Scrope. On the evening of his last day he demanded to know how long he had to live, and he refused to tolerate his doctors' evasions. They gave him two hours. Propped in the arms of his confessor, Thomas Netter of Walden, he now sought the consolations of his religion, reiterated that it had been his intention to rebuild the walls of Jerusalem,[7] and only towards the end did one moment of doubt break through his astounding self-confidence – he was heard to mutter a challenge to evil accusers 'Thou liest, thou liest! My portion is with the Lord Jesus Christ.' At the last, embracing the crucifix, his final words were loudly proclaimed – 'in manus tuas, Domine, ipsum terminum redemisti.'[8]

Throughout his life Henry V had shown a very shrewd appreciation of the value of display – as we would say today, his sense of theatre was acute – and at his death his entourage proved that they had learnt the same lesson. In an age when few could read or write, and when there were no means of mass communication except the traveller's tale and the minstrel's lay, display was the most effective form of propaganda. It was over two months before Henry was at last buried in Westminster Abbey – those two months saw a funeral procession unparalleled for impressive pomp and a final interment of a magnificence never surpassed in a period when pomp and circumstance were major arts. The glorious legend of Henry V began when his body left Vincennes for St Denis.

The preparations for the final journey took a week. Apparently the corpse was dismembered and the flesh separated from the bones by boiling. Flesh and bones were then embalmed in a leaden casket. It is remarkable that Henry's remains were never taken into Paris, and it was an ominous fact that the duke of

Burgundy took no part in Henry's obsequies – the affair of Jacqueline of Hainault had bitten deep and boded ill for the future.[9] At St Denis – the burial place of French kings – Henry lay in state in the choir of the great church. On September 15th an impressive procession began the long journey home.[10]

The coffin was borne on a carriage drawn by four great horses and above it was an effigy, larger than life-size, of Henry made of *cuir bouilli* and dressed in the royal robes with sceptre in the right hand and a golden apple in the left. Above the carriage as the procession moved through towns a canopy of rich silken cloth was held aloft. Behind the coffin came the duke of Bedford, King James I of Scotland, other English lords and the royal household all in black, a striking contrast to the torchbearers and clergy who surrounded the funeral car dressed in white.

On September 19th as the procession approached Rouen the burgesses of Henry's Norman capital came out to meet his body in ceremonial mourning and accompanied the cortège to the castle. It remained there until October 5th, and it was at Rouen that Queen Katherine arrived to join the mourners.

It had been decided that the route home was to be through Abbeville, Montreuil, and Boulogne to Calais, and the slow procession, now including the queen's lengthy train, reached Calais in early November. Unfavourable winds caused some delay but a safe channel crossing was finally made, and over the familiar royal route from Dover by Canterbury, Ospringe, Rochester and Dartford the populace thronged to pay their last tributes to the victor of Agincourt. On November 5th the mayor of London, the aldermen and the craft guilds met the procession at Blackheath and accompanied it over London Bridge to St Paul's. On the next day the procession, now swollen by the citizens of London, reached the abbey of Westminster where on November 7th, 1422, Henry V was buried – and 'in that same yere deiden the moste partye of alle the lory trees thorugh all England'.[11]

It was a truly magnificent funeral. Monstrelet, the French chronicler, maintained that 'greater pomp and expense were made than had been done for two hundred years, and even now, as much honour and reverence is daily paid to his tomb, as if it were certain he was a saint in Paradise'.[12] The mourners were led by James I king of Scots and Queen Katherine, and Henry's three favourite chargers were led up to the altar.

It was not until about 1441 that Henry's tomb and chantry chapel were finally completed.[13] It is an instructive memorial. Henry himself had pre-arranged its siting, and the proud mood of his planning was carried to even greater arrogance. At the expense of Queen Katherine the tomb was surmounted by an effigy of solid English oak plated with silver-gilt and with the head and hands of solid silver. Nothing remains of this effigy save its headless and mutilated oak core. But above the tomb is Henry's superb chantry chapel. It pushed aside the sacred relics, stole much of the glory from the tombs of Queens Eleanor and Philippa and towered above the Plantaganet graves and the shrine of the Confessor beneath. It was deliberately planned to be high enough for congregations far down the nave to see the priests officiating in it, and masses were to be for ever offered up for the soul of the first of our kings who thought it appropriate to have his own separate chantry. The elaborate sculptures on the exterior are still excellently preserved. The founders of the abbey, and, in the statuettes of St George and St Denis, the glories of the two kingdoms, theoretically united under Henry's son, are suitably commemorated. But the chief interest of the sculptures [see plates 4, 11b] is that two portraits of Henry on his charger are included and two scenes of his coronation. Both crowning scene and oath-taking scene are surrounded by statuettes of the assembled peers in their coronation robes, and behind one of the spirited sculptures of Henry at full gallop is the significant portrayal of a row of prisoners hung from the battlements of a captured castle. The corpses are taller than the castle wall, which suggests that the sculptor may have felt strongly about the incident; in approval or disapproval there is no means of knowing.

The sculptured heraldry of the chapel is also of interest. The swans derive from Henry's de Bohun ancestry, but the antelope and the flaming beacon or cresset light are garbled versions of Henry's personal badges. The antelope was supposed to be drawing a horse-mill and to represent the first part of the motto, which is not inappropriate, 'after busie labour cometh victorious reste'. The cresset light is supposed to refer to Henry's alleged change from the darkness of his wild youth to the illumination of his riper years – 'his virtues now shine as the light of a cresset, which is no ordinary light'.

On a beam above the chapel, and visible from the choir, were hung Henry's shield, saddle and helmet [see plate 11a] – a fashion begun with the tomb of the Black Prince at Canterbury – and they are still there. The shield was emblazoned, and the helmet is a tilting helmet and not, as was once thought, 'the bruised helm' he brought back from Agincourt.

There is sad significance too in the altar slab. It is now the tomb of Henry's Queen Katherine. But Henry himself made no provision for her. As he lay dying at Vincennes he had no thought for her, and, about three years after Henry's death, she married Owen Tudor by whom she had a son who was to become the father of King Henry VII. She died very much in retirement in the year 1437.[14] Her tomb was a rough coffin laid in Westminster's Lady Chapel with the corpse 'badly apparelled' and open to public view. When her Tudor grandson became king of England the Lady Chapel was destroyed to make room for his own magnificent chapel, and Katherine's remains were placed on the right side of her husband's, where they could still be seen, 'the bones being firmly united' and thinly clothed with flesh like 'scrapings of fine leather' when, on February 24th, 1668, Samuel Pepys recorded that he had had the perverted pleasure of kissing the lips of a queen![15] It was not until 1878 that Henry V's queen was a last decently interred beneath the altar slab of her first husband's chapel. It is a sorry sequel to the story of the elaborate obsequies for and arrogant memorials to England's hero king.

EPILOGUE

IN HENRY THE FIFTH 'the dying energies of medieval life kindle for a short moment into flame'.[1] 'In the long line of able English kings since Alfred, he alone inspired at once the admiration and affection of his people'.[2] 'A special charm and pathos must always attach to the memory of that princely hero who, through the splendour of his achievements, illumined with the rays of his glory the decline of the medieval world'.[3] 'Indisputably the greatest Englishman of his day – more forceful in arms, more discreet in council, more steadfast in purpose, and, with all his imperfections, more honourable in life'.[4] Such encomiums are typical of many modern English historians, and we know from Shakespeare how Elizabethan England worshipped the memory of Henry of Monmouth. To his French enemies his outstanding love of justice was his abiding claim to honour, and even to a Dauphinist he was acknowledged as *'tres fort justicier'*.[5] To the English people Henry of Monmouth will always be the hero of Agincourt. To the French people he will always be known as 'Henri le Conquérant'. It is time for a new assessment.

When Henry died he was only thirty-five years of age. His reign had lasted a short nine years, and of these only a bare four were spent in England. His youth and young manhood had been spent in cruel border warfare, and had included a bitter taste of civil war. The hardships of campaigning had probably been compensated by some over-indulgence in the licenses of a soldier's leave in London, but even before he ascended the throne he had shown a lively interest in politics and a shrewd sense of his own diplomatic powers. In his father's time England was of little weight in the European scale – Henry IV was a usurper faced with a divided baronage, a hostile Wales, an aggressive Scotland where the ghost of Richard II still walked, and an English Church more preoccupied with revolutionary Lollardy at home than with the Schism abroad. As prince of

218

Wales, Henry had thwarted Glendower, helped to crush a formidable baronial revolt, and shown his orthodox zeal in persecuting heretics. As king, Henry had suppressed a rising of the Lollards and nipped another dangerous baronial and dynastic conspiracy in the bud. He had won against overwhelming odds one stupendous victory over the French at Agincourt. He had conquered the whole of Normandy and taken victorious English arms as far south as the Loire. He had enforced a treaty with Burgundy and Charles VI of France which made him regent of France and heir to the French throne. He had been visited and courted by the Holy Roman Emperor, and his embassies had been instrumental in ending the Schism. He had taken scores of French towns and successfully besieged such formidable strongholds as Caen, Rouen, Falaise, Melun and Meaux, and he had never suffered a single defeat in person. In spite of his long absences abroad, he had never had overmuch cause to worry about support and supplies from clerical or lay sources at home. Although the son of a usurper, he had consolidated his throne, kept England safe and established her fame and reputation abroad. It is a formidable catalogue of achievement.

But it is legitimate to inquire whether all of this achievement was really worth while or truly a success. Lollardy survived both the disaster at St Giles's Fields and the barbarous execution of Sir John Oldcastle. Before the end of the reign. Sir John Mortimer was in the Tower suspected of a conspiracy which links the usurpation of 1399 with the Wars of the Roses.[6] The victory of Agincourt was due to the folly of the French rather than the generalship of Henry. The conquest of Normandy and the defence of Paris displayed Henry as an ingenious and painstaking master of siege-craft, but his trek to Calais from Harfleur had been military folly and his landing at Calais on his last campaign a doubtful move. On the other hand, his strategy on his second campaign was masterly and well rewarded – it was probably the first time that the notion of generalship and overall strategy had appeared in medieval Europe. When the French adventure began, there had been some attempt to colonize conquered towns, but it was an experiment of very short duration, and in the final reorganization of his conquests French laws and customs were strictly preserved and only a ruthless military occupation superimposed – it is questionable whether any merely military occupation can survive for long. On his last campaign, when the siege of one town took seven months, the ultimate futility of so much misery and loss of life may have weighed on the dying king. In the later Middle Ages, a battle did not necessarily win a country. France in fact was not a country. It was a territory which had a king as its overlord, but its economy was truly medieval – it was based on local self-sufficiency. A royal army could suffer overwhelming defeat, but the resistance of every city in the kingdom, strengthened by the garrisons of their superbly placed fortresses, could still remain unimpaired. As Henry lay dying at Vincennes he could only see an endless succession of sieges of Meaux if his dreams that he or his heir were to be truly king of France were to be realized. The prospect was appalling.[7]

And yet there are apologists who have held that Henry's dreams were reasonable. An English Normandy which could easily have included Paris and the Ile de France could have re-mained linked to the English crown as a viable buffer state between Dauphinist France south of the Loire and a revival of Charlemagne's Middle Kingdom of Burgundy and Flanders on the east.[8] Such fictional empire-building ignores the burgeoning spirit of nationality, and all the forces of geography. Henry's dreams, like Henry's claims to the French crown, were looking backwards to the days of Edward III – the future was inevitably with a dauphin who, a mere seven years later, was to be crowned king of France at Rheims with Joan of Arc as his standard bearer. There are defenders of Henry who plead that, if he had lived a more reasonable span, he might at least have consolidated his conquest of Normandy. But Henry did not leave behind him nonentities. His French conquests were left in the very capable hands of his brother John, and his armies were still the men of Agincourt. But Agincourt had been dimmed by Baugé, and there was a growing malaise at home and in Normandy in the face of a war which seemed to have no end and very little purpose. It is true that if Henry had lived another two months he would by virtue of the treaty of Troyes have become king of both England and France – Charles VI died on October 11th, 1422.[9] But, a few years later, a regenerated France was to begin a war that in thirty years regained all she had lost, and left England to an internal war of faction[10] which equalled in savagery anything ever recorded of the strife between Burgundian and Armagnac. It is not unfair to judge a king partly by reference to the heritage he handed on to his successor, and in such a judgement the ghosts of his mad and murdered son, and of a long procession of slain and executed barons, are tragic and pertinent witnesses.

Of Henry the man it is difficult to draw a dispassionate picture. There are several portraits by unknown hands which are alike, and therefore perhaps reliable,[11] in showing a pale lean face with the long Plantagenet straight nose – a mask rather than a face, betraying no warmth of character but only a firm efficiency about lips and jaw. No contemporary ever expatiated on Henry's kindliness, beauty or gaiety, although there is ample evidence that he was very fond of music and wherever he went his minstrels accompanied him.[12] Henry's only other relaxation seems to have been the chase – a passion shared by most of our medieval kings – and for reading we are told he loved the histories of chivalry and in particular the life-story of Godfrey of Bouillon.[13] Of his physique there is conflicting evidence. He had once been seriously ill as a youth, but there was no talk of illness throughout his French campaigns until very near the end, and as a younger man his athletic prowess had been legendary.[14]

Of Henry's religious orthodoxy and devotion there is no shadow of doubt. When in England, he spent time and money on ecclesiastical endowments; when abroad, he was at pains to protect clergy and monks; wherever he went his chaplains were close at hand, and his first duty after victory was to render thanks to God in the nearest church. His religiosity is one of his least appealing qualities to a modern view. He lived and acted as a soldier, but his soldiering was God-driven. His claims to the French crown were based not only on the arguments of his lawyers but on the undoubted goodwill of his Deity. His victories were the judgement of God, and yet, when faced with the threat of fire at the siege of Meaux, he could make the charmingly cynical and homely comment 'as to fire it is the usage of war, and war without fire is no more worth than sausages without mustard'.[15] To modern eyes, Henry's invasions of France were 'unscrupulous and hypocritical aggression' tempted by the obvious weakness of a divided country, but to Henry himself from first to last he was the instrument of a divine purpose.[16]

Of Henry's personal bravery there is no question. At Shrewsbury when he was only sixteen he had fought like a man, and made light of a painful wound. At Agincourt, when his brother the duke of Gloucester had been wounded and overthrown by the duke of Alençon, he had rushed into the mêlée and saved his brother's life – at the cost of a dented helmet and a chipped coronet. At the siege of Melun he had not hesitated to share the single combats in the mines.

Both friend and foe paid tribute to Henry's passion for justice,[17] and no one criticized his ruthlessness. But even by the brutal standards of his own day there are deeds in his record which besmirch his name. The episode of the burning of Badby is not to his credit. The order to execute the prisoners at Agincourt in cold blood was at best the act of a general so scared that his own men could not believe it, and his own bodyguard had to carry out the gruesome order. The treatment of the refugees in the ditch of Rouen, the hanging of Alain Blanchard, the execution of the Scottish defenders of Melun, these are savageries which can possibly be excused by medieval standards although they have their modern apologists too. But the crucifying of the gunners of Louviers, the hanging of the hostages at Montereau, the execution of the trumpeter after the siege of Meaux, and the fate of the unknown soldier who had insulted him from the walls of Rouen were unworthy of any great general in any age. On the other hand, there are several letters which tell of Henry's kindness and care for old friends and retainers, and, like most able soldiers, he was ever mindful of the welfare of his troops.[18] Henry, as Capgrave wrote, 'steadfastly observed the paths of justice', and if his justice was stern it was applied to high and low;[19] it is a pity that so clean if so severe a record is blotted with some unpardonable spites.

Only once in the chronicles does a touch of normal feeling reveal itself – it appears that in an age when a royal marriage was always a convenience and a matter of high policy Henry was moved by the beauty and charm of the princess who was to

be his queen. And yet it was a fatal marriage – the blood of
France was tainted, and the madness of Henry VI was the
product of the insatiable ambition of Henry V.[20] On his death-
bed Henry never gave a thought to his queen, although he spent
much time planning the future of her son. In every ceremonial
occasion of his life, Henry remained cold and aloof – he permitted and arranged rejoicings and celebrations, he allowed
none to see that he may have enjoyed them. His enthusiasms
were for the details of siege-craft and the complications of
strategy and diplomacy, his passions were only released for cold
justice, his character seems as chilly as his face.

But how did this strange aloof soldier leave his England? If the
Paston letters are a guide, the state of lawlessness in the countryside was worse than it had ever been. Constitutionally, his reign
was of little importance. It is true that the commons were slowly
increasing their authority, but England's immediate future was
to be at the mercy of an unscrupulous and unbridled aristocracy.
The lords had helped one of their peers to usurp the throne of
England. In 1404, when Northumberland had been clearly
guilty of treason in the previous year, they were powerful
enough merely to find him guilty only of 'trespass', and his open
rebellion had been passed over lightly as just another exercise of
that private war (in this instance between him and the earl of
Westmorland) which they considered one of their rights. In
France for a while the English lords found exercise enough, but
they were soon to be back in England at the head of men
brutalized by a warfare which had lost all the glamour and
grace of chivalry, unaccustomed to the arts and crafts of peace
and ready for any selfish and internecine adventuring at home.
Contrasted with the poverty of the crown, the lords were becoming rich. They had claimed their pensions and annuities for
helping the Lancastrian dynasty to the throne, they were adept
at engrossing offices and lands, and they had been clever
enough to become among the greatest wool-producers and
sometimes the greatest wool merchants in the kingdom. In the
reign of Henry's son they were to consolidate their power as the
chief estate of the realm, their blood ruled through spiritual
lords closely related to them, their wealth gave them hosts of

retainers who could thwart local justice, their vast estates gave them far more local power than the monarch at Westminster, and only when they began to quarrel between themselves did the commons at last achieve power, and only when king and commons saw the identity of their interests did the throne of England at last achieve real independence.[21] The kingdom of England gained little from the French conquests in terms of money and lost much treasure and many men. Henry's legacy to his own country was 'a false ideal of foreign conquest and aggression, a reckless contempt for the rights and feelings of other nations, and a restless incapacity for peace in spite of exhaustion which had begun to show itself even in his own lifetime' – that is the verdict of a gentle historian who was not blinded by the glitter of trophies.[22] Henry's son was cursed with a heritage which compelled his advisers to squander still more men and treasure in a losing cause, and an England where the seeds of the Wars of the Roses were quickly sprouting.

The arts are frequently pointers to the way of the world. The reign of Henry V was culturally a barren period referred to in the scathing words of a modern critic as 'the sad and desolate years of the early fifteenth century, a time when the pulse of English art almost stopped'.[23] To the greatness of Chaucer succeeded the banality and sycophancy of Hoccleve and the prosaic drivelling of Lydgate.[24] There was no worthy successor to Yevele in the arts of architecture, the brasses of the period, after their short and brilliant hey-day, began their sad and rapid decline; and alabaster was the cheap and easy substitute for the hard stone of earlier sculptors; the great achievements of 'Opus Anglicanum' were already in the past. In music and in painting there were no dramatic developments, although Agincourt gave us one of our first great English songs, and Henry himself composed competent music for his Chapel Royal.[25] For lyric poetry, we have only the minor work of two foreign princes, James of Scotland and Charles of Orléans, both of whom, significantly enough, wrote as Henry's captives. The arts of peace rarely go well with the arts of war, but it is only fair to add that France, suffering from similar disabilities, was in like case – Monstrelet for example was but a poor shadow of

. The tilting helm,
dle and inner face
Henry V's shield.
e saddle was of blue
vet powdered with
d fleurs-de-lys. The
eld shows part of
 arms of Navarre
enry's step-
ther's). The sword
s possibly Henry's
d certainly of his
iod.

b. Henry V on his
arger: from the
rth side of his
antry Chapel in
estminster Abbey.
rpses hang from the
ttlements of the
tle on the right.

12. Part of the Syon Cope showing St George killing the dragon. An outstanding example of fourteenth century English needlework.

the brilliant Froissart. There is no doubt that the military court of Henry V compares sadly with the galaxy of talent which surrounded Richard II, and the backwardness of Lancastrian England is in grim contrast to the artistic achievements of contemporary Flanders and Italy. In the Middle Ages, and in the Renaissance which followed, culture depended very much on patronage – Henry V was too busy harking back to the dreams of his great-grandfather to have the time, even if he ever had the inclination, to emulate the virtues of the despised Richard II who had welcomed Froissart, patronized Chaucer, and propounded a policy of peace which might have carried England from the pit of the Peasants' Revolt to the efflorescence of the Tudors without so much tragedy and bloodshed in between.

The day of St Crispin and St Crispianus was the day of Agincourt; it was also the day of Balaclava. The two battles are now part of the same mystique – the mystique of patriotism. And there is no doubt that in Henry of Monmouth England found its own patron saint of national glory. Like most idols it has feet of clay. The Elizabethans, after the brutalities of the Wars of the Roses, found their *preux chevalier* in the legendary virtues of 'Harry of Monmouth', and the genius of their Shakespeare disguised the shallowness of patriotism with the magic of immortal verse. It is sad that history must also record the cold, priggish, ruthless efficiency of the father of that legend, the barrenness of his glory and the futility of his achievement, yet it cannot forbear tribute to an organizing genius who was a hero to his own day, an upholder of the hard logic of implacable justice, and a heroic myth for generations to come.

APPENDIX

The Siege of Rouen
by
John Page

The Siege of Rouen is a rhyming chronicle written by a certain John Page at some time between the death of Clarence (March 1421) and the death of Henry V (August 1422). In the Great Roll of 1417 there is a John Page listed in the retinue of Sir Philip Leche of Chatsworth, but nothing definite is known about the author other than what he tells us himself – he was a soldier with Henry V at the siege of Rouen. His work became popular in the London of his own day, was used by several later English chroniclers, but was lost until rediscovered in 1827. Portions were printed then and in 1828 (and later in 1908) but the whole text was first edited and printed by the Camden Society in 1876 and had been translated into French by Professor M. L. Puiseux of Caen in 1867.

As an eye-witness account of great events it has undisputed authority, as vivid reporting it is unique in our early literature, but it is of course written in the English of the early fifteenth century and is therefore not readily available or acceptable to twentieth century readers. It has therefore seemed worth while to offer a free translation into modern English prose.

It is illuminating that this ordinary soldier's language is coloured throughout by religious references, whereas in modern times sport or perhaps science would colour a similar narrative from a similar author. The religiosity of medieval characters, which the modern mind finds it difficult to appreciate, was quite natural to an age when religion was so much a part of everyday living.

All the available printed texts have been consulted – J. J. Conybeare in *Archaeologia* XXI, London 1827, 43 – 78; F. Madden in *Archaeologia* XXII, London 1828, 350 – 398; James Gairdner in *The Historical Collection of a Citizen of London in the Fifteenth Century*, Camden Society 1876 x – xvi and 1 – 46; *Brut*, II 394 – 422; the French free translation by Professor Puiseux in his *Siège et Prise de Rouen par les Anglais*, Caen 1867, 235 – 272, which is acknowledged with gratitude and admiration; and finally the impressive critical annotated edition of Professor H. Huscher in *John Page's Siege of Rouen* (Kölner Anglistische Arbeiten I) Leipzig 1927.

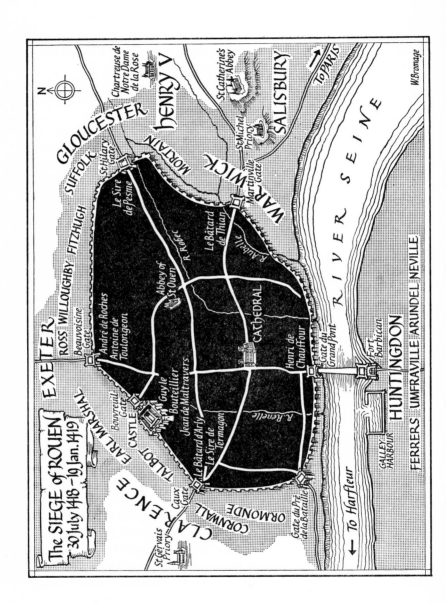

The SIEGE of ROUEN
30 July 1418 – 19 Jan. 1419

N

GLOUCESTER

SUFFOLK

Chartreuse de
Notre Dame
de la Rose

HENRY V

MORTAIN

St Hilary's
Gate

St Catherine's
Abbey

St Michael
Priory

SALISBURY

WARWICK

Martinville
Gate

To Paris

RIVER SEINE

W. Bromage

EXETER

ROSS WILLOUGHBY FITZHUGH

Beauvoisine
Gate

Le Sire
de Pesme

R. Robec

Abbey of
St Ouen

Le Bâtard
de Thian

R. Aubelle

CATHEDRAL

André de Roches
Antoine de
Toulongeon

Henri de
Chauffour

Gate du
Grand Pont

Fort
Barbican

HUNTINGDON

EARL MARSHAL

Boupreuil
Gate

CASTLE

Guyle
Bouteillier
Jean de Maltravers

Le Bâtard d'Arly
Le Sire de
Tormagon

R. Renelle

GALLEY
HARBOUR

FERRERS UMFRAVILLE ARUNDEL NEVILLE

CLARENCE

TALBOT

Caux
Gate

St Gervais
Priory

CORNWALL

ORMONDE

Gate du Pré
de la Bataille

To Harfleur

THE SIEGE OF ROUEN

> May God who died on the cross
> and bought us all with His
> blood, so generously shed,
> grant His blessing to those who
> listen to my story . . .

Often, both in prose and in verse, we hear stories of adventure, assault, siege and doughty battle in the days of old. Now I will tell you, if you will listen to me, a story of our own time; of how our liege-lord Henry V with his royal forces laid siege to that rich city of Rouen which he coveted as his own. There has been no siege more famous since the sieges of Troy and of Jerusalem. Never have so many troops been involved; never was there such a siege – of that I am certain. Now listen to me a while and I will tell you how it was. I can tell you all the better because I was actually there with my lord the king, and I carefully set down everything that came to my notice.

After the successful siege of Pont de l'Arche and when the crossing of the Seine had begun, the king sent forward that most devoted lord, the duke of Exeter, together with heralds, to the city of Rouen to inquire whether it was prepared to surrender. At the same time they were to reconnoitre the approaches, and discover how best the city might be besieged if the citizens refused to submit.

When the duke of Exeter – of great renown – arrived before the city gates, he unfurled his many banners and sent his heralds to warn the citizens on pain of death to receive our king in peace, never to thwart his rights, and to surrender the city forthwith. Moreover, he told them to make it clear that the king was determined to take Rouen, and that he would not move on until by God's grace he had it.

231

To this the citizens made no answer, told our heralds to depart and urged us by signs to wait no longer but to retire immediately. They then opened fire with their guns and staged an attack of great ferocity – a troop of knights in great fettle and gleaming armour made a sortie to such effect that the duke had to withdraw suffering considerable losses in killed and prisoners. This action over, he returned immediately to the king, who was still at Pont de l'Arche, and told him how matters stood at Rouen, and of how fiercely the citizens had reacted.

Now, if you will bear with me, I will tell you of a cursed and sinful deed committed by the French before our king reached the city. All the suburbs of that beautiful city – churches as well as houses – they destroyed. Issuing from the St Hilary Gate they destroyed the church whose patron saint had given the gate its name. At the Cauchoise Gate they demolished the church of St Andrew, and also the Priory of St Gervais where later the duke of Clarence took up his quarters. At the Bridge Gate they razed the churches of Nôtre-Dame, of St Catherine (that sweet virgin), of St Sauveur and of St Matthew – they left neither stick nor stone standing. At the Martinville Gate they mined the beautiful church of St Michael and another not far from it dedicated to St Paul. The hedges of their gardens and the trees were all cut down and stored within the walls, while the branches, briars and brushwood were all burned so that the area was as bare as my hand.

That beautiful city was now a proud sight – it was very well prepared for action and had every imaginable engine of defence. The walls were manned ready; the moats were deep and easy to defend. The great fosse which ringed the city walls was broad and deep and in addition was protected with trenches on each side. These trenches had very steep sides and were to defend the approaches to the fosse so that no man could get near to it save at the risk of his life. Anyone who got into the fosse could not escape unharmed, for the ground was sown with wolf-traps. Every trap was a lance-length in depth, so that if a man fell into it he could not defend himself or even see whether any enemy was approaching. The ground between these traps was studded with obstacles and entanglements and in addition strewn with 'caltrops'[1] like a coat of mail. Within the town they had built up earthen breastworks against the walls strong enough and hard enough to provide a road for laden carts – this was to enable them to repair the effects of artillery fire. And, truly, the besieged had invented many other ingenious stratagems.

This fair city has only five main gates, but round it I reckon there were many scores of towers spaced at intervals of about thirty-three yards. In each tower there were three guns aimed to three different quarters. On the wall between each tower was a great cannon mounted low in the earth and ready to fire. There were wall-guns at regular intervals on the walls set to shoot at close or long range, and between each tower on the parapet were eight small guns for rapid fire. At each gate there was a kind of engine or 'trypgette'[2] and at some gates more than one; for example at the St Hilary Gate. This was how the besieged had made ready their defence – with masses of materials and ample ordnance.

But let us cease describing all these defence works and tell of Henry our king.

On the Friday before Lammasday our king, richly dressed and with a numerous entourage, reached the city and took up his quarters not far off. On the Saturday he assigned his commanders to various positions surrounding the city. On the Monday our king gave orders that every man should take up his position, and he himself took up his quarters towards the east of the city in the Charterhouse, and with him were many lords. But of all that great flock of nobility and chivalry our king was the bell-wether – no tongue can tell of his renown, yet if you rank all princes according to their worth then place King Henry at their head.

At the edge of the city towards the west, the duke of Clarence was lodged in that ruined abbey near the Cauchoise Gate which had been mined – and there he contained the besieged to great effect, won a warrior's fame and found great honour. He might be called a flower of princehood and in a gathering of all princes Clarence deserves a place next to the greatest.

Between the king and Clarence that zealous knight Exeter was stationed – in front of the Beauvoisine Gate. Every day the French made sorties here; but, by his vigorous resistance, he drove them back inside and won for himself a great reputation. For bravery amongst princes let Exeter share pride of place.

Between him and Clarence was that valiant knight the earl marshal. He took up his position near the Castle Gate and watched it night and day. A little farther on on this side the king positioned the Lord Harrington. Later, Talbot, on his arrival from the capture of Domfront, camped alongside this worthy lord, and, when Sir William Harrington was killed, Talbot took over his command.

The earl of Ormonde with a very sizeable body of retainers took up his post next to Clarence. As for that brilliant knight Cornwall he was at Clarence's side night and day, as well as a bevy of other knights of the first rank whose names slip my memory.

Between Exeter and the king were posted the lords of Ross and of Willoughby and with them the Lord Fitz-Hugh who was reckoned a good true knight.

Sir William Porter's position was in front of the St Hilary Gate. There there was as bitter fighting as has ever been seen. Whenever the French made sorties there he drove them back inside – he gained infinite honour here; this valiant knight was well worthy of his fame.

As long as St Catherine's resisted, the brave earl of Mortain, who was posted between that abbey and the city, smote the French hip and thigh and won for himself a great reputation which lasted as long as he lived. The earl of Salisbury was camped on the other side of the abbey, and from the beginning of this action he earned for himself great renown. There was also a brilliant knight Sir John Grey who was posted at the foot of the hill of St Michael – may he receive honour and glory for his deeds there. Carew, that bold baron, held the ground above him to such purpose that his fame was established far and wide. Finally, there was a worthy esquire called Janyco who was posted higher up still.

On the south bank of the Seine was Huntingdon facing the town to stop sorties on this side – he contained them very effectively and won himself much honour. That comely knight Neville, that brilliant Lord Umfraville and Sir Richard Arundel were there to help him, and Lord Ferrers was also there. All in royal array were at the Bridge Gate where daily they performed great feats of arms.

Towards the town of Pont de l'Arche (up-stream) our king ordered a great chain to be placed across the Seine anchored to great stone piles to prevent ships getting through. Above the chain he made a bridge for both cavalry and infantry so that they could make speedy contact across the river whenever it was necessary.

When Warwick returned from the siege of Domfront he reported to the king and was ordered to besiege Caudebec. As soon as he arrived before this town the inhabitants hastened to come to terms. They agreed to abide by the fate of Rouen, and meanwhile sealed a treaty that would allow our ships with their supplies to sail unmolested up the Seine. After this, our ships went up-river and cast anchor beneath the walls of Rouen. There were so many ships so close together in the Seine that Rouen seemed besieged as much by water as by land.

When Warwick had completed his task, he returned to Rouen and was posted between St Catherine's and the king for so long as the abbey resisted and until by the Grace of God it fell. Soon after that, he was posted to the Martinville Gate where bitter fighting took place – the besieged made ceaseless sorties at this spot but every time they were driven back by Warwick's fierce and brave assault.

Meanwhile Salisbury had been sent off on a special mission, but soon he was back, and he took up his quarters with Gloucester and there remained until the end of the siege. As for Gloucester, after his arrival from the siege of Cherbourg this worthy lord was posted close in front of the St Hilary Gate where he bravely won fame because his position was two hundred yards nearer the enemy than that of any of the other English lords. When one talks of princes, Gloucester must surely rank as one of the bravest. The brilliant earl of Suffolk and that brave knight, Bergavenny, were with him and daily won great honour.

At this time the prior of Kilmainham in Ireland entered the estuary of the Seine and disembarked at Harfleur with 1,500 of his men as well equipped for war as their country could afford. He lost no time in joining the besiegers, and was very welcome to our king.

It was now rumoured that the French king and the Burgundians were approaching our army from the north – the side of the city which caused us the most anxiety. Our king ordered Kilmainham and his men to take up positions alongside the woods, to keep the approaches clear and to scout through the forest of Lyons and keep the French at bay. They therefore posted themselves in the woods and there stood guard and kept their watch in good heart some three leagues from our army – they were ordered to keep at this distance. The prior readily obeyed these orders and bravely they set out ready to withstand the first assault if the French should arrive by this route. The prior won much renown there – and elsewhere.

So, our siege of that fair city was all set – to the glory of our king. I propose now to speak not of the city but of those captains who defended it.

Sir Guy le Bouteiller was the commander-in-chief both of the city and of its castle – he was a very famous man. De Termagon was captain at the Cauchoise Gate; de Roches was captain at the Beauvoisine Gate with Sir Antoine, a fine soldier, as his lieutenant; Henri Chauffour was captain at the Bridge Gate; Jean de Maltravers, that noble fellow, was captain at the Castle Gate; de Pesme was captain at the St Hilary Gate; the Bastard de Thian was at that time captain at the Martinville Gate; the great Jacques, a clever and very able soldier, was captain of the men of Caen – and of the men of all other towns from round about.

Each of these captains had under his orders 10,000 men and more. But if one were to include the inhabitants there must have been 410,000 people – men, women and children – in Rouen.[3] It was, therefore, a proud array of people well worthy of the siege-craft of our king. Added to that they were as brave on foot as on horseback; they were the most intrepid men I ever met and able to prove it in every kind of fighting. When they wished to make a sortie they issued not out of one gate, of two gates, or of three gates, but out of every gate at the same time. Moreover, as I live and speak truth, each group of 10,000 men was handsomely equipped for the fight, proud and wonderfully nimble. It must have been a great joy to lead them, but it was terrible to encounter them; not merely because of their bravery in defending themselves, but also because of the guns and cross-bows which at the same time were firing on us from the walls. To tell you the truth of what I have never experienced before, the moment they made a sortie at least a hundred canons would fire from the walls and towers within the space of an hour, and no tongue can tell how many cross-bow shafts were loosed at us at the same time.

Always the besieged were trying to break out – though many of them fell in action. At other times they would ride out into the open armed with lances and shields. Then our king would order that every man should keep sharp watch. And he ordered a trench to be dug, filled with sharp pointed stakes and palisaded, right round that fair city. Sir Robert Babthorpe was our king's engineer in this enterprise – and much renown he won for it.

Now they had to make their sorties on foot because the fosse was impassable for horses. Both by land and by water our men were always ready to withstand them hand to hand, though often our soldiers were killed. They would charge up to the walls, and if a man escaped with his life it was by the grace of God, for guns and cross-bows shot so fast, 'trypgettes', slings and other engines wrought such havoc – especially on the men of Gloucester, that popular prince, who were posted so close to the enemy.

News now arrived that the Burgundians were approaching to rescue the city, and when the news reached the citizens they set all their bells ringing with great gladness. Apart from this occasion they were never rung from the beginning of the siege until the city was taken.

Now came the news that the Burgundians were at hand. Then said our king with great good cheer 'Comrades, be merry now all of you, for we shall soon be in action'.

However, it was not to be – it was reported that the Burgundians had gone to Paris. A few days later it was said they were at Pontoise, and that 400,000 fighting men were with the duke. Our king ordered that every man should sleep in his battle-kit. Outside the perimeter of the camps a trench was dug at great expense protected above by sharp palisades to spear the horses with sharp and deadly spikes, and guns trained to every quarter. The engineer who supervised this work was a worthy and busy knight.

A little while later it was said that the Burgundians were within twenty miles. The news broke on the Thursday that they would really arrive on the Friday, and the same news also reached the city. The king too was well aware of it. Early on the Friday, our king rode to the earl of Huntingdon and there he planned a stratagem – a *ruse de guerre*, and a noble one too. He posted a corps in battle array with their backs to the city. At the same time he ordered another corps to advance out of the woods in order of battle displaying what appeared to be the banners of the arms of Burgundy. These two corps pretended to join battle in order to provoke a sortie by the besieged. But the besieged did not dare – they were in doubt, suspecting some hidden trick and fearing that they might be slain. Afterwards, they continued to fight on with fury, and made bold and brave sorties as they had before.

For long they counted on the Burgundians, until, towards Christmas time, victuals began to get scarce in the city. Bread, drink and all kinds of provisions began to fail, except that they had enough water and enough vinegar to add to it.[4] It was difficult to put your hand on a loaf. They had no meat save horse-meat. They also ate both dogs and cats, both rats and mice. A quarter of a horse lean or fat was worth 100 shillings; a horse's head 10 shillings, a dog 10 shillings of good money; a rat sold for 40 pence, a cat for 2 nobles, a mouse for 6 pence – and there were few left in any house. A morsel of bread as small as the half of one's hand was worth a French franc, and it was hard to find. It was not made with flour or oats but with bran and husks. Turnips and leeks were a luxury meal – for a leek was worth a shilling – no less: if you could find one. An egg sold at 9 pence and an apple at 10 pence. Such was their shopping. Many hearts were full of woe because the market was so bad. It was not so much the expense as the lack of nourishment, and the difficulty of finding it which grieved them so. And then they took to eating rotten food and any vegetable peelings they could find – they even ate dock roots.

And now the people in the city began to die. Every day many died and found no burial. There, where at one time all was pride and joy, now was grief and sad sorrow. There, where once was meat, drink and song, now was hunger and bitter wailing.

If a child was dying the mother would give it no bread – instead of sharing with it the little they had left, she would hide it far from the bread-bin so that the child could not find it, and she could eat it by herself in secret. Neither would a child share with its mother – it preferred to eat by itself. All love and kindness were forgotten. Each one hid from his neighbour any food he might have; people avoided each other so that they could eat in secret. For hunger overrules all the bonds of kindred and of affection – these folk certainly proved that.

However, on the walls they fought bravely so that our men should not suspect their distress. Many tried to escape to go in search of food, and whenever they were captured they told us of the misery that ruled in the city; yet we could not believe that they were in such desperate straits – so well did they fight.

A little while later, all the poor folk of that city were expelled from every gate – many hundreds at a time. It was a piteous sight to see women with their infants in their arms begging on their knees to save their lives. And old men knelt beside them, and one and all set up a doleful wail 'Have mercy on us, you English men'. Our soldiers gave them some of their own bread, although they had fought us so bitterly. We did them no harm but we did make them go back into the fosse – and there we kept them at a distance so that they could not pass through our outposts. Many said they would rather be killed than return to the city of Rouen again. They went off grumbling and ceaselessly cursing their own nation, for the city would not have them back. In this the citizens committed a very deadly sin, for many died of cold whose lives could have been saved.

This happened at Christmas time. And I can now tell you of a most graceful gesture and of a great act of kindness on the part of our good king. On Christmas Day, our king sent into Rouen his heralds in rich array to proclaim, in honour of this high feast of great and small and because of the scarcity of victuals, that he would provide food and drink for all within the city and also for the poor folk outside, with safe conducts to come and go. They replied 'Thanks a lot' in an off-hand way as though they set little store by the offer. They would scarcely allow any mercy to the poor folk who had been expelled, except that two priests (and no more, would be permitted to take them food – 'but if more come with them, truly we shall shoot them'.

The refugees were sitting in a queue and the priests brought them provisions. They ate, they drank, they were happy and thanked our king with all their hearts. And as they were sitting eating their food thus they spoke to one another, 'Oh Holy Jesus, English men have tender hearts, for see how this excellent king, whom we have always rejected and whom we have never wished to obey and to whom we have refused to render homage, nevertheless now shows us more mercy than do our own country-men. So, Jesus, as thou art full of mercy, grant him grace to win his right in heaven'.

Thus spoke the poor folk at that time – and it was taken good note of. But, after they had eaten and gone back, the truce ended and fighting began again. The English continued with siege-works and every kind of attack, and carefully continued watching the city night and day holding in both great and small.

But hunger breaches even hard stone walls. All the leaders of that fair city now took counsel with a view to a parley – they were in the direst straits of famine, that is why they began to parley.

On the night of New Year's Eve at every gate a knight called out – but no one heard. He therefore returned without answer except on the side of the city watched by Huntingdon. When they called out at the Bridge Gate they were soon answered. A knight asked them what they wanted, and they replied 'We wish to talk to a knight of our own lineage or else some lord of the Baronage'. 'Forsooth', he said, 'I am a knight'. And they asked his name. 'My name' said he 'is Umfraville'. Then they thanked God and the good St Giles; 'For you' they said 'are of the ancient blood of Normandy.[5] Help us then to make a good end between us and this worthy king'. The knight answered them again 'What is your will?' They said 'To cut a long story short, at every gate before which your lords are posted we have called out time and again. First for Clarence – that most excellent lord – we called often before giving up. Then for Gloucester – that lord so good – often we called and long we waited. For Exeter we also tried; but no one wanted to hear us.

Also to Warwick – that generous earl – we have appealed more than three times, and the same to the earl marshal – but no one wanted to hear us. Now that we have appealed to you, for the love of God help us to excuse ourselves; beg all these lords, as they are dukes of great dignity and the leaders of all chivalry, that, in honour of God who made Heaven the earth and all the universe, they will speak for us to the king so that we may find him merciful to us. We pray you now to lead us to the king; beg him for Christ's love and Heaven's king who in six days made all things by his wisdom (for he must be praised above all princes), beg him that, in the name of his royal dignity his courage and his high chivalry, he may be willing to receive us. We will obey him rather than any other king on earth – except God Almighty – for in his own person he is emperor, royal king and conqueror. Beg him that he may show us his great favour and grant us life and liberty so that we may come into his presence – twelve of us – to tell him of our intentions. And, if by the power of God we are allowed to see him, we will inform him forthwith of matters which will give him great pleasure.'

'To this,' quoth Umfraville, 'I gladly agree'. He took his leave and went off to see Clarence, that popular duke, and they discussed the affair. Clarence thanked God and Mary that their enemies were brought so low. He said that with the greatest pleasure he would intercede for them with the king. And immediately that boon he undertook, never forgetting his customary humility. He was a prince well worthy of praise – we find few such Lords nowadays, manful while war's afoot and merciful when it's over. Such courage kindness wit and grace were contained in so small a space. He lacked not any of the gifts that a Lord ought to have – may God save his soul.[6]

Then Umfraville took his leave of them and departed to take the news further. He visited all the earls in turn and told them his story. How quickly these lords of chivalry inclined themselves to mercy – therefore Lord Jesus, for thy Holy Grace, send them Godspeed everywhere!

On the morning of New Year's Day Umfraville came to the king, told him everything and made intercession for the city. Our king, wise in his counsel and priceless in his wisdom, replied 'I grant that city something of what they ask – that twelve of them may come before us.' Of all the lords present not one had anything to say against the king's decision.

Behold that prince, principally worthy, of all earthly kings the leader, now he proves himself merciful as well as courageous. For although those in the city had so often harassed him, so often caused him so much expense and so many casualties, and although they had thwarted him from seizing that which belonged to him, now that they are in his power, and he could if he wished do them terrible injuries, he deigns to listen to their pleas. It is most charitable and merciful of our king to grant them permission to treat, seeing that they had caused so much trouble and had spilled the blood of so many of his men. To grant them such a favour is, it seems to me, an act of great mercy. I think firmly that this king is the true child of God – for he returns good for evil. So, Lord, by your holy passion, receive the soul of King Harry into Thy Kingdom.

And when the king had granted what I have told, then said Umfraville, that knight so bold, 'My liege, when shall this be?' 'Tomorrow let me see them,' replied the king. Then Umfraville immediately took leave of the king and departed to deliver his message. And when he came to the gate of Rouen he found the 'Estates' of Rouen waiting for him. He said 'I have been with my king and he has granted what you ask. Tomorrow early, make ready; for twelve of you must go before him. Do not fail to be there, and, I promise you, tomorrow you will see the worthiest prince of Christendom. But with such a lord you have never before spoken nor with anyone who is so ready to say so. Reflect in your hearts before giving rein to your tongue – for fear that your speeches may be too lengthy. Talk little and choose your words when you meet that prince, for a word out of season might bring you all to disaster. So be wise in what you say, and say nothing without good reason.'

They thanked him most courteously and said to him, 'Sir, many thanks for the good counsels you have given us before we begin treating with this king.' Umfraville then took his leave and went his way.

Early on the Sunday following New Year's Day, Umfraville went out accompanied by the squires of the king and the yeomen of the crown who were appointed as his escort. They went to the St Hilary Gate and twelve men came out – four knights, four clerics, and four leading burgesses from the guilds all clothed in black, of smart appearance and well spoken. When they arrived at the Charterhouse our king was then at Mass. They waited in the audience chamber until Mass was over. The king then came forth without delay as he had made his devotions in his private chapel. He had the bearing of a chieftain and the mien of a great lord. His manners were polished and affable – it was pleasure to look at him.

When the Frenchmen saw the king they fell on their knees before him and with humble words presented to him a petition. The king commanded Exeter to look at it. Then the duke spoke with the king for several minutes. I have heard it said that this petition contained a plea for a treaty at any cost. They besought him for God's sake, that made Heaven and earth and all things both east and west, north and south, 'That we may speak with you by word of mouth.' The king replied, 'Say what you wish.'

They were full of gratitude, and, still kneeling in front of the king, said, 'We pray and beseech you, in the name of Him who died on Good Friday and for the love of His Blessed Mother, to grant your mercy to us and to the poor folk outside who die in the fosse. Have mercy and pity on them and grant them leave to go home.' The king stood silent all this time with a cold countenance. He would not smile, and yet, while they were in his presence, he maintained his dignity and showed himself neither too soft nor too hard: not for a moment did his expression change – he remained brooding still. When at last he made reply he said, 'Who put them there in the ditches of this city? It was not me, that you know well. Let them have what they want, for they have been there too long. As for you, you know well that you have offended me with your misdeeds, you have kept me from my own city, which is my rightful heritage, when you ought to be my true liege-men.'

And then they answered and said 'As for this city that we defend, we are charged – and heavily charged – by our sovereign liege to defend it from assault and siege; for we are born his liege men and we have sworn fidelity to him. We have also received a pressing charge from the duke of Burgundy. But would you, of your great mercy, grant us life and liberty so that some of us may go to inform our king of our distress, so that they may excuse us before him in that many of us must refuse him our allegiance – we are ceding our town to you and most of us will be your liege-men.' The king replied, 'I am going to put an end to any uncertainty. My city I will not go without, and, as I have said, you know this well, you have greatly offended me in keeping me from this my own city which is my free heritage. As for your French sovereign he knows well that I am besieging you, and so does the duke of Burgundy – they both know that full well. All the time I have been here we have been exchanging messages, and if they wish to meet me they know they can find me here: they know well that I shall not depart without my rights, neither for friend nor foe. As they have known for so long that I am here, it would be pointless to send stale and yet staler news – that would merely mean delay and superfluity. Such a message I will *not* send – it is not necessary, and what we have done suffices.'

When the king had given this answer there was no more to be said. However, a knight began to speak, 'It is fine to win Rouen and all the people there . . .' The king interrupted, 'Rouen is my own ground. I will have it in spite of all those who withstand me: as for the men who are within it I shall deal with them so that they will speak of me till the Day of Judgement.'

At these words they were frightened. Then a cleric began to speak and said 'My sovereign lord, if you will listen to me, what I am going to say is written in story and it is there that I have read it – how that two chieftains had appointed a day for battle and were arrayed with their armies. The two corps were ranged in the field and were about to come to blows. Then one saw the corps which had the fewer men take bread and wine to signify to the stronger that they ought to have mercy and pity on them. Here, *you* are that chieftain, and we bring you today bread and wine, together with Rouen – which is so beautiful a city!'

The king replied, 'Rouen is my heritage; I will have it by right of lineage. I counsel you to conduct yourselves in such a way that one can grant you mercy. But, for the love of God Almighty and of the Virgin his mother, I am willing to grant you a truce. Act therefore so that you may find mercy.' 'Good Lord,' they said, 'For Holy Charity what will you do for our poor folk who suffer so grievously in the ditches where they lie like swine. Have some pity on them and give them leave to go home.'

Our king answered most shrewdly, 'I will take advice on this subject and as God counsels me so will I do in pity for them.' And with these words the king said 'Adieu'.

All the Frenchmen then retired with the lord of Umfraville, and as they were returning to the city they spoke of our king's worthy princehood. They said 'In our opinion, of all the powers of the earth he must take the prize for his courtesy, the distinction of his person, the beauty of his countenance, his deep discretion, his disposition, his great princeliness and his surpassing manhood. He is merciful in battle and asks for nothing but what is his by right – with all the virtues that shine in him what other king could compare? Now he should be held in great honour, for he is a worthy conqueror. We can well believe that God loves him – that is quite obvious.' Thus the Frenchmen spoke of our king, chatting as they went on their way to Rouen. Then they took leave of Umfraville and returned into the city.

Early on the morrow, our king ordered marquees to be pitched, one for the English and the other for the French – both were sited in Gloucester's lines – so that however bad the weather they could all negotiate dryheaded. When both tents were erected the negotiators got down to business. They were Warwick (that wise and worthy earl) who was the leader for our side, Salisbury (that earl so true) and also the Lord FitzHugh and Hungerford, steward to the king – I can't remember the other names. From the city there came to meet them twenty-four distinguished citizens.

It was a solemn sight for both sides to see – the marquees in all their panoply, the citizens crowded on the city walls, our soldiers outside parading round in great numbers, and the brilliant heralds who went from one tent to the other. The king's heralds and pursuivants displayed their appropriate blazonries – the English, a leopard; the French, a lily; the Portuguese, castles and towers; the others, the various insignia of their several lords. Their costumes glittered with gold as bright as the sun which shone on them.

But this was a bitter sight for the poor folk in the fosse who were nearly dead of sorrow and pain. They had scarcely a few rags to cover their nakedness, and a few tatters on their backs to protect them against the weather; it had rained during the whole period of their agony. There one could see a piteous spectacle – one could see wandering here and there children of two or three years of age begging for bread, for their parents were dead. These wretched people had only the sodden soil under them, and they lay there crying for food – some starving to death, some unable to open their eyes and no longer breathing, others cowering on their knees as thin as twigs. A woman was there clutching her dead child to her breast to warm it, and a child was sucking the breast of its dead mother. There one could easily count ten or twelve dead to one alive, who had died so quietly without call or cry as though they had died in their sleep.

Here were two contrasting sights – the one of joy the other of sorrow; as though Hell and Heaven had been shared between them – these were the happy ones, those the wretched. No king, however ruthless, could look on such a scene without emotion. He only had to glance about him to turn sorrowful and pensive. There, men might learn what it is to fight against the right. For while our enemies were in their strength they were truly cruel, God knows, and showed no pity until they were forced to ask for it on their own behalf. But now let us leave these folk and tell of the parleying . . .

We then challenged and accused them; they answered and made excuses. We asked much and they offered little – which was not a likely way to peace. If they had parleyed for a fortnight thus they could not have settled their differences. Negotiations were precipitately broken off and both tents were struck. But the French realized that they were only doing themselves injury, and, just as they were taking their leave, they addressed the following plea to our negotiators: 'For the love of Almighty God continue this parleying until midnight, and if we fall asleep be pleased to speak to us so that before then you can hear our pleas.' The English lords replied, 'To that we agree.' Both took their leave and departed. Our lords went to the king and quickly told him what had happened, how they had parted and what ensued and how they had taken upon themselves to agree to continue the truce. The king was in a merciful mood, and in no way disagreed with what had been decided.

The French therefore returned to the city in a body reasonably content. Soon it was noised in the city that the truce was over. Then the poor folk cried out everywhere against the rich saying, 'False traitors, assassins and ruffians, do you take no notice of us who have suffered so much and are dying day by day. We could well say that you recoup yourselves at our expense, and that it is your fault that we are doomed. We pray God that one day you will be forced to answer before that Judge who suffered so cruelly on Calvary's Cross and bought us with His blessed blood. It is you who are guilty in this matter – we charge you so before His face. If you were to obey the king then he would raise the siege. But you refuse because of the love of your own goods that you are hiding. Because of your pomp and pride you will never bow to this king – you prefer to let us perish of hunger. Unless you do as we wish we shall kill you instantly, and the king shall get his rights. If you oppose this we shall fight rather than lie here all to be destroyed by famine.'

Thus they spoke, and they seemed to be serious about it; but amongst themselves they said, 'All that we do is to get into the good graces of this king, and therefore we shall pay as little as possible!'

All the citizens then assembled in the city, and each man agreed in his turn that there was no need for further talk. 'There are only two choices left; either to deliver up the keys of this city or to die here. There is no other choice.'

They went off then to the St Hilary Gate and called out with one accord. Immediately a knight called Sir John Robsart answered them: 'Sirs,' he said, 'What do you want?' They answered and said to him, 'We beseech you, for charity and the honour of chivalry, that you will speak for us to the duke of Gloucester and beg him to ask the king on our behalf that negotiations may be reopened. We will submit ourselves to his will; our persons, our possessions – all shall be at his disposal and discretion.'

When Robsart had informed the duke, the duke agreed immediately to speak for them to the king – who forthwith granted a new parley.

The archbishop of Canterbury was at this time lodged at St Catherine's. When he heard of this business he was very much concerned. He hastened to the king, and with the best of intentions begged him to allow him to go into the city and confer with its clergy in order to join the parleying and help to conclude a final peace. The king immediately granted him his wish. The two marquees were again pitched within the fosse where they had been before. The archbishop had his own pitched between the other two, so that the Church might bring them to agreement.

They parleyed by day, they parleyed by night by the light of candles and bright torches; they parleyed four days there. At last by the Grace of God they came to a conclusion. The French, when they saw that agreement was near, made a petition to save their honour. They asked for eight days in which they might send word to the French king and to the duke of Burgundy as to how they stood and ask them for rescue. This was a point of chivalry, and the king granted it willingly so that they might know how and when help might arrive.

Now, if you will listen to my story, I will tell you what they agreed:

In eight days, as I told you, if no rescue came they must surrender the city, and all its burgesses would become English and would pay to our king in good coin 50,000 pounds. Furthermore, they would agree to build a castle for our king within half a year without fail – and it must be built on the banks of the Seine. On these conditions the inhabitants could keep their liberties and franchises as they had existed in time past. No person would have the right to sell in the city except domiciled citizens. As for anyone born a Norman who had previously sworn fidelity to the English king he would be the king's prisoner to be held for ransom. All soldiers in the city must abandon everything they possessed and depart naked, apart from their doublets, out of the city. However, our king gave each of them a cloak. Such was the agreement reached by fair bargaining.

Then the great Jacques was sent immediately to ask for rescue. He carried out his mission to the letter but did not himself return to Rouen – he sent a messenger thither, bade them finish and make an end, and would have them know (I tell you truly) that he knew of no possibility of rescue for them.

The eighth day, to tell you the truth, was the feast of St Wulfstan – it was a Thursday. On that day our king, seated like a conqueror, took his place in his ceremonial royal robes inside the Charterhouse to receive the keys of the city. Sir Guy le Bouteiller and a company of the burgesses brought the keys to the king, and begged him to receive their allegiance. Our sovereign king ordered Exeter to accept the keys, and to become the captain of the city. He charged him to take possession of that rich city and enter it in his name that same night, taking with him many knights as escort.

Then the duke of Exeter without delay mounted his horse and rode to the Beauvoisine Gate – that strong gate in front of which he had fought for so long. He soon reached the gate and with him many valiant men-at-arms – there was the neighing of many steeds, there was the brilliance of many gay costumes, there was many a colourful banner in that brave display. And when the gate was opened and they were all set to enter, trumpeters sounded their brass trumpets, and there were many pipes and clarions I assure you. And as they went through they shouted loudly, 'St George, St George! Hail to our king's own right.'

The French people of the city were gathered in their thousands to see them pass by, and they all shouted, 'Welcome; enter safely now, and please God we shall have peace and unity.' It was a pitiful sight to see the people. Many of them were mere skin and bones with hollow eyes and pinched noses. They could scarcely breathe or talk. Their skin was dull as lead, like the dead rather than the living; they looked like those effigies of dead kings that one sees on tombs. There one could realize how lack of food destroys a people. In every street were corpses, and hundreds of citizens crying out for bread. For many days afterwards they died – quicker than the carts could carry them to burial. May God guide them to his Holy House that they may live in bliss; Amen.

Now I will tell you further of the duke of Exeter. First he rode to the castle. Then he made a tour of inspection right through the city and set up gay banners at every gate. On the St Hilary Gate a banner of the Trinity, on the Beauvais Gate a banner of the image of the Queen of Heaven, on the Martinville Gate a brilliant banner of St George, on the castle he unfurled the banners of France and of England.

On the Friday morning our king made his entry into the city with four bishops in their vestments and seven abbots carrying their jewelled crosses. There were forty-two crosses carried by both the regular and the secular clergy of the city; and all went out to welcome the prince outside the walls. The king kissed each cross in turn with due reverence while the English arch-bishop sprinkled holy water. At the great Cauchoise Gate the king passed in – without pomp, without pipe or trumpet blast. Our king advanced with dignity as a conqueror into his own kingdom ever thanking God Almighty. And all the people of that city cried out 'Welcome, our most generous lord, welcome into your own right; it is the will of God Almighty!' And with that they all shouted 'Hail' as loudly as they could.

The king rode upon a brown horse with housings of black damask, a breast-cloth of bright gold hung down from his collar and his train was so long it hung down behind him and reached to the ground. Those who had never seen him before instantly recognized him in his glory. He went straight to the cathedral and dismounted. At the door he was met by his chaplains, who preceded him in procession singing the glorious response 'Quis est magnus Dominus'. He heard Mass, made his offering and then went straight to the castle, which is a regal building and a palace of great beauty. There he was lodged in that city in great estate. The city itself was soon amply supplied with bread with wine with fish and with meat: and so our gracious liege made an end of his siege.

John Page wrote this story without fable or falsehood in rough and not in polished rhyme (because he had no time to do this). However, when this war is ended, and if he is alive and has the inclination, he will put this right. May He that died for us upon a tree bring His blessing to those who have heard this reading; for charity's sake let us all say,

'Amen'.

NOTES

I have not thought it necessary to include a bibliography – there are excellent ones readily available in Professor E. F. Jacob's *The Fifteenth Century,* Oxford 1961, and in the *Cambridge Mediaeval History,* volume VIII – and the notes include a mention of the majority of books that would have been included.

Throughout the notes certain references are abbreviated as follows:

Annales   *Annales Ric II et Hen IV* in *Chronica Johannis de Trokelowe*, ed. H. T. Riley (Rolls Series), London 1866.

Archaeologia Miscellaneous Tracts, pub. by the Society of Antiquaries of London, London 1770, etc.

Bourgeois   *Journal d'un Bourgeois de Paris,* ed. A. Tuetey, Paris 1881.

Brut   *The Brut* or *The Chronicles of England,* ed. F. W. D. Brie, part II, Early English Text Society, London and Oxford 1908.

Cal. Pat.   *Calendar of the Patent Rolls,* London 1903–11.

Capgrave   J. Capgrave, *Liber de Illustribus Henricis,* ed. and trans. F. C. Hengeston (Rolls Series), London 1858.

Chastelain   G. Chastelain (1405–75), *Chroniques,* ed. Kervyn de Lettenhove, Brussels 1863, etc.

Chron. Lond.   *A Chronicle of London 1189–1483,* ed. N. H. Nicolas, London 1827.

Chron. R   *A Chronicle of the reigns of Richard II, Henry IV, V and VI (1377–*
II – H VI   *1461),* ed. J. S. Davies, Camden Society, London 1856.

C.M.H.   *The Cambridge Medieval History,* Vols. VII and VIII, Cambridge 1932, etc.

Creton   *French Metrical History of the Deposition of Richard II,* ed. and trans. J. Webb, in *Archaeologia,* XX, 1–423, London 1819.

Delpit   J. Delpit, *Collection générale des documents français qui se trouvent en Angleterre,* Paris 1847.

D.N.B.   *Dictionary of National Biography,* London 1903, etc.

E.H.R.   *English Historical Review,* London 1886, etc.

Ellis   H. Ellis, *Original Letters illustrative of English History,* 3 series, London 1824–46.

'Elmham'   *Vita et Gesta Henrici Quinti,* ed. T. Hearne, London 1727. Wrongly attributed to T. Elmham. Probably written 1445.

Evesham   *Vita R. Ricardi II* by a monk of Evesham, ed. T. Hearne, Oxford 1729.

First Life   C. L. Kingsford, *The First English Life of Henry V,* Oxford 1911. Written 1513 by an unknown and based on Livius and partly the work of the 4th Earl of Ormonde (1392–1452). The introduction by Kingsford is invaluable.

Gesta   *Gesta Henrici Quinti,* ed. B. Williams for the English Historical Society, London 1830 – it also includes a *Chronique de Normandie* by Sir George Chastelain, Herald of the Order of the Golden Fleece of Burgundy. The *Gesta*'s author was an unknown chaplain to Henry V, and his chronicle appears in translation in Nicolas's *Agincourt* (LXXXVII–CCXLVII).

Giles	*Incerti Scriptoris Chronicon Angliae,* ed. J. A. Giles, London 1848.
Hardyng	John Hardyng (1378– c. 1470), *Chronicle* ed. H. Ellis, London 1812. A rhyming chronicle – Hardyng fought at Agincourt.
Hist. Angl.	T. Walsingham, *Historia Anglicana,* ed. H. T. Riley (Rolls Series) London 1863–4.
Livius	T. Livius de Frulovisiis, *Vita Henrici Quinti,* ed. T. Hearne, London 1716. Livius was an Italian in the household of Humphrey duke of Gloucester, and wrote some time after 1437.
Memorials	*Memorials of Henry V,* ed. C. A. Cole (Rolls Series), London 1858; comprising (1) *Vita* by R. Redmayne (16th century) (2) *Versus Rhythmici* by a Benedictine monk of Westminster (3) *Liber Metricus* by Thomas Elmham.
Monstrelet	Enguerrand de Monstrelet, *Chroniques.* References give chapter numbers for all editions and page numbers for the English translation by T. Johnes, London 1853.
Ord. Priv. Co.	*Proceedings and Ordinances of the Privy Council,* ed. N. H. Nicolas, London 1834–7.
Otterbourne	T. Otterbourne, *Chronica Regum Anglicae,* ed. T. Hearne, Oxford 1732.
Pell	*Issues of the Exchequer* (Pell Rolls) Henry III–VI, ed. F. Devon, London 1837.
Rot. Norm.	*Rotuli Normanniae,* ed. T. D. Hardy, London 1835.
Rot. Parl.	*Rotuli Parliamentorum,* London 1767, etc.
Rymer	Thomas Rymer, *Foedera, Conventiones et Litterae,* London 1709, etc.
St Albans	*The St Albans Chronicle 1406–1420,* ed. V. H. Galbraith, Oxford 1937. The great contemporary work of Thomas Walsingham of St Albans.
St Denis	*Chronique du Réligieux de Saint-Denys,* Latin with French translation by M. L. Bellaguet, Paris 1841.
St Rémy	*Chronique (1408–35) de Jean le Févre, seigneur de Saint-Rémy,* ed. F. Morand, Paris 1876. He was present at Agincourt with the English.
Stat.	*Statutes of the Realm,* London 1810–22.
Strecche	*The Chronicle of John Strecche for the reign of Henry V (1414–1422),* ed. F Taylor, Manchester 1932. He was a canon of Kenilworth and his work was contemporary.
T.R.H.S.	*Transactions of the Royal Historical Society.*
Ursins	Jean Juvénal des Ursins, *Histoire de Charles VI,* ed. Michand et Poujoulet in *Mémoires relatif à l'histoire de France,* Paris 1850.
Usk	Adam of Usk, *Chronicon 1377–1421,* ed. and trans. by E. M. Thompson (2nd edition), London 1904.
Waurin	Jehan de Waurin, *Receuil des croniques et anchiennes istories de la Grant Bretaigne à present nomme Engleterre,* ed. W. Hardy and E. L. C. P. Hardy (Rolls Series), London 1864, etc. Waurin was a Fleming present with the French army at Agincourt.

NOTES

pp. 15–23 (1) See C. L. Kingsford, *Henry V*, 2nd edition, London 1923, 13 note 1 and *E.H.R.*, XXV, 62.

(2) Exhibit D 48, see E. E. Barnett, *Cradles of the Past*, *The Connoisseur* XXXII (1912) no. 129, 93. Later Johanna was granted an annuity of £20 by Henry – *Ord. Priv. Co.* III, 190, June 5th, 1415; *Cal. Pat.*, 264; C. L. Kingsford op. cit., 13–14.

(3) See below p. 74 and note 7 (chapter VI) p. 259.

(4) *Hardyng*, 1, note 2.

(5) *Memorials*, 64–5.

(6) Henry 'delighted in songe and musical Instruments', *First Life*, 17; and see J. E. Tyler, *Henry of Monmouth*, London 1838, I, 15–16. His chapel music was celebrated – *Memorials*, 68; but cf. F. Le. Harrison, *Music in Medieval Britain*, London 1958, 22 and 220–3.

(7) J. R. Magrath, *The Queen's College*, Oxford 1921, I, 83, and see the wishful thinking of Tyler, op. cit. I, 21–27.

(8) J. H. Wylie and W. T. Waugh, *The Reign of Henry V*, Cambridge 1929, III, 427.

(9) *Pell*, 269.

(10) *Creton*, 30 and 299. Also cf. *Memorials*, 65 and *First Life*, 8 – Henry was 'nourished in the Kings Courte right honourably in all things'; he 'obtained the favour and love of the Kynge'.

(11) *Otterbourne*, 205.

(12) *Pell*, 281.

(13) *Usk*, 29 and 180 suggests that Humphrey may have been poisoned by Lord Despenser. He also adds the information that the prince brought with him Sir William Bagot in chains. Bagot had been one of Richard II's closest officials, and it is remarkable that, having escaped the fate of his fellows, he survived to die peacefully in retirement a few years later. cf. *Archaeologia*, XX, 278.

(14) This was Henry IV's first installation of his new Order of the Bath.

(15) *Rymer*, VIII, 148; *Usk*, 36–7 and 190–1.

(16) For the mighty power of Lancaster see S. Armitage-Smith, *John of Gaunt*, London 1904, cap X *passim*.

(17) *Annales*, 323 ff.; *Traison et Mort de Richart II*, ed. B. Williams (English Historical Society), London 1846, 77 and 229 ff; *Creton*, 402–4. Just prior to the discovery of the conspiracy the whole royal family were suffering from suspected poisoning – but it may of course have been merely food poisoning.

(18) *Monstrelet*, I, 239–40 (cap CI).

(19) For a detailed description of a medieval coronation cf. *Hist. Angl.*, I, 332 ff. and *The Anonimalle Chronicle*, ed. V. H. Galbraith, Manchester 1927, 107 ff.

HENRY V

CHAPTER 2

pp. 24–33 (1) For the general reader there is no better guide to Medieval Europe than H. A. L. Fisher's wholly readable *A History of Europe*, London 1936, I caps, XVII to XXXV. Students may prefer W. T. Waugh, *A History of Europe from 1378–1494* (3rd edition), London 1949. For greater detail but suffering from a multiplicity of authors, see *C.M.H.*, VII and VIII – comprehensive bibliographies and maps are included.

(2) 'Steel yard' is probably a mistranslation of 'stal hof' or sample hall. cf. J. Stowe, *A Survey of London*, ed. C. L. Kingsford, Oxford 1908, I 232–5 and II 318–21; and E. Power and M. M. Postan, *Studies in English Trade in the Fifteenth Century*, London 1933, 91–114.

(3) 'Certes Jacke Strawe, and his meinie, Ne made never shoutes half so shrille Whan that they wolden any Fleming kille, As thilke day was made upon the fox!' Chaucer, *Nun's Priest's Tale*, 4580.

(4) See below p. 221. It is significant of this transition period that Gower wrote in French, in Latin and in English. Chaucer wrote for his royal and baronial patrons in English, and we are told that Richard II (who had been complimented on his French by Froissart) chatted with his Cheshire archers 'in materna lingua': see M. V. Clarke, *Fourteenth Century Studies*, Oxford 1937, 98; *Traison*, op. cit. 293 note 1; V. H. Galbraith, *The Literacy of the Medieval English Kings*, British Academy XXI, London 1935.

(5) E. F. Henderson, *Select Historical Documents of the Middle Ages*, London 1912, 435–7. For the persistence of Lollardy see K. B. McFarlane, *John Wycliffe and the Beginnings of English Nonconformity*, Oxford 1952, and J. A. F. Thomson, *The Later Lollards, 1440–1520*, Oxford 1965.

(6) For the arts in medieval England see Lawrence Stone's *Sculpture in Britain; The Middle Ages*, Geoffrey Webb's *Architecture in Britain; The Middle Ages* and Margaret Rickert's *Painting in Britain; The Middle Ages*, all in The Pelican History of Art series, London 1955. See also Joan Evans, *History of English Art 1307–1461*, Oxford 1949, and note 10 Chapter VI below.

(7) C. W. C. Oman, *A History of the Art of War in the Middle Ages*, New York 1924, II, *passim*.

(8) E. Curtis, *A History of Mediaeval Ireland*, London 1938.

(9) For the social background general readers are recommended to G. M. Trevelyan, *English Social History*, London 1944; G. G. Coulton, *Mediaeval Panorama*, Cambridge 1943; and E. Rickert, *Chaucer's World*, Oxford 1948.

(10) J. H. Clapham, *Concise Economic History of Britain*, Oxford

254

pp. 33–7 1949; M. McKisack, *The Fourteenth Century*, Oxford 1959, cap. XI.

(11) The pungent phrase comes from a fourteenth-century abbot of Burton.

(12) E. Lipson, *Economic History of England*, London 1937, I, 471–86; Eileen Power, *Mediaeval English Wool Trade*, Oxford 1941, 66–123.

(13) cf. *Fasciculi Zizaniorum*, ed. W. W. Shirley (Rolls Series), London 1858, *passim*. The origin of the name 'Lollard' is obscure, but there is no doubt as to the origin of the sect – they were the followers of John Wyclif, who, in the time of Edward III and Richard II, had given theoretical and theological principles to a reform movement whose roots were as honest as William Langland and as mundane as John of Gaunt. Wyclif's theory of 'dominium' translated into everyday speech involved the right of every man to call his soul his own without need of go-betweens, and his theory of 'consubstantiation' was a subtle criticism of established Catholic doctrine. Lollards, in their own crude language, objected to 'eating a God' every time they partook of the wafer of the Mass. See H. Knighton, *Chronicon*, ed. J. R. Lumby (Rolls Series), London 1895, II, 151–98; K. B. McFarlane, *John Wycliffe and the Beginnings of English Nonconformity*, Oxford 1952, *passim*.

(14) S. Armitage-Smith, *John of Gaunt*, London 1904, 149–52 and 160–83.

(15) H. F. Hutchison, *The Hollow Crown – A Life of Richard II*, London 1961, 198–210.

(16) Nevertheless the author of the theory must be read – W. Stubbs, *The Constitutional History of England*, Oxford 1880, III, cap. XVIII.

(17) The 'magnates' of the Middle Ages were the chronicler's technical Latin for the greater barons, whereas the modern word usually describes, in a rather pejorative sense, the industrial wealthy.

(18) See note 7 chapter VII below.

(19) Typical examples are William of Wykeham, Michael de la Pole and Edmund de Stafford. Stafford's able service to Richard II was even recognized by that king's usurper – he was re-employed by Henry IV.

CHAPTER 3

pp. 38–9 (1) *Creton*, 204 and 394–5.

(2) *Ord. Priv. Co.*, II, 42.

(3) Or 'The Statute of Wales', 12 Ed. I. I owe much to J. E. Lloyd, *Owen Glendower*, Oxford 1931, for my references to Welsh affairs. See also his cap. XVII in *C.M.H.*, VII; and see

pp. 39–50 Glanmor Williams's *Owen Glendower*, Oxford 1966, for an attractive summary of the latest research.

(4) *Annales*, Hen. IV, 333; *Hist. Angl.* II 246.

(5) N. H. Nicolas, *The Scrope and Grosvenor Roll*, London 1832, I, 254.

(6) *Evesham*, 171.

(7) *Ord. Priv. Co.*, I, 146 note 1.

(8) *Ellis*, 2nd series I, 4–6.

(9) *Rot. Parl.*, III, 457.

(10) See above p. 217.

(11) *Usk*, 70–1 and 237–9.

(12) *Hist. Angl.*, II, 250.

(13) *Usk*, 70 and 237.

(14) *Giles*, 31–2;

(15) *Usk*, 71 and 238, but cf. Glanmor Williams *op. cit.* 52: it may have been the red dragon of Cadwaladr or the four lions rampant of Gwynedd.

(16) *Ellis*, 2nd series I, 14; M. D. Legge, *Anglo-Norman Letters and Petitions*, Oxford 1941, 321–3.

(17) *Legge*, op. cit., 290.

(18) *Rymer*, VIII, 291–2.

(19) *Usk*, 72 and 239.

(20) *Annales*, Hen. IV, 338–9; *Evesham*, 177; *Usk*, 78 and 247; *Rot. Parl.* III, 487; *Ellis*, op. cit. 9 note.

(21) *Evesham*, 182; *Hist. Angl.*, II, 250 and 253–4.

(22) *Ellis*, op. cit 24–6.

(23) *Hist. Angl.* II, 250–1.

(24) *Ellis*, op. cit. 33–4. 'Sowes' were protective shelters for miners and trench diggers, with wood above and hide at the sides.

(25) *Ellis*, op. cit. 10–13; J. O. Halliwell, *Letters of the Kings of England*, London 1848, I, 70–72; and cf. *Usk*, 61 and 226.

(26) *Legge*, op. cit. 359–60.

(27) See J. W. M. Bean, *Henry IV and the Percies*, in *History*, XLIV, (1959), 212–27 and R. L. Storey, *The Wardens of the Marches of England towards Scotland 1377–1489*, in *E.H.R.*, LXXII (1957), 602–4.

(28) *Hist. Angl.*, II, 257; *J.H.* Ramsay, Lancaster and York, I, 64.

(29) *Annales*, 367–8; *Livius*, 3–4; 'Elmham', 7–8.

(30) The phrase 'Wars of the Roses' is unknown to contemporary chronicles – it was probably invented by Sir Walter Scott.

(31) 'Destitutus' is the Latin word, *Hist. Angl.*, II, 259.

(32) *Rot. Parl.*, III, 525.

(33) *Usk*, 86 and 257; and *Rymer*, VIII, 356.

(34) *St Denis*, III, 164–8.

(35) The duke was tried on March 1st, 1405, and later returned to favour – *Rymer*, VIII, 386–8; cf. *Annales*, 398–9, *Capgrave*, 288–9 and Wylie, *Henry IV*, II, 35–53.

(36) *Ellis*, op. cit. 27–8; *Giles*, 39–42; *Lloyd*, op. cit. 93–95.

(37) For this episode see Wylie, *Henry IV*, II, 192–244. The earl

pp. 50–3 marshal was the son of that duke of Norfolk who had been Henry Bolingbroke's opponent in the Lists of Coventry.

(38) *Giles*, 52–53; *Hist. Angl.*, II, 273; E. W. M. Balfour-Melville, *James I, King of Scots*, London 1936, 35. Henry received James 'libenter' and treated him well according to his rank. The pirates were from the Norfolk ports of Great Yarmouth and Cley.

(39) *Ellis*, op. cit. 43, note b.

(40) *St Denis*, III, 322–8; *Monstrelet*, I, 28–29 (cap. XV); *Waurin*, II, 92; *Annales*, 415.

(41) *Rot. Parl.*, III, 569; *Cal. Pat.*, III, 164–5; *Rymer*, VIII 436.

(42) *Annales*, 399.

(43) *Rot. Parl.*, III, 611.

(44) '*Elmham*', 9–10.

(45) *Usk*, 129 and 313 and note; '*Elmham*', 10.

CHAPTER 4

pp. 54–61 (1) Wylie, *Henry IV*, II, 245–52 and IV, 151–5; *Giles*, 47–48; J. Capgrave, *The Chronicles of England*, ed. F. C. Hingeston (Rolls Series), London 1858, 291, who reports that Henry IV's condition became 'evyr fowlere and fowlere' after his execution of Archbishop Scrope; *C.M.H.*, VIII, 375 and note; *Monstrelet*, I, 239 (cap. C I).

(2) *First Life*, intro, xxvii–xxix and 12–16.

(3) See Genealogies, pp. 14 and endpapers

(4) *Rymer*, VIII, 93, 99, 571 and 585.

(5) The quotation is from John Stowe, *Survey of London*, ed. C. L. Kingsford, Oxford 1908, I, 236. cf. *Tyler* op. cit. I 258; Wylie, *Henry IV*, III, 304 note; *Rymer*, VIII, 628.

(6) *Monstrelet*, I, 196–200 (cap LXXXI); *Chron. Lond.*, 93; *Giles*, 61; *Hardyng*, 369; *Hist. Angl.* II, 286; *Brut*, II, 371 where it is mentioned that Sir John Oldcastle was with the expedition.

(7) *Hardyng*, 369; *Rymer*, VIII, 753.

(8) *Rymer*, VIII, 745; *St Denis*, IV, 704 and 720; *Waurin*, II, 153 and 160; *Giles*, 61–2; *Monstrelet*, I, 225 and 227 (caps XCV and XCVI). The French chroniclers are especially severe on the English savageries.

(9) *Rot. Parl.*, IV, 298.

(10) *Giles*, 62–3 – 'Princeps desideravit a patre suo regni et coronae resignationem'.

(11) *Monstrelet*, I, 43 (cap XXVI).

(12) *Rot. Parl.*, III, 647; *Giles*, 62.

(13) *St Alban*, 65–7; *Chron. Lond.* 94; *First Life*, intro. xxvii–xxix and 11–16.

(14) The prince, who arrived 'with great company of Lords' had 'disguised himself in a gown of blue satin or damask made full

pp. 61–5 of iletts or holes and at every ilett the needle wherewith it was made hanging by the thread of silk and about his arm he wore a dog's collar set full of S.S. and the teretts of the same also of fine gold'. *First Life,* intro. xx–xxiv and 11–12. For 'S.S.' see note 20 chapter XII below. See also *Otterbourne,* 271.

(15) *Stat.,* II, 125. For trans. see G. B. Adams and H. Morse Stephens, *Select Documents of English Constitutional History,* New York 1935, 168–71.

(16) For details of Arundel's intervention in Oxford's affairs see H. Maxwell Lyte, *History of the University of Oxford to 1530,* London 1886, 295; and *Snappe's Formulary,* ed. H. E. Salter, Oxford 1924, 101–15 and 181–6; cf Hastings Randall's *Mediaeval Universities,* ed. F. M. Powicke and A. B. Emden, Oxford 1942, III, 132–6, 270–1.

(17) The scene is graphically described in Gregory's chronicle in *Historical Collections of a Citizen of London,* ed. J. Gairdner (Camden Soc.) London 1876, 105–6; *Hist. Angl.,* II, 282; *Capgrave,* 122 note. 'The tailor showed higher heroism than that which won Agincourt,' C. W. C. Oman, *History of England 1377–1485,* 223. But 'a prince had come to a tailor to save if it were possible his life in this world, and, as the prince thought, his life in the world to come': H. Maynard Smith, *Pre-Reformation England,* London 1938, 280.

(18) *Brut,* II, 372; *Capgrave,* 123.

CHAPTER 5

pp. 66–7 (1) *Monstrelet,* I, 240 (cap CI) followed by E. Hall, *Chronicle,* ed. H. Ellis, London 1809, 45, and Grafton *Chronicle* (1569) London 1809, I, 506. cf. *Waurin,* II, 166–7 and *St Denis,* IV, 770–3 who expresses doubts as to the unanimity of the English lords. The legend can have had a very innocent origin if the Monstrelet version is accepted. The attendants, having decided that the king was dead, covered his face, and quite correctly the prince, as the dead man's successor, took care of the crown which by custom was at the bedside. It was a visible symbol of legitimate inheritance. But the king was not quite dead – he rallied to discover the crown missing.

(2) *Paston Letters,* ed. J. Gairdner, London 1900–1, III, 89. This was Sir John Fastolf of Caister (see *D.N.B.*). There was also a Sir John Fastolf of Nacton near Ipswich; but neither can be confused with Shakespeare's fiction.

(3) *Brut,* II, 494 and 594–5; *Hist. Angl.,* II, 290; *First Life,* 17–19; R. Fabyan (d. 1513), *New Chronicles of England and France,* London 1811, 577. The confusion is made worse by the two surviving references to Oldcastle in Shakespeare – Henry IV,

pp. 67–70   Part I, act I scene 2, 'my old lad of the castle', and Henry IV Part II, act V epilogue, 'for Oldcastle died a martyr and this is not the man'.

(4) *Memorials*, 11.

(5) *First Life*, xxxviii–xli; Stowe, op. cit. I, 217. See F. Solly-Flood, *The Story of Prince Henry and Chief Justice Gascoyne*, London 1886, *passim*, and L. W. Vernon Harcourt in *T.R.H.S.*, 3rd series, IV, 47–62.

(6) '*Elmham*', 13.

(7) *First Life*, 17; *Livius*, 4–5.

(8) *Hist. Angl.*, II, 290; *St Albans*, 69.

(9) *Brut*, II, 594–6 to be read in conjunction with *First Life*, 17–19. The reference to Katherine Swynford is an error, see *First Life*, xxxi, note 2. *Hardyng*, 371–2.

(10) 'Justice, continence, humility and from the time of the death of his father his virtue was never doubted' – *First Life*, 5.

CHAPTER 6

pp. 71–7   (1) '*Elmham*', 16; the probable door of this cell, in what is now Poet's Corner, has recently been revealed thanks to the researches of Mr Lawrence E. Tanner, Librarian of the Abbey: see Lawrence E. Tanner, *The History and Treasures of Westminster Abbey*, London 1953, 92–93.

(2) *Memorials*, xxxv – vi, 65–66 and 71; '*Elmham*', 12–16; *First Life*, 16–17; *Gesta* 'aetate juvenis sed maturitate senex'.

(3) *St Albans*, 69; *Hist. Angl.* II 290; *Livius*, 24.

(4) *St Denis*, IV, 770–3.

(5) *Cal. Pat.*, Hen. V, I, 35.

(6) C. L. Kingsford, *Henry V*, op. cit. 100.

(7) Professor J. Simmons of the University of Leicester points out that this surviving effigy may have been of Henry's nurse. See J. Nichols, *History and Antiquities of the County of Leicester*, London 1795, I, plate xxix and 339; J. H. Wylie, *Henry V*, I, 232–3; *Pell*, 20th May 1413.

(8) *St Denis*, IV. 770; *Hist. Angl.*, II, 327 where Walsingham reports that Oldcastle as late as 1417 alleged that Richard was still alive in Scotland.

(9) *Memorials*, 65, 72 and above pp. 19–20.

(10) The nuns of Syon left England in the reign of Elizabeth and emigrated to Flanders, France and later to Portugal taking their precious cope with them. It came back to England in 1830. cf. A. G. I. Christie, *Mediaeval English Embroidery*, Oxford 1938, 142–6.

(11) *Memorials*, 70–3; *Capgrave*, op. cit. 307–8; Wylie, *Henry V*, op. cit. I cap XV *passim*; Ramsay, op. cit. I, 307–8. For his father's conscience see *Capgrave*, II, 124 note 2. An excellent

pp. 77–83 summary is in M. D. Knowles, *The Religious Orders in England*, Cambridge 1955, II, 175–82.

(12) *Hist. Angl*, II, 344.

(13) *Rot. Parl.*, IV, 13.

(14) See note 13, cap II, above and especially K. B. McFarlane op. cit. 160–82.

(15) W. T. Waugh, *Sir John Oldcastle* in *E.H.R.* xx (1905) 434–56, 637–58; and cf. *D.N.B.*

(16) *Hist. Angl.*, II, 291; *Capgrave*, II, 125–7 and note 3.

(17) Wylie, *Henry V*, op. cit. I, 245–6.

(18) *Rymer*, IX, 61–6; *St Albans*, 70–6; *Capgrave*, ibid.

(19) 'Daemonis artis ope' suggests Elmham in *Memorials*, 97.

(20) *Hist. Angl.*, II, 299.

(21) *Rymer*, IX, 170–1; *Rot. Parl.*, IV, 15.

(22) It is significant that only seven of the condemned were burnt – the rest were hung. The Lollards in this instance were mostly treated as rebels not as heretics. See *Usk*, 121 and 301 and note 2.

(23) Wylie, *Henry V*, op. cit. I, 280–1.

CHAPTER 7

pp. 84–7 (1) *Rot. Parl.*, IV, 15, 24.

(2) *Writings and Examinations of Brute, Thorpe, Cobham, etc. with The Lantern of Light*, Religious Tract Society, London 1831. Its simplicities were of course loaded with potential upheaval, e.g. 'we understand that the soul of the righteous man is the seat of God'; it is wrong 'to deceive men's eyes with curious buildings and many vain staring sights in their churches'; the best pilgrimage is when we 'visit the needy', etc. etc.
Rot. Parl., IV, 22. 'No thyng he enacted to the Peticions of his Comune that be contrarie of his askyng wharby they should be bounde withoute their assent. Savyng alwey to our liege lord his real Progatyf...' cf. Adams and Stephens, op. cit. 181–2.

(3) See Howard L. Gray, *The Influence of the Commons on Early Legislation*, Harvard 1932, 261–87, and S. B. Chrimes, *English Constitutional Ideas in the Fifteenth Century*, Cambridge 1931, 159–64: for a modern assessment which corrects the over-enthusiasm of Bishop Stubbs.

(4) cf. J. Froissart, *Chroniques* (Globe edition), cap ccccxxviii, 295, and G. M. Trevelyan *History of England*, London 1942, 223.

(5) Adams and Stephens, op. cit. 180–1.

(6) But cf *Brut*, II, 495.

(7) Lords could overawe local justice by the presence of armed retainers wearing the livery of their lords. The final cure for baronial Livery and Maintenance was when the livery and

NOTES

pp. 87–93 maintenance of the crown – the king's uniform and the king's justice – obtained a monopoly of that force which is one sanction of justice. See R. Higden, *Polychronicon*, ed. J. R. Lumby (Rolls Series), London 1886, IX, 189–92.

(8) *Ord. Priv. Co.*, III, xxv.

(9) See endpapers. For England's claim to the throne of France there is no better summary than in E. Perroy, *The Hundred Years War*, London 1959, 69–167.

(10) *First Life*, xliii–xliv; *Capgrave*, 129–30; *Brut*, II, 374–6 where, in describing the siege of Harfleur, the chronicler refers back to his previous story 'and there he played at tenys with his hard gune-stones'; *Strecche*, 11, 12 and 16; *Memorials*, 101; *Chron. Lond.*, 216–17; *Otterbourne* 275; *Duo Rerum Anglicarum Scriptores*, ed. T. Hearne, London 1732, 274. Shakespeare, *Henry V*, Act I scene 2.

(11) *Ord. Priv. Co.*, II, 140–2; *Rot. Parl.*, IV, 34; *Hist. Angl.*, II, 302.

(12) Henry's career in the lists of marriage was long and varied: it was first proposed that he should marry Isabella the child widow of Richard II (1400); in 1402 he agreed to marry Katherine, the sister of the young King Eric of Denmark; in 1406 there were negotiations for a marriage with 'one of the daughters' of the king of France; in 1411 it was proposed that he should marry Anne, the daughter of the duke of Burgundy.

(13) *Rymer*, IX, 208–15.

CHAPTER 8

pp. 94–7 (1) *Rymer*, IX, 215–16.

(2) See two comments on the problems of feudal military service by C. Warren Hollister and J. C. Holt in *Economic History Review*, 2nd series, XVI, 104–20. The period of service was limited to 40 days and exceptionally to 60 days.

(3) *Oman;* op. cit. I, 119–23; *C.M.H.* VIII, cap XXI; N. H. Nicolas, *History of the Battle of Agincourt*, London 1827, 45–48; G. G. Coulton, *Mediaeval Panorama*, Cambridge 1943, 506–18; H. W. C. Davis, *Mediaeval England*, Oxford 1924, 125–40. I am deeply indebted for all my references to military affairs to Professor R. A. Newhall's *The English Conquest of Normandy, 1416–1424*, Yale 1924, especially caps. V and VI.

(4) cf. J. Fortescue, *The Governance of England*, ed. C. Plummer, Oxford 1885, 137 and 282–3.

(5) W. Stubbs, *Select Charters*, Oxford 1913, 363–5.

(6) *Stat.* 12 Ric. II c6 and 11 Hen. IV c4; *Rot. Parl*, III, 643.

(7) Wylie, *Henry V*, op. cit. II, 150–3 and notes. *Plummer* ibid.

(8) *Oman* op. cit. II, 205–29; J. R. Partington *A History of Greek Fire and Gunpowder*, Cambridge 1960.

261

HENRY V

pp. 99-103 (9) *Rymer*, IX, 232.

(10) Wylie, *Henry V*, op. cit. I, 448. The names of Henry's ships were *The Thomas, The Trinité Royale, The Marie, The Philip, The Katherine, The Gabriel* and the *Red Cog*, all 'de la toure'. cf. C. F. Richmond, *The Keeping of the Seas during The Hundred Years War, History* XLIX (1964), 283–98; Ellis *Original Letters* (series I) 18; *Rymer*, IX, 223–39; *The Black Book of the Admiralty*, ed. T. Twiss, (Rolls Series), London 1871, I, 12–13.

(11) Nicolas, op. cit. 373–89; J. H. Wylie, *Notes on the Agincourt Roll*, in *T.R.H.S.* V (1911), 105–40; *Gesta*, 9 note 1 and 35–36; *Rymer*, IX, 260; A. H. Burne, *The Agincourt War*, London 1956, 36.

(12) Nicolas, op. cit. 386–9; *Rymer*, IX, 253–60; C. Hibbert, *Agincourt*, London 1964, App. III.

(13) 'In ingenio suo mirabili rex disposuit et sagaciter ordinavit', *Strecche*, 16.

(14) *Rymer*, IX, 241, 268–9, 284–5. In 1454 Sir John Fastolf was still claiming arrears due to him for services at Harfleur in 1415 – *C.M.H.* VIII, 386.

(15) *Usk*, 129 and 313, but see Wylie, *Henry V*, I 483 and note.

(16) *Monstrelet*, I, 328–32 (caps CXXXVIII to CXL).

(17) *Rymer*, IX, 208–15.

CHAPTER 9

pp. 104–9 (1) Murdoch had been taken prisoner at the battle of Homildon Hill (1402). Henry Percy had accompanied his grandfather, the earl of Northumberland, to Scotland in 1405, and after the old earl's death he was detained there as an honoured prisoner.

(2) 'Scrope whom he greatly loved and who many times had slept with the king and in his chamber', *St Rémy*, I, 224, *Monstrelet*, I, 332 (cap CXLI); *Hist. Angl.*, II, 305.

(3) *Waurin*, II, 177–182.

(4) Ellis, op. cit. I, letters XVI and XVII, 44–49.

(5) *Plummer*, op. cit. 8; *Rot. Parl.*, IV, 64 ff.

(6) *Rymer*, IX, 303.

(7) *Brut*, II, 375–6; *Hist. Angl.*, II, 305–6.

(8) *Memorials*, 41.

(9) *Rymer*, IX, 289–93: *Wills of the Kings and Queens of England*, ed. J. Nichols, London 1780, 227 and 236–8.

(10) Cambridge and Scrope had mooted the possibility of setting fire to the fleet. cf. Wylie, *Henry V*, I, 525 and note.

(11) '*Elmham*', 37.

NOTES

CHAPTER 10

pp. 110–5 (1) 'La clef de la mer', *Monstrelet*, I, 332 – 4 (cap CXLI); *Waurin*, II, 181.

(2) *Gesta*, 16; *Memorials*, 107; E. Dumont, *L'Abbaye de Montivilliers*, Le Havre 1876. This famous abbey was just to the north of Harfleur.

(3) *St Rémy*, I, 225; *Waurin*, II, 181.

(4) *Memorials*, 42.

(5) *Memorials*, 41; *Gesta*, 15; *Black Book*, op. cit. I, 283.

(6) *Black Book*, I, 289, 456, 464.

(7) *Rymer*, X, 107.

(8) 'Absque sopore tenens noctes' *Memorials*, 109; 'The Kinge daylie and nightlie in his owne person visited and searched the watches orders and stacions of everie part of his hoast . . . and whome he founde dilligent he praised and thanked, and the negligent he corrected and chastised', *First Life*, 38; *Livius*, 10; '*Elmham*', 46; *St Rémy*, I, 226.

(9) *Strecche*, 18; *Hardyng*, 375; *Hist. Angl.*, II, 309.

(10) He died in September as a result of his experiences, *Hist. Angl.*, II, 309.

(11) 'Without hosen or shoes', *First Life*, 40. The citizens' deputation was clad in 'sheets of penitence with ropes about their necks', *Usk*, 125 and 307.

(12) *Brut*, II, 377.

(13) *Halliwell*, op. cit. I, 80; *Rymer*, IX, 313.

(14) *Halliwell*, op. cit. I, 83.

(15) *Usk*, 126 and 308; *Memorials*, 114; Nicolas *Agincourt*, op. cit. CXL.

CHAPTER 11

pp. 116–18 (1) *Gesta*, 34; *St Denis*, V, 544; *St Rémy*; *Waurin*, II, 186.

(2) J. H. Wylie, *Henry V* op. cit. II, 76 and note 6. Nicolas in *Agincourt*, CCC, writes of 'almost incredible' recklessness.

(3) *Livius*, 12.

(4) The prose version is in *Gesta*, the metrical version in *Memorials*, 77–165. See Wylie, op. cit. II, 77–88 and C. L. Kingsford, *The Early Biographies of Henry V* in E.H.R., XXV (1910), but the identity of this writer, once firmly accepted as Thomas Elmham, has been disputed in recent years; but see the forthcoming edition of the *Gesta Henrici Quinti* (Clarendon Press) by F. Taylor. and J. S. Roskell

(5) *St. Rémy*, I, 231; *Waurin*, II, 158.

(6) *First Life*, 44; *St Denis*, V, 550; *St Rémy*, I, 233; *Waurin*, II, 189.

pp. 118–24 (7) 'The chaplain' was in despair: see *Gesta*, 39–40.

(8) *Gesta*, 41 note 3; *St Rémy*, I 234; *Waurin* I, 192.

(9) *First Life*, 44; *Gesta*, 41; '*Elmham*', 53. Shakespeare used the incident, *Henry V*, Act III, scene vi.

(10) *St Denis*, V, 544 and 552.

(11) *Livius*, 14; '*Elmham*', 55; *St Rémy*, I, 237.

(12) *Gesta*, 45, 51 and 53; Nicolas, *Agincourt* CLIVCL-V and CLXX

(13) *St Rémy*, I, 241.

(14) *Gesta*, 46.

(15) *St Denis*, V, 554; *St Rémy*, 251–2; *Gesta*, 34–5; '*Elmham*', 63; *Waurin*, II, 208–9; *Ursins*, 518. Some authorities time this incident for the morning of the battle.

(16) *First Life*, 54; *Gesta*, 47; Nicolas, *Agincourt*, CLXXVI-CLXXVII; *Giles*, 41; *St Rémy*, I, 245; *Waurin*, II, 203. And in *Halliwell*, op. cit. I, 85–8 is the so-called 'letter of proclamamation' which Henry made to his men. It is a superb speech and contains the warning that the French had threatened to cut off the thumbs of every archer they captured. See also *St Denis*, V, 554 and *Brut*, II, 377–8 and 555.

(17) But *Monstrelet*, I, 339 (Cf. CXLV) has a different version – in his account it is the English who were noisy and reckless as they expected certain death on the morrow. In *First Life*, 52, although the story of the French dicing is confirmed, the chronicler states that the English kept up their music all night while the French camp was silent.

(18) He and his army had marched about 250 miles, and see *Gesta*, 45, 'multum animose et humaniter animavit exercitum suum'.

(19) *Hist. Angl.* II, 311 says 'newly-sewn wheat' and *St Rémy*, I, 255 agrees.

(20) *First Life*, 54 describes his 'shininge armour' and his bright helmet 'marvelous rich'.

(21) *First Life,* 57.

(22) *First Life*, 55; *Gesta*, 42; Nicolas, *Agincourt*, CLX; *Giles*, 37; *Brut*, II, 378 and 555. It is not clear whether this was suggested by the duke of York or whether it was the duke who carried out the king's suggestion.

(23) 'God and our archers made hem sore to stomble', *Brut*, II, 378 and 596. cf. R. Fabyan (d. 1513), *New Chronicles of England and France*, London 1811, 579: 'But at those dayes the yemen had their lymmes at lybertie; for theyr hosyn were than fastened with one poynt, and theyr jackes were longe and easy to shote in, so that they myght drawe bowes of great strength and shote arowes of a yerde longe besyde the hede'.

(24) The duke of Brabant, who was a younger brother of the duke of Burgundy, was a late arrival at the scene of battle, and at the same time Henry's rear had been attacked by pillagers – both facts help to justify Henry's anxiety if not his action. *St*

NOTES

pp. 124–8 *Rémy*, I, 258; *Waurin*, II, 216; *Gesta*, 55–6; *First Life*, 60–1; *Giles*, 45; *Brut*, II, 597.

(25) E. Halle (1498–1547), *The Union of the Two Noble and Illustre Families of Lancaster and Yorke*, London 1809, 70.

(26) *Hardyng*, 375.

(27) 'And that was a myghty losse to Engelond', *Brut*, II, 597. The French chroniclers (e.g. *Monstrelet*, I, 342–3 (cap CXLVI) tend to blame Brabant (see note 24 above) rather than Henry, and in no case censure him, cf. *St Rémy*, I, 258.

(28) *St Rémy*, I, 260; '*Elmham*', 70.

(29) E. F. Jacob, *The Fifteenth Century*, Oxford 1961, 156; Wylie, *Henry V*, II, 182–6.

(30) *Livius*, 20; *First Life*, 60.

(31) We are fortunate in having accounts of the battle of Agincourt by eye-witnesses. 'The chaplain' watched the scene from the baggage lines and wrote his account (*Gesta*) within two years of the event. *John Hardyng* fought under Sir Robert Umfraville but did not write his account until twenty-five years later. *Jean le Févre of St Rémy* fought on the English side, and *Jean Waurin* on the French side, but did not write till forty years later by which time they had the chronicle of *Monstrelet* (who was a native of Picardy) as a basis. *Gilbert de Lannoi* was also on the French side and he was consulted by le Févre. *Thomas Walsingham* wrote within three years of the battle and probably based his account on 'the chaplain's' story. *Livius* was attached to the household of the duke of Gloucester who was wounded in the battle. The monk of *St Denis* gives us the official Paris version, while *Jean Juvénal des Ursins* gives us the Armagnac view.

(32) *Rot. Parl.*, IV, 69 and 91; *Usk*, 127 and 309; Adam and Stephens, *Select Documents*, 182–3.

(33) *Waurin*, II, 222; *St Rémy*, I, 263.

(34) 'Without accumbrance and dis-ease of his stomach', *First Life*, 64; *Livius*, 22; '*Elmham*', 70.

(35) *Memorials*, 48 and 125–9; *Gesta*, 61 ff.; '*Elmham*', 72; *Livius*, 22–3. It was to this occasion that is ascribed the earliest and most famous of English songs '*Owre Kynge went forth to Normandye*': see words and music in Nicolas, *Agincourt* app. 67–8 and T. Percy, *Reliques of Ancient Poetry*, series II no. 5.

(36) *Chron. Lond.*, 103.

(37) As earl of Rutland there is good evidence to support the view that at least twice he betrayed Richard II; see *Traison*, 65 and 216 and *Creton*, 211–12.

(38) *Strecche*, 13; *Rymer*, IX, 558.

pp. 131–9 (1) N. de Baye (1364–1419), *Journal*, ed. A. Tuetey, Paris 1885–8, II, 224. The French chroniclers record defeat but not national disaster – 'La malle aventure', *Waurin*, II, 230; 'la douloureuse aventure', *Monstrelet*, I, 347 (cap CXLVIII); 'cette malheureuse et douloureuse journée', *St Rémy*, I, 232.

(2) He had lost two brothers at Agincourt.

(3) *St Denis*, VI, 81.

(4) *St Denis*, V, 750; *Ursins*, 522.

(5) *Rot. Parl.*, IV, 70.

(6) *Rymer*, IX, 244 and 458; *Hist. Angl.*, II, 300.

(7) *Gesta*, 79–80 note 2.

(8) *Hist. Angl.*, II, 314; *St Denis*, V, 252; *Strecche*, 22–3.

(9) Norman Chronicle in *Gesta*, 174; *St Rémy*, I, 285; *Monstrelet*, I, 361–2 (cap CLXIII); *Strecche*, ibid. The second fight is known as the battle of Cany (*Gesta*, 72).

(10) *Gesta*, 73.

(11) *St Denis*, VI, 12; *Memorials*, 137; *Gesta*, 80; *St Rémy*, I, 281.

(12) This engagement is sometimes known as the Battle of the Seine. See *Hardyng* (who was present), 377; *St Denis*, VI, 40–2; '*Elmham*', 81–2; *Gesta*, 87–8; *Hist. Angl.*, II, 316; *St Rémy*, I, 282; *Waurin*, II, 236.

(13) 'King of the Romans' was the title of an emperor-elect. Papal coronation was normally the authority for the full title of Holy Roman Emperor. In Sigismund's case in view of the Schism he assumed the full title by declaration and was not actually crowned Emperor by Pope Eugenius IV until May 31st, 1433.

(14) See E. Perroy, *L'Angleterre et le Grand Schisme d'Occident*, Paris 1933.

(15) John Hus was burnt in the cathedral square of Constance, 6th July, 1415.

(16) *St Denis*, V, 774; *Ursins*, 529; *Monstrelet*, I, 352 (cap CLIII) – Sigismund gave great offence by exercising his imperial right to confer knighthood – he knighted a litigant in a case he was helping to decide in the Paris court.

(17) *Rymer*, IX, 339. All knights throughout England were summoned by means of letters to sheriffs and to the chancellor of the County Palatine of Lancaster to muster in London.

(18) This story was considered apocryphal until the publication of *First Life*, 67–86. See C. L. Kingsford, '*A legend of Sigismund's visit to England*', in *E.H.R.* xxvi (1911), 750–1; Wylie, *Henry V*, III, appendix Z2; *Memorials*, 49.

(19) 'Abode a long tyme in the land on the Kynge's cost', *Brut*, II, 381 and 559; *Strecche*, 21; 'at the great cost of the realm', *Usk*, 130 and 314; '*Elmham*', 75–6; *Waurin*, II, 228.

NOTES

pp. 139–41 (20) No one has satisfactorily explained 'the S.S. collar'. Clearly it was one of the symbols of the Lancastrian lords, but why 'S.S.'? See Wylie, *Henry IV*, IV, 116–17. For its wearing by the Emperor see *Gesta*, 78 note; *Hist. Angl.*, II, 316; *Rymer*, VIII, 165 and IX, 434 – 'a glad Syghte to 'alle your Lyge Men to se'.

(21) William, count of Holland, came to London – he had married Margaret, the daughter of Philip the Bold and their child Jacqueline was the widow of the Dauphin Jean.

(22) *Rot. Parl.*, IV, 96; *Rymer*, IX, 377–82; *First Life*, 72.

(23) *Gesta*, 89–90.

(24) *Rymer*, IX, 394–6.

(25) Gloucester's rudeness to the count de Charolais is related in *Monstrelet*, I, 358–9 (cap CLIX) but *Waurin*, II, 230, ignored it. See also *First Life*, 67–8. The 'Good Duke Humphrey' was to become a nuisance in the next reign. His only 'goodness' was his contribution to what became the Bodleian Library at Oxford.

(26) On November 11th, 1417, the Cardinal Oddo Colonna became Pope Martin V and the Schism was ended see above cap XVII.

CHAPTER 13

pp. 142–5 (1) *Rot. Parl.*, IV, 95; *Gesta*, 106.

(2) *Hist. Angl.*, II, 317.

(3) See the learned and comprehensive note to Wylie, *Henry V*, III, 39.

(4) *Rymer*, IX, 430 – 'ye shall pray my Brother that he suppose not that for any Tretee that they will make, that I wol leve my Voyage, with Godds Grace; for sekirly, with his Mercy, I shall not faile' (written by Henry with his own hand).

(5) For Henry's finances at this time see R. A. Newhall, *The English Conquest of Normandy 1416–1424*, Yale 1924, cap IV, and his, *The War Finances of Henry V and the Duke of Bedford* in *E.H.R.* xxxvi (1921), 172–198.

(6) *Rymer*, IX, 436–7; *E.H.R.* xxix, 512.

(7) N. H. Nicolas, *History of the Royal Navy*, London 1847, II, 402 and note (a) and Appendix 515. There is a masterly summary of the evidence on Henry's naval affairs in Wylie, *Henry V*, II, cap XLV. See also C. L. Kingsford, *The Beginnings of English Maritime Enterprise*, History (new series), XIII (1928) 97–106 and 193–203, especially 99–100 and C. F. Richmond, *The Keeping of the Seas during the Hundred Years War*, History, XLIX (1964), 283–98, and Newhall, op. cit. 195–200.

(8) *Ellis*, op. cit., 2nd series, I, 69–72.

(9) *The Black Book of the Admiralty*, ed. T. Twiss (Rolls Series), London 1871–6; Nicolas, *Agincourt*, op. cit. Appendix 31; Nicolas, *Navy*, op. cit. II, 489.

267

pp. 145-7 (10) In the 'Libel of English Policy' (*Political Songs*, II, 202) it urges 'kepe than the see, that is the walle of England'; cf. Plummer, *Fortescue*, op. cit. 200 and 234-6. Cf. *The Libelle of Englyshe Policye*, ed. G. Warner, Oxford 1926 and G. A. Holmes, *The Libel of English Policy* in *E.H.R.* LXXVI (1961), 193-216.

(11) *St Denis*, VI, 96; *Ursins*, 536; *Livius*, 31; '*Elmham*', 93-5; *First Life*, 78; Nicolas, *Navy*, op. cit. II, 432-3.

(12) *Wills of Kings*, op. cit. 236 ff.; *Cal. Pat.*, 1416-22, 118.

(13) 'Tripgettis' were for catapulting stones and arrows; 'sowes' were hoardings to cover those attacking a fortress as they approached the walls; 'bastilles' were wooden towers for attacking ramparts without climbing; 'brygges' were pontoons of hide on wicker frames; 'mallis' were mallets, 'pykys' were picks and 'pavys' were body shields for archers. *Brut*, II, 382.

(14) The estimate of 16,400 is in *Livius*, 31 ff. and followed by '*Elmham*', 92. The so-called Roll of Agincourt belongs correctly to this expedition. See R. A. Newhall, *The English Conquest of Normandy*, op. cit. and J. H. Wylie, *Notes on the Agincourt Roll*, in *T.R.H.S.* (3rd series) V, 1911, 105-40, also his *Henry V*, III, 51 and W. T. Waugh, ibid. 52 note. The only larger overseas expedition of the Middle Ages was possibly that of Edward IV in 1475: cf. Jacob, *The Fifteenth Century*, op. cit. 375.

(15) We have the names of Henry's four master-gunners – all Germans. Nicolas, *Agincourt, 386*.

CHAPTER 14

pp. 148-53 (1) It is a surprising fact that Paris is even north of St Malo.

(2) '*Elmham*', 96; *Livius*, 33.

(3) *Ursins*, 533; *Livius*, 34; '*Elmham*', 99.

(4) Robert of Avesbury, *De Gestis Mirabilibus Edwardi Tertii*, ed. E. M. Thompson (Rolls Series), London 1889, 359; L. Puiseux, *Siège et Prise de Caen par les Anglais en 1417*, Caen 1858, *passim*.

(5) Both abbeys miraculously survived the Anglo–American invasion of Normandy in 1944. For Clarence's exploit cf. *Hist. Angl.*, II, 322-3; *Livius*, 35 ff.; '*Elmham*', 102.

(6) *First Life*, 89.

(7) *First Life*, 86; '*Elmham*', 105; *Brut*, II, 383.

(8) Henry was 'a prince from whome all avarice was fair exiled' – *First Life*, 92.

(9) *First Life*, 91-2; *Brut*, II, 384.

(10) Cf. R. A. Newhall, op. cit. 59 ff.

(11) *Rymer*, IX, 511-16; *Livius*, 45.

(12) *First Life*, 102-4; *Livius*, 46 ff.; '*Elmham*', 129-30.

NOTES

pp. 153–5 (13) On the other hand a brave and stubborn Welshman, Edward ap Griffith, who had fought to the last was tried and executed and his quarters fixed to the gates of Caen, Lisieux, Alençon and Verneuil; *Rot. Norm.*, 364.

(14) *Rymer*, IX, 571, 573, 739–40.

(15) 'In substance there is no man of estate come in to the king's obeisance; the which is a thing that causeth the people to be full unstable, and there is no wonder'. *Ord. Priv. Co.*, II, 350.

(16) Salt and spices helped to keep food through the winter.

(17) *Rymer*, IX, 583–5.

(18) *First Life*, 130 ff. which incorrectly dates this incident during the siege of Rouen; *Otterbourne*, 280.

CHAPTER 15

pp. 156–9 (1) Wylie, *Henry V*, op. cit. III, 77; cf. *Monstrelet*, I, 377 (cap CLXXIII) – Henry 'found no difficulties in adding to his conquests – from the effect of these internal divisions he met with scarcely any resistance'.

(2) *Bourgeois*, 78; *Ursins*, 533, 537; *St Rémy*, I, 242.

(3) *Monstrelet*, I, 384 (cap CLXXVII); *Ursins*, 537.

(4) *Monstrelet*, I, 385–6; *St Rémy*, I, 318.

(5) *Bourgeois*, 98, he was in Paris at the time; *Monstrelet*, I, 394–7 (cap CLXXVII); *St Denis*, VI, 232 ff.; *Ursins*, 540 ff.; *St Rémy*, I, 332 ff.

(6) *Bourgeois*, 114; *St Denis*, VI, 278 ff.

(7) *Livius*, 58; '*Elmham*', 169; *Strecche*, 29. Orsini's protégé was nevertheless imprisoned for life.

(8) '*Elmham*', 172; *First Life*, 120–1.

(9) For a romantic incident during the attack see *Monstrelet*, I, 400 (cap CXCI) and *Strecche*, 30–3; *Livius*, 57.

(10) John Page, *The Siege of Rouen* in *Historical Collections of a London Citizen*, ed. J. Gairdner (Camden Society), London 1876, 2; *Strecche*, 33–4; *Brut*, II, 387 and 394. See appendix below pp. 228–50.

(11) *Usk*, 129 and 313 and note 3.

(12) Oldcastle was taken, after a violent struggle in which he was wounded, on the Welsh border. Before parliament he still maintained his detestation of priests and his belief in the existence of King Richard in Scotland. He was hanged in chains, roasted alive, and died without a cry at St Giles's Fields. *Memorials*, 156 ff.; *Capgrave*, 122–3 and 141–2; *Strecche*, 14–15; *Usk*, 131 and 317; *Brut*, II, 386.

(13) *Rot. Parl.*, IV, 107–11.

(14) For the 'Foul Raid' see *Livius*, 56; *Hardyng*, 380–1; *Hist. Angl.*, II, 325; *First Life*, 115–16.

269

HENRY V

pp. 160–8 (1) *First Life*, 114.
(2) 'As bare as my honde', *Page*, op. cit. 3–4, who calls it a 'cursed deed', but see L. Puiseux, *Siége et Prise de Rouen par les Anglais*, Caen 1867, 56.
(3) See an impressive list in *Brut*, II, 390, including 'Graunt Jakes' a celebrated condottiere from Lombardy.
(4) The quotations are from *First Life*, 122 ff.
(5) See Appendix *Page* was used by *Strecche*, 34 ff.; *Gesta*, 127; *Livius*, 65 and '*Elmham*', 195.
(6) Caltrops were spiked iron balls to maim cavalry horses. *Page*, 6; *First Life*, 123.
(7) *Monstrelet*, I, 403–4 (cap CXCIV); *St Rémy*, I, 345; *Waurin*, II, 249.
(8) *Cal. Pat.*, 14, 16–22, 204.
(9) *Page*, 7, 10. For details of the curious capitulation terms see *Rymer*, IX, 620.
(10) *Page*, 10; *Livius*, 61 ff.; *Strecche*, 35; *First Life*, 124; Brut, II, 388; '*Elmham*', 182; *Gesta*, 189 and 240.
(11) *Page*, 12; *Monstrelet*, I, 404 (cap CXCIV) who says the kernes 'did infinite mischiefs'; *Brut*, II, 389 and 397 – they rode without saddles; *St Rémy*, I, 345; *Waurin*, II, 249 who very much exaggerated their numbers. For Henry's discipline see *Gesta*, 125.
(12) *First Life*, 126–7.
(13) *Monstrelet*, I, 404 (cap CXCIV); *Gesta*, 189; *Otterbourne*, 128; *Waurin*, II, 243 who remarks of the single combats 'but such passages of arms could profit neither the besiegers nor the besieged except for the renown of their valiant nobility'.
(14) *Page*, 15, 'For schot of goone and quarelle bothe Sawe I nevyr gretter wrothe'; *Brut*, II, 398–9.
(15) *Page*, 16; *Livius*, 65.
(16) *Brut*, II, 400.
(17) There is no lack of evidence for the miseries of this siege. See especially *Page*, 18–21; *St Rémy*, 352–3; *Brut*, II, 400–1; *Brut*, II, 400–1; *Monstrelet*, I, 409 (cap CXCIX).
(18) *Page*, 22; *Brut*, II, 404–6; *Strecche*, 38; *St Rémy*, I, 356.
(19) *Page*, 34–6.
(20) *Monstrelet*, I, 410 (cap CC); *St Rémy*, I, 356; *Waurin*, II, 261.
(21) *Rymer*, IX, 664 ff.; *Ramsay*, op. cit. I, 266, calculates that the ransom equalled £50,000 in late nineteenth century currency.
(22) *Page*, 44–5 and *Monstrelet*, ibid.

NOTES

CHAPTER 17

pp. 169–72 (1) See below, Chapter XXIV, p. 214 and note 7.

(2) For details, M. Creighton's *History of the Papacy*, London 1899, is still indispensable. The general reader will find in H. A. L. Fisher, *A History of Europe*, London 1936, 348–61 a useful summary. See also J. H. Wylie, *The Council of Constance*, London 1900, and W. T. Waugh, *A History of Europe 1378–1494*, London 1960, 171–87.

(3) See note 20, Chapter XII above.

(4) *Rymer*, IX, 472; *Hist. Angl.*, II, 319.

(5) J. Stevenson, *Letters and Papers Illustrative of the Wars of the English in France* (Rolls Series), London 1861, 4, II, 441; cf. K. B. McFarlane, *Henry V, Bishop Beaufort and the Red Hat 1417–1421*, in *E.H.R.*, LX (1945), 316.

(6) *Rymer*, IX, 680 and 806–7.

CHAPTER 18

pp. 173–7 (1) *Brut*, II, 391.

(2) *Otterbourne*, 282; '*Elmham*', 200; *Monstrelet*, I, 411 (cap CC). Others 'escaped punishment by dint of money'; *Livius*, 68.

(3) *Monstrelet*, ibid.; *Waurin*, II, 256 and 264.

(4) *Rymer*, IX, 667.

(5) *Rymer*, IX, 664 – 7; *Livius*, 68.

(6) Puiseux, *Rouen*, op. cit. 208, 211 and 213; *Monstrelet*, I, 412 (cap CC).

(7) *Monstrelet*, ibid., describes how some citizens threw their valuables into the Seine 'to avoid being plundered'.

(8) *Rymer*, IX, 691. In *St Denis*, XL, 9 it is reported that Henry at this time struck coins at Caen stamped 'Henricus, rex Franciae'.

(9) *Ursins* (545) at the dauphin's court says that very few of the Norman nobility ever submitted, but cf. *Monstrelet*, ibid. where he says 'the inhabitants' but not those 'of great authority' wore the English red cross of St George. For the clergy see *Rymer*, IX, 684.

(10) C. L. Kingsford, *Henry V*, op. cit. 249.

(11) *Rymer*, IX, 632 ff.

(12) *Rymer*, IX, 654 ff.

(13) *Rymer*, IX, 656 ff.

(14) *Waurin*, II, 252; *St Rémy*, I, 348 – 'it pleased him very well'; *Monstrelet*, I, 415–16 (cf. CCV).

(15) *Ellis*, series II, I, 76; *Rymer*, IX, 704. For Henry's assessment of the diplomatic situation see the remarkable document addressed to his council in *Ord. Priv. Co.*, II, 350–8.

271

pp. 176–80 (16) *Rymer*, IX, 759; *Monstrelet*, I, 415 (cap CCV); *Brut*, II, 423–4.

(17) *Monstrelet*, ibid., 'she was very handsome, of high birth, and of the most engaging manners'; *Waurin*, II, 258–60, 'she was a very handsome lady to look at, of graceful figure and pleasing countenance'; *Livius*, 74; '*Elmham*', 220 ff.; *Gesta*, 130; *Ursins*, 550.

(18) 'Except the flame of love some deale fired the heart of this Martiall Kinge' – *First Life*, 143–4.

(19) *Monstrelet*, I, 416 (cap CCV); *St Rémy*, I, 362–3.

(20) *Rymer*, IX, 775 ff.; *St Denis*, VI, 328, 32; *Monstrelet*, ibid.

CHAPTER 19

pp. 181–5 (1) Finally Bedford at the age of thirty-four married Anne, daughter of John the Fearless, duke of Burgundy, in 1423.

(2) He had been given the title of count of Longueville by Henry V as a reward for his services in the previous June (*Rymer*, IX, 706); his French title was Captal de Buch.

(3) Henry, as *Monstrelet* put it, 'was not very well pleased' at the treaty between Burgundy and the dauphin – the somewhat shady capture of Pontoise was his bitter answer. The English 'did innumerable mischiefs' adds *Monstrelet*, I, 419 (cap CCVII). Cf. *St. Denis*, VI, 352–4; *St Rémy*, I 366–7; *Ursins*, 552; *Waurin*, II, 274; *Livius*, 76–77.

(4) *Hist. Angl.*, II, 330; *Delpit*, 227.

(5) Mutineers in Rouen were beheaded, *First Life*, 146; '*Elmham*', 226.

(6) W. Forbes-Leith, *The Scots Men-at-arms and Life Guards in France*, Edinburgh 1882, I, 153 and II, 193–9.

(7) *Livius*, 7; '*Elmham*', 231; *Gesta*, 130.

(8) The most vivid account is in *Monstrelet*, I, 422–6 (cap CCX), but see also G. du Fresne de Beaucourt, *Histoire de Charles VII*, Paris 1881 – 92, I, 144–89

(9) But see R. Vaughan, *John the Fearless*, London 1966, 263–86, for the view that the dauphin was in the plot. The only flaw in an otherwise convincing argument is that it assumes an extraordinary precocity in a mere boy.

(10) Apparently the cords of its only well had worn out – *Monstrelet*, I, 421 (CCIX).

(11) See Wylie and Waugh, *Henry V*, op. cit. 250 note 1; *Rot. Norm.*, 332–71; *Rymer*, IX, 852–88, L. Puiseux, *L'Emigration Normande et la Colonisation Anglaise*, Rouan 1866.

(12) '*Elmham*', 238; *Rymer*, IX, 821 ff.

(13) *Gesta*, 198.

NOTES

pp. 186–92 (1) There was an unpleasant quarrel at Roye – *Monstrelet*, I, 432–3 (cap CCXVI).

(2) *Ursins*, 556; *St Denis*, VI, 398.

(3) *Rymer*, IX, 877 ff.

(4) 'Populo civitatis inspectante et ut apparuit valde gaudente' – *Hist. Angl.*, II, 334; *Bourgeois*, 139.

(5) *Livius*, 83; '*Elmham*', 250–1; *Monstrelet*, I, 438 (cap CCXXIII).

(6) *Chastelain*, I, 131–3.

(7) For the treaty terms see *Rymer*, IX, 895–904 and X, 916–20; *St Denis*, VI, 410 ff.; *Gesta*, 137 ff.; *Monstrelet*, I, 439–42 (cap CCXXIII).

(8) *Rymer*, IX, 901 ff.

(9) *Rymer*, IX, 906 ff.

(10) *Hist. Angl.*, II, 335.

(11) *Chastelain*, I, 133–4; *Monstrelet*, I, 439 (cap CCXXIII) who says that Henry looked 'as if he were at that moment king of all the world'; *Waurin*, II, 303; *St Rémy*, II, 1–2; '*Elmham*', 267; *Ursins*, 557.

(12) *Bourgeois*, 140.

(13) *Monstrelet*, I, 443–4 (cap CCXXIV) adds another revealing note – 'The king likewise hanged a running footman, who always followed him when he rode, holding the bridle of his horse. He was a great favourite of the king's, but having killed a knight in a quarrel, was thus punished.' Cf. *Chastelain*, I, 146; *St Rémy*, II, 12.

(14) But the 'joint' forces were kept apart to avoid friction – *Livius*, 89; '*Elmham*', 277.

(15) The chronicler was Jean Juvénal des Ursins; his brother was Louis – *Ursins*, 558 ff.

(16) 'Six or eight English clarions and divers other instruments' – *Waurin*, II, 312–13; '*Elmham*', 275; *Monstrelet*, I, 446 (cap CCXXVI).

(17) *Monstrelet*, ibid.

(18) *Monstrelet*, I, 449 (cap CCXXIX); *St Rémy*, II, 18; *Ursins*, 560; *Waurin*, II, 339; '*Elmham*', 282.

(19) *Scotichronicon*, ed. T. Hearne, Oxford 1722, IV, 1217; *Waurin*, II, 342; A. Hellot, '*Les Chroniques de Normandie*', Rouen 1881, 62.

(20) *Monstrelet*, I, 450 (cap CCXXIX); *St Rémy*, II, 24; *Waurin*, II, 343; *Ursins*, 561.

(21) In the *First Life*, 167–71, it is clear that it was Barbazan who appealed to the heralds for his 'mercy' – Henry would have had him executed. Cf. '*Elmham*', 286.

(22) 'Carols were sung in all the squares through which they passed' – *Monstrelet*, I, 450 (cap CCXXX); *Chastelain*, I, 187.

p. 192 (23) *Monstrelet,* L, 451 (cap CCXXX); *Chastelain,* I, 192 ff.;
Bourgeois, 144.

(24) *Bourgeois,* 145–6; *Ursins,* 374.

CHAPTER 21

pp. 193–7 (1) *Rymer,* X, 31, 110.

(2) *Ursins,* 562.

(3) *Monstrelet,* I, 415–2 (cap CCXXX); *Chastelain,* I, 194–5;
Ursins, 562; *Rymer,* X, 33–35.

(4) *Monstrelet,* ibid.; *Chastelain,* I, 198 ff.

(5) *Bourgeois,* 147 and 164.

(6) *Rot. Parl.,* IV, 123 and 125.

(7) *Rymer,* X, 58 and 85; '*Elmham*', 294.

(8) For my summary of the re-organization of Normandy I am
wholly in debt to W. T. Waugh in his chapter LXCII, pp.
255–64 of vol. III of Wylie and Waugh *Henry V* and to Prof.
R. A. Newhall in his *The English Conquest of Normandy 1416–
1424,* Yale 1924 and his *Henry V's Policy of Conciliation in
Normandy 1417–1422* in Anniversary Essays in Mediaeval
History by students of C. H. Hoskins, New York 1929; cf.
Puiseux, *L'Emigration Normande,* op. cit., *passim.*

(9) *Rymer,* X, 224.

(10) 'He was received in England as if he had been an angel from
God' – *Monstrelet,* I, 453 (cap CCXXXIII); *Brut,* II, 425;
'*Elmham*', 295 ff.

CHAPTER 22

pp. 198–201 (1) '*Elmham*', 296 ff.; *Hist. Angl.,* II, 336–7; *Brut,* II, 426–7;
Strecche, 49.

(2) For the menu see *Brut,* II, 447 and R. Fabyan (d. 1513),
New Chronicles of England and France, London 1811, 586 ff.
For 'sotelties' see *Chron. Lond.,* 164 ff.

(3) At Kenilworth he stayed at his manor of 'Plesantmaris,
which the king himself had reclaimed from a bog' – *Strecche,*
50.

(4) '*Elmham*', 300; *Monstrelet,* I, 453 (cap CCXXXIII) who says
bluntly that Henry needed 'money and men'.

(5) '*Elmham*', 303–4; *Northern Chron.,* 290.

(6) *Rot. Parl.,* IV, 123–8.

(7) *Rot. Parl.,* IV, 135.

(8) *Usk,* 133 and 320.

(9) Cf. *Rot. Parl.,* IV, 306 – all foreigners in Joanna's household
were expelled on the grounds that they were betraying England.

NOTES

pp. 201–3 (10) The queen was accused on the confession of her chaplain of having 'compassed and imagined the king's death in 'the most treasonable and horrible manner that could be devised' – *Rot. Parl.*, IV, 118; *Brut*, II, 422 and 444; *Hist. Angl.*, II, 331, and see A. R. Myers *The Captivity of a Royal Witch*, Bulletin of the John Rylands Library, Manchester 1940, XXIV, 2, 1–17.

(11) *Rot. Parl.*, IV, 148; *Stat.*, II, 206.

(12) The conference was summoned by Henry himself – *Hist. Angl.*, II, 337–8 and cf. M. D. Knowles, *The Religious Orders in England*, Cambridge 1955, II, 182–4.

(13) *Rymer*, X, 123 ff.

(14) *Rymer*, X, 127–8. Bourbon was even persuaded to agree that the treaty was 'good, reasonable and just' – ibid., 85.

(15) *Rymer*, X, 120.

(16) P. H. Morice, *Memoires pour servir de preuves a l'Histoire de La Bretagne*, Paris 1742, 6; II, 1091 ff.

(17) *Monstrelet*, I, 454 (cap CCXXXIV); *St Rémy*, II, 31–2.

CHAPTER 23

pp. 204–8 (1) *Ursins*, 561; *Beaucourt*, op. cit. I, 333–5.

(2) For the numbers engaged in the battle of Baugé see Wylie and Waugh, *Henry V*, op. cit. III, 304 note 3.

(3) 'Al was because they wold not take Archers with them' – *Brut*, II, 427 and 492; *Ursins*, 389–90; *Chastelain*, I, 224 ff.; *St Rémy*, II, 35; *St Denis*, VI, 456; *Bourgeois*, 151; '*Elmham*', 301–4; *Hardyng*, 334–5; *Hist. Angl.*, II, 338–9; *Monstrelet*, I, 458–9 (cap CCXXXVIII).

(4) When the news of Baugé was reported to Pope Martin V he is reported to have remarked 'verily the Scots are the antidote of the English' – *Scotichronicon*, op. cit. IV, 1216.

(5) *Rymer*, X, 131.

(6) *Delpit*, 231.

(7) *Chastelain*, I, 238; 'very unwillingly' says *Monstrelet*, I, 461 (cap CCXLII).

(8) The lord de l'Isle Adam, suspected of Dauphinist sympathies, was imprisoned and remained a prisoner until after Henry's death – *Monstrelet*, I, 458 (cap CCXXXVII). For the story of de l'Isle Adam boldly 'answering back' to Henry see *Monstrelet*, I, 448–9 (cap CCXXIX).

(9) '*Elmham*', 313 ff.; *St Denis*, VI, 464; *Ursins*, 566; *St Rémy*, II, 39.

(10) '*Elmham*', 314; *St Denis*, VI, 464; *Scotichronicon*, op. cit. IV, 1217.

(11) The king lodged a mile from Meaux at the castle of Ruthile while the duke of Exeter commanded the English camp – '*Elmham*', 315–16.

pp. 208–10 (12) *'Elmham'*, 318; *Bourgeois*, 160.
(13) *Hist. Angl.*, II, 340; *St Denis*, VI, 448; *Ursins*, 562.
(14) 'Also throughout the kingdom was perfect joy more than there had been seen for a long time' – *Waurin*, II, 361.
(15) *Monstrelet*, I, 472 (cap CCLV); *Bourgeois*, 16 ff.; *'Elmham'*, 320.
(16) *Monstrelet*, I, 475 (cap CCLIX); *'Elmham'*, 322 ff.
(17) *Rymer*, X, 212–14; *Waurin*, II, 370–3; *St Denis*, VI, 450; *Ursins*, 563 who repeats the St Denis story of Henry's fury at an English soldier who fled – he was taken, buried up to the neck and starved to death. *Monstrelet*, ibid.
(18) *Bourgeois*, 170.

CHAPTER 24

pp. 211–16 (1) *Brut*, II, 493; 'Which created much sorrow in the hearts of all loyal Frenchmen, and not without cause' – *Monstrelet*, I, 478 (cap CCLXI).
(2) *Bourgeois*, 174 ff.; *Monstrelet*, I, 479 (cap CCLXIII).
(3) Master John Swanwyth, *Issue Rolls* 10 Hen. V, July 14th, 1422.
(4) The death actually took place very early in the morning of September 1st – *Rymer*, X, 253; *'Elmham'*, 331–2; *Livius*, 95; *Brut*, II, 493; *Monstrelet*, I, 483 (cap CCLXIV).
(5) *Hist. Angl.*, II, 343; *St Denis*, VI, 480; *Ursins*, 567; *Waurin*, II, 389; *Monstrelet*, I, 484 (cap CCLXIV). In *Hall*, 113, it is said that Basset, who was Henry's chamberlain, maintained that death was due to pleurisy, but the contemporary authorities are more or less agreed on dysentery; cf. Wylie, *Henry V*, III, 416 and note 2.
(6) For the deathbed scene the best authorities are *'Elmham'*, 332 ff. and *Monstrelet*, I, 483 (cap CCLXIV); cf. *Waurin*, II, 386 ff.
(7) A year before his death Henry had actually dispatched Sir Gilbert de Lannoi, a Burgundian, to investigate the chances of war in the eastern Mediterranean. He arrived back after the king's death. See his report in *Archaeologia*, XXI (1527), 281–444; cf. *Brut*, 496.
(8) *Psalms*, XXI, 6.
(9) *'Elmham'*, 336 ff.; *St Denis*, VI, 482; *Bourgeois*, 176.
(10) *Brut*, II, 430 and 493; *'Elmham'*, 337; *St Rémy*, II, 65 ff.; *Monstrelet*, I, 484 (cap CCLXIV).
(11) *Brut*, II, 430. For the funeral scenes and chapel see W. H. St John Hope, *The Funeral Monument and Chantry Chapel of King Henry V* in *Archaeologia*, 2nd series, LXV (1914), 129–86.
(12) *Monstrelet*, I, 484 (cap CCLXIV).
(13) See Dean A. P. Stanley, *Historical Memorials of Westminster Abb y*, London 1882, 127–134; *Archaeologia*, XLVI, 281–93;

276

pp. 216–17   *Rymer* IX, 289; C. W. Scott-Giles, *Heraldry in Westminster Abbey*, Westminster 1954, 16–20.

(14) Her second marriage to Owen Tudor was clandestine but was recognized later. She retired to Bermondsey Abbey and took no part in affairs of state.

(15) Samuel Pepys, *Diary*, 24th February, 1668.

EPILOGUE

pp. 218–22   (1) W. Stubbs, *Constitutional , History*op. cit. III, 100.

(2) R. B. Mowat, *Henry V*, London 1919, 320.

(3) C. L. Kingsford, *Henry V*, 2nd edition, London 1923, 402.

(4) W. T. Waugh, *Henry V*, III, 426.

(5) P. de Coquy, *Chronique des Ducs d'Alençon*, ed. H. Moranville. Paris 1892, 126.

(6) *Rot. Parl.*, IV, 160. He was Sir John Mortimer of Hatfield and presumably was plotting on behalf of the earl of March who, so Grafton says, was his uncle. Twice he escaped from the Tower but in 1424 he was finally recaptured and was hung drawn and quartered at Tyburn. *Brut*, II, 31 and 564; *Rot. Parl.*, IV, 202 and 260.

(7) 'In the last analysis he was an adventurer, not a statesman' – E. F. Jacob, *The Fifteenth Century*, Oxford 1961, 202.

(8) See R. B. Mowat, op. cit. 295–6.

(9) Henry's son Henry VI, a mere boy of 10, was crowned king of France in Notre-Dame on December 16th, 1431. For the fantastic celebrations in Paris see *Monstrelet*, I, 596–7 (cap CIX).

(10) 'The unhappy genius of Henry of Monmouth was mainly responsible', C. W. C. Oman, *The Political History of England (1377–1485)*, London 1920, IV, 286.

(11) There is a portrait at Windsor Castle which dates from the time of Henry VIII. Similar portraits are in the National Portrait Gallery, at Eton and at The Queen's College, Oxford.

(12) In October 1420 he paid £8 13s. od. for harps for himself and his queen; in September 1421 he paid £2 13s. 8d. for a harp which was to be sent to him in France – *Pell*, 367. When abroad, his chapel contained six 'organists' or instrumentalists.

(13) In November 1421, he paid £12 8s. od. for twelve books on hunting – *Pell*, 368. Apparently he borrowed books and sometimes delayed long in returning them – *Rymer*, X, 317.

(14) See above p. 72.

(15) *Ursins*, 561.

(16) C. Plummer, *Fortescue on the Governance of England*, Oxford 1885, 2. For Henry's 'religiosity' cf. my introduction to Page's *Siege of Rouen*. Appendix, above p. 229.

pp. 222–4 (17) E.g. 'Grand justicier qui sans acception des personnes faisoit aussi bonne justice au petit que au grand' – *St Denis*, VI, 126; 'Above all thyng he keped the lawe' – *Hardyng*, 388.

(18) Cf. *supra*, p. 53; *Gesta*, xxiv – 'and in especial see that the porer partye suffre no wrong'.

(19) 'The principle reason that he was feared was that he punished with death without any mercy those who went contrary to and infringed his commands or orders and he fully maintained the discipline of chivalry as the Romans did of old' – *Waurin*, II, 391.

(20) 'Henry V did not, in the eager fulfilment of his designs, reckon with the far-reaching power of hereditary disease' – S. B. Chrimes, *Lancastrians Yorkists and Henry VII*, London 1964, 48. 'He killed himself in following his own selfish ends . . . and thus left a defenceless minor not quite nine months old to succeed him, one too, in whom his ambitious marriage with Katherine of France had implanted the seeds of insanity' – K. H. Vickers, *England in the Later Middle Ages*, London 1937, 383.

(21) Cr. J. E. A. Jolliffe, *The Constitutional History of Mediaeval England*, London, 1937, V, 409–95. For the growth of the commons, see J. S. Roskell, *The Commons in the Parliamen of 1422*, Manchester 1965, and *The Speakers in English Parliaments 1376–1523*, Manchester 1965. For the aristocracy, see K. B. McFarlane, *The Wars of the Roses*, in *Proceedings of the British Academy*, vol. L (1964).

(22) C. Plummer, op. cit. 8; and see K. B. McFarlane in *C.M.H.*, VIII, cap XI, 384–5 – 'It is the tragedy of his reign that he gave a wrong direction to national aspirations which he did so much himself to stimulate, that he led his people in pursuit of the chimera of foreign conquest, an adventure from which they recoiled exhausted and embittered after more than thirty years of useless sacrifice.'

(23) J. H. Harvey, *Henry Yevele*, London 1944, 71; Joan Evans, *The Oxford History of English Art*, vol. V (1307–1461), Oxford 1949. On the other hand Henry gave 1,000 marks per annum during his pleasure for the completion and repair of the nave of Westminster Abbey – *Rymer*, IX, 78 and C. Plummer, op. cit. 245.

(24) Perhaps Lydgate's lines on Henry V are a sufficient sample:
The V Henry, of knyghthoode lode starre,
Wyse ande manly playnly te termyne,
Ryght fortunate provyde in pes and yn warre,
Gretely experte and marcyall dyssepleyne,
Spousyde the daughter of Fraunce, Katerynne,
Raynyd X yere, who lyste to have rewarde,
Lythe at Westmynster, not far fro Synt Edwarde.
(*Historical Collections of a Citizen of London in the XVII Century*, ed. J. Gairdner, Camden Society, London 1876, 53.)

NOTES

p. 224 (25) Cf. Percy's *Reliques*, note to Series II, 5, and Nicolas, *Agincourt*, op. cit. 77. For the superiority of Henry IV in music see Frank Le Harrison, *Music in Mediaeval Britain*, London 1958, 22 and 220–3.

APPENDIX

pp. 232–41 (1) 'Caltrops' were spiked iron balls to maim cavalry horses.

(2) Probably 'le trébuchet' which was a huge mechanical catapult for throwing great stones.

(3) This is of course an exaggeration. 80,000 inhabitants would be nearer, but the city had accepted thousands of refugees from the English invasion of Lower Normandy.

(4) Either as a sanitary precaution or as a substitute for wine and cider; perhaps both.

(5) The Umfravilles originally came from Amfreville in the Cotentin.

(6) It looks as though Page was writing soon after Clarence's death at Baugé in March 1421.

INDEX

INDEX

INDEX

INDEX

INDEX

Suffolk, earls of, *see* Pole
Switzerland, 24
Swynford, Lady Katherine, 17, 56, 69, 75
Sycharth, 40, 45
Syon, 76, 77

Talbot, Sir Gilbert, 52, 234
Tamerlane, 26
Tanneguy, du Chatel, *see* Chatel
Taxation, 77–8, 101, 126, 132, 142, 199–200
Ternoise, river, 120
Thomas, duke of Clarence, 60, 85, 108, 113, 139, 146, 149–51, 158, 162, 175, 182, 192, 195, 199, 204–5, 233–4, 241
Tiptoft, Sir John, 154, 195
Touques, 147–9
Tonnage and Poundage, *see* Taxation
Tours, 157, 204
Tower of London, 73, 80–1, 198, 209
Towns, medieval, 29, 34
Tramecourt, 120, 122
Trim, 20
Tripartite Indenture, 49–50
Trotton, 122
Troyes, 184, 186–7, 189
Troyes, treaty of, 188–9, 93–5, 200, 202
Tudors, 42, 52, 217
Turks, Ottoman, *see* Bayazid

Umfraville, Sir Gilbert, 117, 119, 166, 205, 234, 240–2
Umfraville, Sir Robert, 105
Universities, medieval, 28
Urban VI, Pope, 136–7
Usk, Adam of, 42, 200

Valmont, battle of, 134, 139
Vaurus, Bastard of, 209
Vere, Richard de, earl of Oxford, 75, 117
Vernon, 175
Vincennes, Bois de, 211–12
Voyennes, 119

Walden, Thomas Netter of, *see* Netter
Wales, 32, 38–53
Waring, Johanna, 15, 77
Warwick, earl of, *see* Beauchamp, Richard
Wenzel, Emperor, 135
Westminster Abbey, 64-5, 71–2, 73–4, 76, 127, 202, 214–15, 217
Westminster Palace, 61, 77, 126, 128, 132, 139, 142, 198–9
Westmorland, earl of, *see* Neville, Ralph
Whitelock, John, 73
Whittington, Sir Richard, 76
Winchester, 102–3
Winchester, bishop of, *see* Beaufort, Henry; Wykeham, William of
Windsor, 21, 79, 139, 208
Woodbury Hill, 51
Worcester, earls of, *see* Beauchamp; Richard; Percy; Thomas
Wyclif, John, 30, 62, 84
Wykeham, William of, bishop of Winchester, 91–2

Yevele, Henry, 17, 224
York, 48, 50, 73
York, archbishop of, *see* Scrope, Richard le
York, duke of, *see* Edward Plantagenet

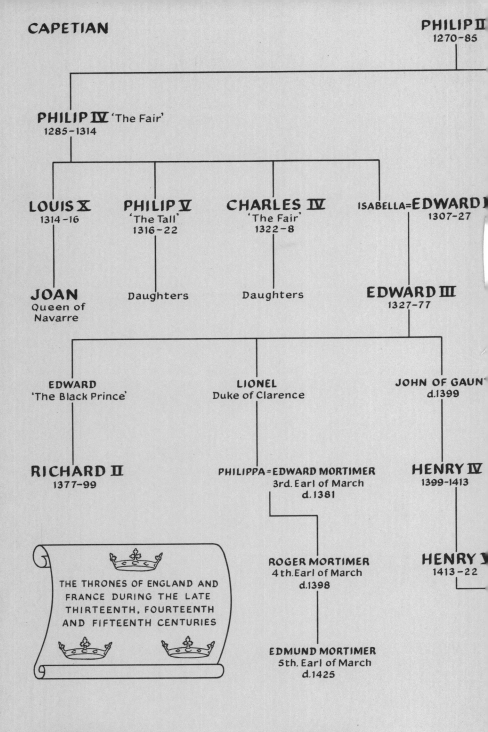

CAPETIAN

PHILIP III
1270-85

PHILIP IV 'The Fair'
1285-1314

LOUIS X
1314-16

PHILIP V
'The Tall'
1316-22

CHARLES IV
'The Fair'
1322-8

ISABELLA=**EDWARD II**
1307-27

JOAN
Queen of
Navarre

Daughters

Daughters

EDWARD III
1327-77

EDWARD
'The Black Prince'

LIONEL
Duke of Clarence

JOHN OF GAUNT
d.1399

RICHARD II
1377-99

PHILIPPA=EDWARD MORTIMER
3rd. Earl of March
d.1381

HENRY IV
1399-1413

ROGER MORTIMER
4th. Earl of March
d.1398

HENRY V
1413-22

THE THRONES OF ENGLAND AND
FRANCE DURING THE LATE
THIRTEENTH, FOURTEENTH
AND FIFTEENTH CENTURIES

EDMUND MORTIMER
5th. Earl of March
d.1425

PLANTAGENET

MORTIMER